An Outline of Chinese Literature II

Different from previous researches weighted toward historical description and individual writer and work, this book establishes a general analytical system and a multi-angled methodology to examine Chinese literature.

In ancient China, there was no definite concept of pure literature. Considering both modern ideas of literature and the corresponding traditional concept, this book broadly discusses *Shi* and *Fu* poetry, *Ci* poems and *Qu* verses, novels and essays. The four chapters deal with the origins, evolutions, structures and styles of the various genres respectively, analyzing some representative works. It's worth mentioning that the book is written from an individual perspective. Based on his own appreciation as a reader, the author expresses the depth of his various related impressions on Chinese literature. In addition, it conveys many fresh points of view, which will enrich and inspire related researches.

This book will appeal to scholars and students of Chinese literature and comparative literature. People who are interested in Chinese literature and Chinese culture will also benefit from this book.

Yuan Xingpei is a professor of Department of Chinese Language and Literature, Peking University. His research focuses on Chinese classic literature, especially Chinese poetical art.

China Perspectives Series

The *China Perspectives* series focuses on translating and publishing works by leading Chinese scholars, writing about both global topics and China-related themes. It covers Humanities & Social Sciences, Education, Media and Psychology, as well as many interdisciplinary themes.

This is the first time any of these books have been published in English for international readers. The series aims to put forward a Chinese perspective, give insights into cutting-edge academic thinking in China, and inspire researchers globally.

For more information, please visit www.routledge.com/series/CPH

Existing title:

Beyond the Iron House: Lu Xun and the modern Chinese literary field
Sun Saiyin

Forthcoming titles:

Literature and Literary Criticism in Contemporary China
Zhang Jiong

Literature and Literary Theory in Contemporary China
Zhang Jiong

An Outline of Chinese Literature I
Yuan Xingpei

An Outline of Chinese Literature II
Yuan Xingpei

Seven Lectures on Wang Guowei's Renjian Cihua
Florence Chia-Ying Yeh

An Outline of Chinese Literature II

Yuan Xingpei

Translated by Paul White

LONDON AND NEW YORK

First published 2018
by Routledge

2 Park Square, Milton Park, Abingdon, Oxfordshire OX14 4RN
52 Vanderbilt Avenue, New York, NY 10017

Routledge is an imprint of the Taylor & Francis Group, an informa business

First issued in paperback 2020

British Library Cataloguing-in-Publication Data
A catalogue record for this book is available from the British Library

Library of Congress Cataloging-in-Publication Data
A catalog record for this book has been requested

ISBN: 978-1-138-24255-5 (hbk)
ISBN: 978-0-367-52893-5 (pbk)

Typeset in Times New Roman
by Apex CoVantage, LLC

Contents

Foreword to the Chinese edition

In September 1987 I was invited by Professor Nagashima of Japan's Aichi University to teach an outline course in Chinese literature. On my way back home via Hong Kong personages in Hong Kong's publishing circles, on seeing my lecture notes, decided that they deserved to be published, and so they were sent to the printer. Due to their kind care, this small volume came to be presented to the readers.

Although this book was written for foreigners who wish to study Chinese literature, the requirements of the Chinese reader have also been fully taken into account. For a long time our research into Chinese literature has been weighted toward historical description and discussions of individual writers and works, and too little attention has been paid to many other aspects of the subject as well as to an overall analysis. The style of writing literary history has hardened into a rigid model – one it is not easy to break away from. In these circumstances, it is hoped that this attempt to expound on Chinese literature using the method of an outline can provide the readers with fresh perspectives and awaken in them a deeper interest in the subject.

In the course of compiling this book I have consulted a wide range of authorities and studies, and duly noted where I am indebted to them. Some have pointed me in the direction of deeper consideration, and some have furnished me with clues for my research. Although I am not able to cite them one by one, let me take this opportunity to thank them all here. I may mention for special thanks for their assistance Mr. Guo Shaoyu, author of *A History of Chinese Literary Criticism*, Mr. Chu Binjie, author of *An Introduction to Ancient Chinese Inscriptions* and Mr. Qi Zhiping, author of *A Brief Account of Tang and Song Poetry*. Special thanks also go to Meng Erdong and Ma Zili who helped me with the proof-reading of the whole text. Due to the author's limited scholarship, there are bound to be omissions and errors, and he hopes that the readers will bring them to his attention.

Finally, my heartfelt thanks go out to Aichi University and Prof. Nagashima. If it had not been for their kind invitation and "assignment" perhaps this book would never have been written.

Yuan Xingpei

—December 1987

Preface to the Chinese edition

The word "literature" appeared in China even before the time of the Qin Dynasty (221–206 BC). But it had a different connotation from what we mean by "literature" today. In the Confucian classic known as the *Analects* we find the disciples of Confucius divided into four categories of specialty:

> Virtuous conduct: Yan Yuan, Min Ziqian, Ran Boniu and Zhong Gong. Eloquence: Zai Wo and Zi Gong. Politics: Ran You and Ji Lu. Literature: Zi You and Zi Xia.[1]

Xing Bing, in his *The Analects Annotated*, defines the two characters which make up the Chinese word "literature" as follows: "learned in written works."[2] And Yang Xiong, in his *Discourses on Methods * Gentleman*, says "Zi You and Zi Xia were accomplished at letters."[3] In the *History of the Han Dynasty * Biography of Dong Zhongshu*, it says, "There was a strict ban on literature, and no one could walk around with books under his arm."[4] The word "literature" here originally meant ancient documents. Yang Bojun backs this interpretation in his *The Analects Explained and Annotated* by saying, "Steeped in ancient documents were Zi You and Zi Xia."[5]

The Han Dynasty (206 BC–220 AD) saw a change in the understanding of the word "literature," when it came to mean "learning" in general. As the *Records of the Historian * Chronicle of Li Wu* notes:

> In order to spread the Confucian teachings, he summoned the worthy Zhao Wan and Wang Zang and made them senior ministers on account of their learning. And to discuss ancient matters a special hall was set up in the south of the city where the feudal lords who were attending the court could gather.[6]

Zhao Wan and Wang Zang were leading Confucian scholars. The *Records of the Historian * Biographies of Confucian Scholars* says:

> The emperor dispatched famous Confucianists in high positions like Zhao Wan and Wang Zang to the provinces and summoned to his court upright and worthy men, scholars renowned for their learning.[7]

By comparing these two passages we can clearly see that "literature" at this time meant Confucian learning. Zhao Wan and Wang Zang were scholars, but not in the modern sense. In the *Records of the Historian * Preface by Sima Qian*, it says:

> And so the Han Dynasty flourished. Xiao He put the laws in order. Han Xin expounded on the military disciplines. Zhang Cang enacted the rules and regulations. Shusun Tong arranged the rites and ceremonies. And so it was that literature advanced in elegance, the *Book of Odes* and the *Book of Documents* were issued in several printings.[8]

Here we can see that the law, military discipline, rules and regulations and rites and ceremonies were all included under the heading of "literature."

It is worth noticing that in Han times, besides "wenxue" the word "wenzhang" was also used. The latter denoted non-scholastic writing. In the *History of the Han Dynasty * Eulogy to Gongsun Hong, Bu Shi and Er Kuan*, it says:

> The Han Dynasty had a plethora of talented men. In the field of general erudition outstanding were Gongsun Hong, Dong Zhongshu and Er Kuan . . . and in the field of non-scholastic writing, Sima Qian and Sima Xiangru.[9]

Celebrated for their non-scholastic writings were Liu Xiang and Wang Bao . . . who advocated filial piety and the inheritance of tradition.[10]

"Wenzhang" covered such genres as *cifu* (mixed prose and poetry) and historical accounts, in other words styles of writing displaying elegant wording. As for the difference between "wenxue" and "wenzhang," the clearest definition may be in the words of Xiahou Hui in the *Annals of the Three Kingdoms*:

> Xiahou Hui, in an encouraging tone, said, "A *wenxue* scholar takes care to advance his theme using elaborate detail, while a *wenzhang* scholar takes pride in the close integration of his words."[11]

Moreover, the people of Han times took great care over the meaning of words and stressed their composition and use. This is different from what we today call "literature."

Advancing a little from the difference between "wenxue" and "wenzhang" in the Han Dynasty, during the Southern Dynasties (420–589) there emerged a difference between "wen" (writing) and "bi" (writing brush). In the *History of the Southern Dynasties * Biography of Yan Yan*, we find:

> The emperor once asked Yan Zi about the ability needed by his officials. Yan Zi replied, "The quality of his writing is the measure of an official's literary attainment."[12]

Liu Xie says in his *Carving a Dragon with a Literary Heart * Chronological Sequence*:

> "Yu used his writing to endear people to him; Wen used literature to make his own thoughts more generous."[13]

In his *Chapter on the Arts*, the same author says,

> "It is often said that there is literature and there is writing: The latter is not full of pleasing sounds; the former is."[14]

Using the presence or absence of pleasing sounds as the criterion for distinguishing "literature" from "writing" was a concept which sprang up early in history. Xiao Yi, Emperor Yuan (reign: 552–555) of Liang, in his *The Golden Tower * Eternal Words*, says,

> "In ancient times there were two ways of scholarship; nowadays there are four."[15]

The two ways of "scholarship" of ancient times he is referring to are the "literature" and "writings" of the Han Dynasty; the four ways of "scholarship" of his own day are "Confucian studies" and "learning," into which "Wenxue" was divided, and "literature" and "writings," into which "Wenzhang" was divided. In the *Chapter on Bequeathing Writings to Posterity* there is a further elaboration on the difference between "literature" and "writings":

> Qu Yuan, Song Yu, Mei Cheng, Chang Qing and their ilk confined themselves to writing *cifu*, which they called literature. . . . As for the works of people like Yan Zuan, whose poetry is awkward, and Bo Song, whose talent lay in composing memorials to the throne, they come under the general heading of "bi" or "writings." The chanting of ballads and long-drawn-out dirges were included in the category of "literature." . . . As for "writings," at the very least they would be called incomplete, and at the very most meaningless. They were regarded as mere clever exercises in composition. As for literary works, they had to be elaborate and embroidered, with high-flown phrases and sentiments.[16]

Xiao Yi's demarcation between "wen" and "bi" was not one simply between the presence and absence of pleasing sounds. He in fact recognized that the characteristic of "wen" was its ability to stir the emotions and thereby rouse men to action. "Wen" also had the value of providing enjoyment through its emphasis on the beauty of its diction (rhythm and flourishes, etc.). "Bi" was the writing style used to frame memorials to the throne and suchlike. As Zhang Binglin said, " 'Wen' is used for poetical and *fu* (mixed poetry and prose) works; 'bi' for official documents. That was what they used to say in those days."[17] The "cleverness" in “bi” writings was restricted to the technique of composition, and could not be compared to the qualities of “wen.”

Xiao Yi’s emphasis on the two special characteristics of emotion and diction in “wen” are close to what we today would call “literature.” However, the influence of his *The Golden Tower* was not great; the biggest influence on the theory of literary style in China was exerted by two works which appeared at different times – *Carving a Dragon with a Literary Heart* and *Selected Works of Literature*. These two works did not make clear distinction between “wen” and “bi.” In the category of “wen” they included the forms of applied writing such as edicts, lyrics, summonses and didactics. This situation lasted down to the Qing Dynasty (1644–1911), with the appearance of *A Compilation of Classical Prose* by Yao Nai, an antiquarian of the Tongcheng School. This work contains prose writings in the ancient style dating from the Warring States Period (475–221 BC) to the Qing Dynasty, and includes applied genres.

In traditional bibliographies too the scope of literature is not clear. Xun Xu of the Western Jin Dynasty (265–317) divided writings into four categories, which he labeled A, B, C and D. Li Chong of the Eastern Jin Dynasty (317–420) combined Xun Xu’s B and C categories and divided writings into classics, histories, philosophy and anthologies. But what the bibliographers called anthologies were equivalent to neither what Xiao Yi called collections of “wen” nor what are today called anthologies of literary works. On the one hand, the first included many applied writing genres, some of which could be classified as literature and some of which could not. It is necessary to examine their concrete circumstances before deciding. On the other hand, novels and opera scripts, which today would be regarded as indispensable parts of anthologies of literature, are not included in the ancient collections. Novels written in classical Chinese were included under the heading of history or philosophy. Novels written in colloquial language and opera scripts were basically ignored by the bibliographers.

To sum up: In ancient China here was no strict division between literary and non-literary writing. In fact, there was no definite concept of pure literature as such. What was called literature in the old days included, on the one hand, genres which we nowadays would not consider as belonging to the category of literature at all, and on the other, excluded genres which we would include as literature. Therefore, when we embark on a study of Chinese literature we must not only take into account modern ideas of literature but also the more diverse concept of literature that are traditional in China. Based on this principle, this book broadly discusses poetry (including its *fu*, *ci* and *qu* sub-genres), the novel and discursive writing.

Notes

1 *Commentary on the Thirteen Classics*, World Bookstore photocopy of the Ruan woodblock print, P. 2498.
2 *Commentary on the Thirteen Classics*, World Bookstore photocopy of the Ruan woodblock print, P. 2498.

3 *Collected Works of the Philosophers*, Vol.7, Shanghai Bookstore, 1991, P. 39.
4 [Han Dynasty] Gu, Ban: *History of the Han Dynasty*, Vol.56, Zhonghua Book Company, 1962, P. 2504.
5 Bojun, Yang: *The Analects Explained and Annotated*, Zhonghua Book Company, 1980, P. 110.
6 [Han Dynasty] Qian, Sima: *Records of the Historian*, Vol.12, Zhonghua Book Company, 1959, P. 452.
7 [Han Dynasty] Qian, Sima: *Records of the Historian*, Vol.121, Zhonghua Book Company, 1959, P. 3118.
8 [Han Dynasty] Qian, Sima: *Records of the Historian*, Vol.130, Zhonghua Book Company, 1959, P. 3319.
9 [Han Dynasty] Gu, Ban: *History of the Han Dynasty*, Vol.58, Zhonghua Book Company, 1962, P. 2634.
10 [Han Dynasty] Gu, Ban: *History of the Han Dynasty*, Vol.58, Zhonghua Book Company, 1962, P. 2634.
11 [Jin Dynasty] Shou, Chen: *Annals of the Three Kingdoms*, Vol.21, *Biography of Liu Shao*, Zhonghua Book Company, 1963, P. 619.
12 [Tang Dynasty] Yanshou, Li: *History of the Southern Dynasties*, Vol.34, Zhonghua Book Company, 1975, P. 879.
13 Wenlan, Fan: *Carving a Dragon With a Literary Heart Annotated*, Vol.9, People's Literature Publishing House, 1978, P. 674.
14 Wenlan, Fan: *Carving a Dragon With a Literary Heart Annotated*, Vol.9, People's Literature Publishing House, 1978, P. 655.
15 [The Liang Court of the Southern Dynasties] Yi, Xiao: *The Golden Tower * Eternal Words*, Vol.4, *Collected Works From Lack of Knowledge Studio*, Vol.9, woodblock print, sixth year (1826) of the Daoguang reign period of the Qing Dynasty.
16 [The Liang Court of the Southern Dynasties] Yi, Xiao: *The Golden Tower * Eternal Words*, Vol.4, *Collected Works From Lack of Knowledge Studio*, Vol.9, woodblock print, sixth year (1826) of the Daoguang reign period of the Qing Dynasty.
17 Binglin, Zhang: *Discussing China's Culture * Literary Symposium*, Original Text with Notes, Shanghai Ancient Works Propagation Publishing House, P. 41.

Part 1

Shi and *fu* poetry

The collocation *shi* and *fu* poetry is a very old one. We find in the *Songs of Chu * Great Summons*: "Sixteen girls danced in succession, their gestures coordinating rhythmically with the elegant songs and lyrics." Wang Yi notes "*shi* and *fu* poetry refers to elegant music."[1] As two styles of poetry – *shi* and *fu* – Wang Fu of the Han Dynasty (206 BC–220 AD) has this to say in his *Sayings of a Hermit*: "*Shi* and *fu* poetry, inasmuch as it has the virtue of recounting both the good and the bad, has the quality of being an outlet both for sorrow and joy; thus it has a steady and elegant form while containing deep meanings of stimulus and analogy."[2] Liu Xin, in his *Seven Outlines* has a section on *shi* and *fu* poetry, and in the *History of the Han Dynasty * Records of Art and Literature* we find, "Liu Xin gathered a multitude of records, which he then arranged into *Seven Outlines* for presentation to the emperor. Among them were the "Compilation Outline," "Six Arts Outline," "Philosophers Outline" and "*Shi* and *Fu* Poetry Outline."[3] Cao Pi, in his *Dissertation on Scholarship * On Literature*, divides literature into four branches, of which *shi and fu* is one. He says, "*Shi* and *fu* are marked by beauty."[4] From the above, we can see that *shi* and *fu* were two forms of versification which were often regarded for the purposes of discussion as very closely linked. And so this book will discuss them together, paying attention to their influence upon each other and the mutual connection in their growth and decline.

Notes

1 [Song Dynasty] Xingzu, Hong: *Additional Commentary on the Songs of Chu*, Vol.10, Zhonghua Book Company, 1983, P. 221.

2 [Qing Dynasty] Jipei, Wang: *Commentaries on Sayings of a Hermit*, Vol.1, *Dealing with the Fundamentals*, Zhonghua Book Company, 1979, P. 19.

3 [Han Dynasty] Gu, Ban: *History of the Han Dynasty*, Vol.30, Zhonghua Book Company, 1962, P. 1701.

4 Li Shan, Lv Yanji et al. [Tang Dynasty]: *Selection of the Major Writings of Six Officials*, Vol.52, *Collected Writings of the Four Basic Branches of Literature*

1 The three sources of Chinese poetry and ballads

Book of Odes: songs of the heavenly flute

According to conjectures in written records, a certain kind of primitive songs were produced in China pre-dating the *Book of Odes*. These songs were accompanied by music and dancing. The *Spring and Autumn Annals of Mr. Lv * Section on Ancient Music* says, "In antiquity the musical performances of the Getian tribe involved three people holding ox tails and moving their feet to the 'song in eight *que*'."[1] Described here is obviously a primitive song-and-dance performance. "Holding ox tails" is clear, and "moving their feet" must refer to dancing, but as there is no written record of the "eight *que*," it is not known for certain what kind of song this was.

Doubtless, the songs and ballads of the most ancient times were handed down orally; they were written down at a much later date an example of an ancient song reduced to writing is the "The Catapult Song" from *The Spring and Autumn Annals of the Kingdoms of Wu and Yue*:

> Split the bamboo. Bind the pieces. Let the mud fly. Chase the prey [lit. "meat"].[2]

Liu Xie, in his *Carving a Dragon with a Literary Heart * Inheritance and Innovation*, says, "When the Yellow Emperor sang the song 'Splitting the Bamboo' he was sincere in the extreme."[3] It is not known on what grounds he based his conclusion that this song dated from the time of the Yellow Emperor; however, the simplicity of the language indicates an origin of great antiquity. It depicts the life of a hunter, who splits bamboo and binds the pieces to make some sort of catapult. He then makes pellets out of mud, which he shoots at his prey. In only eight characters four actions are described covering the whole course of making and using a hunting weapon in a natural and unadorned manner.

Vol.11 of the *Comprehensive Categories of Art and Literature* quotes the "Song of the Husbandman," contained in Huang Fumi's *Era of the Monarchs*. It is said to be part of a song titled "Fifty Old Men on their Way to Till the Soil," dating from the time of the legendary Emperor Yao:

> I go to work at sunrise, and rest at sunset. I dig a well and drink. I till the fields and eat. Does the emperor labor as hard as I?

This song is quoted too in the "Commentaries on the Book of Documents" section of the *Book of Rites * Explanation of the Classics*. It reflects the hand-to-mouth existence of the common people in ancient times. The last line – "Does the emperor labor as hard as I?" – is quoted in the "Record of Early Studies," which comments on its primitive thought. However, some people contend that this line is a later forgery, for instance, see Zhu Ziqing's *Three Types of Ancient Poetry and Ballads with Comments and Translations * Collection with Discussions of Ancient Works no Longer Extant*. In addition, there is no way of deciding whether the songs "South Wind" and "My Lord Says," which are said to date from the time of the legendary Emperor Shun, are genuine or not. In *Spring and Autumn Annals of Mr. Lv * First Part of the Section on Music* we find, "Yu [Legendary emperor who tamed the floods] went forth upon his task. He saw the woman of Tushan, but did not go to her. Instead, he went to inspect the territory of the south. The woman of Tushan waited for Yu as his wife on the north side of Mount Tu, where she composed and sang the song 'Waiting for my lord, indeed how wonderful!' This was the true beginning of the southern music." From this we can get a glimpse at least of what the songs of high antiquity were like.

With the invention of writing, the old ballads came to be written down as poems. It is said that in ancient times there was a system for collecting such poems. Ban Gu, in the "Food and Goods" section of his *History of the Han Dynasty*, says, "In the first month of spring, just as the farmers were on their way to the fields, officials beating wooden clappers as a sign of their office would record the songs they were singing, and submit them to their superiors. These songs were then set to music for the consideration of the emperor."[4] As to the reason why they did so, the "Records of Art and Literature" section of the *History of the Han Dynasty* tells us: "In olden times, special officers would collect folk songs so that the ruler would be cognizant of the doings of the common people, know what was going right and what was going wrong, and reflect on his own conduct."[5] It was a way of ascertaining the mood of the people, judging the benefits and defects of policies, and adjusting the focus of government. It is said that many of the poems and ballads contained in the *Book of Odes* were collected and recorded in this way. However, these are restricted to those in the sections titled, "Airs of the States" and "Minor Court Hymns"; those in the sections titled, "Eulogies" and "Hymns" were probably compositions by court ministers and scholars.

The *Book of Odes* was China's first collection of poems and ballads; it was also one of the sources of such poems and ballads. Altogether, it contains 305 pieces collected from the early years of the Western Zhou period (11th century BC) to the middle part of the Spring and Autumn period (sixth century BC) – a time scale of some 500 years. The last edition of the book was probably completed in the sixth century BC, somewhere in the area now occupied by the provinces of Shaanxi, Shanxi, Henan, Hebei, Shandong and the northern part of Hubei. In the Han Dynasty it was held that Confucius had compiled the *Book of Odes*. For instance, according to the section on Confucius in the *Records of the Historian*, "There were over 3,000 poems handed down from ancient times, but Confucius pared them down to only those which were consonant with benevolence and righteousness – some 305 – which Confucius sang to the accompaniment of the zither."[6] It is believable that there were 305 poems which could be set to music, but not that Confucius alone did the editing, because in his time there was already a tradition of the "Three Hundred Poems," which only acquired the title *Book of Odes* in the Han Dynasty. In the pre-Qin period [in which Confucius lived], they were simply known as the *Poems*; it was Han Dynasty scholars who raised them to the level of a classic, and called the collection the *Book of Odes*.

The contents of the *Book of Odes* are divided into three parts – Airs, Hymns and Eulogies. The Airs, or Airs of the States, were collected from 15 states in ancient China. The Hymns are divided into Minor Court Hymns and Major Court Hymns, and the Eulogies into the Eulogies of Zhou, Lu and Shang.[7] The tripartite division is because of supposed differences in the music which originally accompanied the poems: That for the Airs, which were folk songs collected from 15 different regions, had a regional coloring; that of the Hymns, which originated in the area directly ruled by the Zhou king, the overlord of the various states, was the solemn music of the Zhou court. The character *ya*, which occurs in the title of the Hymns section, originally meant "straight" or "correct," as the music of the Zhou court was considered the standard mode. The difference between the Hymns and the Airs was that between "standard language" and "regional language." There are different theories about the division of the Hymns into Minor Court Hymns and Major Court Hymns, but it was probably connected with differences in musical accompaniment. As for the Eulogies, in the "Preface to the Mao Poems" we find "They are replete with beauty and the aspect of virtue, and are ideal expressions of worship." The Qing Dynasty (1644–1911) scholar Ruan Yuan said, "The character 'song' used for Eulogy should be 'rong,' which indicates an attitude of dance."[8] This theory postulates the Eulogies as being part of the music and dancing used in religious rites.

In the past the designations of *feng* (airs), *ya* (hymns), *song* (eulogies), of the *Book of Odes* were classified together with the *fu* (straightforward), *bi* (simile) and *xing* (with introduction) types of poetry, to form the so-called "Six Formats." In the "Preface to the Mao Poems" we find, "There are six formats of poetry – Airs, *Fu*, *Bi*, *Xing*, Hymns and Eulogies." *The Rites of Zhou * Spring Official * Great Master* calls them the "Six Poetics," and lists them in the same order. In his *The Orthodox Mao Poems*, Kong Yingda says,

> The Airs, Hymns and Eulogies are all different ways of composing poetry; *Fu*, *Bi* and *Xing* are all different ways of expressing it in words. The combinations of these diverse forms give the Six Formats: The *Fu*, *Bi* and *Xing* constitute the framework, and the Airs, Hymns and Eulogies the style of the poem. The absorption of the first three into the second three is called "formatting." There is no other mode of doing it.

Concerning *fu*, *bi* and *xing*, scholars through the ages have come up with different explanations, and their divergences on just what is a *fu*, *bi* or *xing* poem are particularly clear. But, in general, it is agreed that they are three methods of expression. "*Fu*" "Elaborates on the subject and describes it directly."[9] An example is the "Airs of Qin * No Clothes" from the *Book of Odes*:

How shall it be said that you are unclad?
I will share my long robes with you.
The king is raising his forces;
I will prepare my lance and spear,
And will be your comrade.
How shall it be said that you are unclad?
I will share my under clothes with you.
The king is raising his forces;
I will prepare my spear and lance,
And will take the field with you.
How shall it be said that you are unclad?
I will share my lower garments with you.
The king is raising his forces;
I will prepare my buffcoat and sharp weapons,
And will march along with you.[10]

This poem extols the comradeship and dedication of soldiers of the State of Qin in opposing the enemy. It is in the *fu* mode, and the reader can almost hear the bold cries of the soldiers as they march off to war.

The *bi* and *xing* modes are often found combined. *Bi* has a clearly metaphorical function, while *xing* introduces the topic of the poem from something seemingly unconnected with it. For instance, "Airs of Wei * Big Rat":

Big rat! Big rat!
Do not eat our millet.
Three years have we had to do with you,
And you have not been willing to show any regard for us.
We will leave you,
And go to that happy land.
Happy land! Happy land!
There shall we find our place.
Big rat! Big rat!
Do not eat our wheat.
Three years have we had to do with you,
And you have not been willing to show any kindness to us.
We will leave you,
And go to that happy State.
Happy State! Happy State!
There shall we find ourselves right.
Big rat! Big rat!
Do not eat our ripening grain!
Three years have we had to do with you,

And you have not been willing to think of our toil.
We will leave you,
And go to those happy borders.
Happy borders! Happy borders!
Who will there make us always to groan?[11]

This poem uses the metaphor of a big rat to point the finger of blame at a parasite who consumes without working (presumably a landlord). The whole poem is in the *bi* mode. Another example is the "Airs of Chen * Willows at the East Gate":

On the willows at the east gate,
The leaves are very luxuriant.
The evening was the time agreed on,
And the morning star is shining bright.
On the willows at the east gate,
The leaves are dense.
The evening was the time agreed on,
And the morning star is shining bright.[12]

This poem is in the *xing* mode. There are repeated syllables in both verses, but the two repeated ones in the first half of each verse, describing the luxuriance of the willow leaves, simply set the scene; they are not a metaphor for the nocturnal tryst. However, there are places where the *bi* and *xing* modes come very close and it is hard to distinguish between them. That is why we often find in Zhu Xi's *Poetry Collection* the comment "*bi* and *xing*." Zheng Zhong said, "*Bi* draws an analogy, while *xing* expresses the thing itself."[13] Liu Xie says, "*Bi* is manifest, while *xing* is obscure, and so *bi* has the meaning attached, while the meaning of *xing* has to be assumed. The former points directly at the object being described, but the latter demands conjecture."[14] Li Zhongmeng of the Song Dynasty (960–1279) says, "Using one's feelings to search for something is called *bi*; the feeling is attached to the thing. Using an object to conjure up a feeling is called *xing*; the object gives rise to the feeling."[15] All these theories give us food for thought.

Most of the poems in the *Book of Odes* are divided into four divisions, each ending in a rhyme. There is a beauty of primitive and balanced simplicity in this. The divisions of each poem echo each other. These are important characteristics of this style. An example is the "Airs of Zheng * Artful Boy":

That artful boy!
He will not speak with me!
But for the sake of you, Sir,
Shall I make myself unable to eat?
That artful boy!
He will not eat with me!
But for the sake of you, Sir,
Shall I make myself unable to rest?[16]

There are two stanzas to this poem, and only two characters different in each stanza – "speak" in the first is changed to "eat" in the second, and "eat" in the first is changed to "rest" in the second – producing an echoing effect.

The contents of the *Book of Odes* are wide-ranging. There are chants used in sacrificial rites to the ancestors, historical poems referring to the Zhou kings, songs of farm life, political allegories, complaints about warfare and conscript labor, and songs of love and marriage. Their value as literature and their appeal to us come from their deep and genuine aroma of real life, and especially of the soil. An example is "Zhounan * Osprey":

Guan-guan go the ospreys,
On the islet in the river.
The modest, retiring, virtuous, young lady:
For our prince a good mate she.
Here long, there short, is the duckweed,
To the left, to the right, borne about by the current.
The modest, retiring, virtuous, young lady:
Waking and sleeping, he sought her.
He sought her and found her not,
And waking and sleeping he thought about her.
Long he thought; oh! long and anxiously;
On his side, on his back, he turned, and back again.
Here long, there short, is the duckweed;
On the left, on the right, we gather it.
The modest, retiring, virtuous, young lady:
With lutes, small and large, let us give her friendly welcome.
Here long, there short, is the duckweed;
On the left, on the right, we cook and present it.
The modest, retiring, virtuous, young lady:
With bells and drums let us show our delight in her.[17]

The girl gathering duckweed by the river awakens love in the young man's breast. Waking and sleeping, he thinks of her. Restless the whole day, she fills his thoughts, sleep is kept at bay. He imagines the day when she will be his wife, welcoming her to his home with the joyous clamor of drums and gongs. Similar is "Zhounan * Plantains":

We gather and gather the plantains;
Now we pluck the ears.
We gather and gather the plantains;
Now we rub out the seeds.
We gather and gather the plantains;
Now we may gather them.
We gather and gather the plantains;
Now we have got them.

We gather and gather the plantains;
Now we place the seeds in our skirts.
We gather and gather the plantains;
Now we tuck out skirts under our girdles.[18]

In Vol.1 of his *Origins of the Book of Odes*, Fang Yurun says, "Reading this ballad in a tranquil and receptive state of mind, one can dimly hear the cheerful farm girls in the patchwork of fields made appealing by the wind and the sunshine, as they chant back and forth to each other. Their voices rise in the air, now far, now near, now broken off, now continuing on. We may not know exactly what gives rise to their buoyant mood or how cheerful their spirit, but it is not necessary to translate this ballad exactly to appreciate its charm."[19] However, Yu Guanying has done an excellent translation into modern Chinese.

Another example is the "Airs of Wei * Bo Xi," in which a wife in her own words describes her longing for her husband away on a far expedition:

My noble husband is how martial-like!
The hero of the country!
My husband, grasping his halberd,
Is in the leading chariot of the king's [host].
Since my husband went to the east,
My head has been like the flying [pappus of the] artemisia.
It is not that I could not anoint and wash it;
But for whom should I adorn myself?
O for rain! O for rain!
But brightly the sun comes forth.
Longingly I think of my husband,
Till my heart is weary, and my head aches.
How shall I get the plant of forgetfulness?
I would plant it on the north of my house.
Longingly I think of my husband,
And my heart is made to ache.[21]

She imagines her husband, hero-like in the front line. She is so proud of him. But at the same time she feels a deep sense of loneliness. Because of this she is disinclined to wash and comb her hair and adorn herself. It is not that she doesn't have cosmetics, but for whom should she make herself pretty? The reference to the rain and the sun is a skillful piece of analogy: She longs for rain, but the sun comes out, meaning that her hopes are constantly disappointed. And so she reigns herself to the pain of separation.

The important legacy of the *Book of Odes* for later generations was not its structure; its four-character-verse became ossified during the Han Dynasty, and was only used for hymns to be chanted at the ancestral shrine. It is true that some fine poems were written after this time in four-character style by poets such as Cao Cao and Tao Yuanming, but on the whole the quality of poems written in this format by later generations was not high. Nevertheless, it goes without saying that the ongoing influence of the *Book of Odes* was strong.

In addition, there is another point worthy of note, and that is the fact that the Confucianists and their successors of the Han Dynasty drew on the *Book of Odes* to elucidate their series of analyses and theories of poetry. Their maxims in this field, such as "poetic words and meaning," "no profane thoughts," "beauty and satire," "stimulus through comparison," and even "gentle and sincere" became virtually the guiding principles for poetic creation and even overall literary creation, and had a deep-going influence on Chinese literature for some 2,000 years. The Han Confucians elevated the *Book of Odes* to the status of a classic, along with their own commentaries on the *Odes*. The actual *Book of Odes* itself became less important than the analyses and theories of the Confucianists as a guide to the creation of poetry and ballads.

The earliest mention of "poetic words and meaning" occurs in the *Book of Shang* * Canon of Yao: "Poetic words and meaning, songs with immortal words, sounds following the chant and rhythm harmonizing the sounds." Here, "meaning" refers to the feelings and thoughts in the heart, and poetry is the means of expressing subjective feelings and meanings using words. As this touches on the basic understanding of literature it is worth paying attention to. "Poetic words and meaning" emphasizes expression, and so is different from the Western imitative theory, and thus is also worthy of attention. "No profane thoughts" is Confucius' judgment on the some 300 poems contained in the *Book of Odes*. In the *Analects * The Practice of Government* it says, "The Master said, 'In the *Book of Odes* are three hundred pieces, but the design of them all may be embraced in one sentence – "Having no profane thoughts." ' "[22] Not profane means "proper," that is, conforming to the scope of virtue as advocated by the Confucians. Therefore, "having no profane thoughts" is a demand of the trend of thought needed for the creation of poems and ballads. "Beauty and satire" was a phrase used by the Han Dynasty Confucianists when discussing the *Book of Odes*. A concept touching on the "beauty and satire" occurs in the "Great Preface to the Book of Odes". It is also used in the minor preface to that work to analyze the poems: In some, the beauty prevails; in others the thrust. In his "Preface to a Manual of Poetry," Zheng Xuan of the latter part of the Han Dynasty sums up this theory as follows: "By discussing merits and lauding virtue one is in line with the beauty therein; by pointing out malfeasance and failures one can correct evil."[23] The importance of the "beauty and satire" lies in the social and political function of poems and ballads, and the fact that it set up a target for later creators of poems and ballads to aim at. When using poetry and ballads to advance the concept of "beauty and satire," especially when the latter half of the formula is predominant, it is necessary that the language be indirect and diplomatic, and that the method be comparative and appropriate: Then the effect will be one of "gentleness and sincerity." These ideas about the *Book of Odes* raised by the Han Dynasty Confucianists had a standardization effect on later poetry and ballad creation, the impact of which was deep and long-lasting.

The folk songs of remote antiquity and most of the pieces in the *Book of Odes* are plain and natural, with nothing pretentious in their creativity. They are full of the scent of real life. They are often referred to as the "Songs of the Heavenly Flute."

Songs of Chu: among the immortals

Another wellspring of Chinese poems and ballads is *Songs of Chu*.

Some 300 years after the poems in the *Book of Odes* were committed to writing, in the third century BC, in the latter part of the Warring States Period (475–221 BC) in China, a new poetic form, full of thick earthy color, emerged in the southern Kingdom of Chu. This was *Songs of Chu*. Several decades of excavations have brought to light archaeological evidence that Chu had a fairly advanced culture of a clearly romantic tinge. As such, the *Songs of Chu* is closely connected with Chu culture. The originator and representative writer of *Songs of Chu* was a renowned poet of that kingdom by the name of Qu Yuan. During the reign (32–8 BC) of Emperor Cheng of the Han Dynasty, Liu Xiang compiled the works of Qu Yuan, Song Yu and others into a book he titled *Songs of Chu*. From this time on, *Songs of Chu* became the name for a general collection of poems and ballads of this type.

Qu Yuan (about 340–277 BC), originally named Ping, was born into an aristocratic family which had fallen on hard times in the Kingdom of Chu. He held two official positions in the government and won the confidence of King Huai. As far as domestic affairs were concerned, he advocated the promotion of the meritorious and able, and in external affairs urged a policy of friendship with the State of Qi in opposition to the State of Qin. However, slandered by the conservatives in the Chu aristocracy, Qu Yuan found himself distanced from King Huai, who finally sent him into exile. On his lonely road to banishment, Qu Yuan came to the conclusion that the Kingdom of Chu was doomed and untold hardships were in store for its people, and their salvation was beyond his power. Not wanting to leave his native land, Qu Yuan drowned himself in the Miluo River.

There is some controversy over the authenticity of some poems ascribed to Qu Yuan. Those that can be confirmed as his are the more important ones such as the "Li Sao," "Asking Heaven," "Nine Songs" and "Nine Pieces."

Qu Yuan's fine character comes out in his poems; for instance his spirit of "inflexible independence" in "Song of the Tangerine Bush," his attitude of "High and low I search alone" in the "Li Sao" and his dedication to "constant self-improvement" also in the "Li Sao." His ardent love for his homeland is without comparison. In the midst of political strife he strictly adhered to his principles, and never allowed himself to drift with the tide. He was passionately fond of the truth, which he pursued doggedly. He clung to his fine political ideals, and was never tainted by the forces of corruption. His magnificent poems, resplendent and colorful, flowing and subtle are filled with a lofty and infectious attraction.

In his "Li Sao," Qu Yuan focuses on two themes – the right way ahead for the Kingdom of Chu and the right way ahead for himself. Early on in this poem he points out the dangers on the road ahead for Chu. He expresses his hope that the king will follow the highroad of good government and the welfare of the people. The king, however, instead of appreciating his loyalty and sincerity gave ear to slanderous tongues, and sent Qu Yuan into exile. Qu Yuan composed this long poem to express both his faithfulness and his grief. He was unwilling to give up the struggle but at the same time refused to be sullied by court politics. Remembering past wrongs and vexed in his innermost heart, Qu Yuan was torn by a tangled web of all sorts of painful emotions. But he took heart from the story of the legendary Emperor Shun to formulate his own political ideas, and decided to make one more effort to save his homeland. Buoyed up with new hope he embarked on another long search, and it was then that his poetic creation reached a new and more brilliant stage:

> I ordered Xi Ho to stay the sun-steeds' gallop/
> To gaze on Mount Yanzi, and not go in/
> Long, long had been my road/
> And far, far was the journey/
> I would go up and down to seek/
> My heart's desire/
> I watered my dragon steeds at the Pool of Heaven/
> And tied the reins to the Fusang tree/
> I broke a sprig of the Ruo tree/
> To lash the sun with/
> I wanted to roam a little at leisure/
> I sent Wang Shu ahead to ride before me/
> The Wind God went behind as my outrider/
> The Bird of Heaven gave notice of my coming/
> And the Thunder God told me when all was not ready/
> I caused my phoenixes to mount on their pinions/
> And fly ever onward, by night and by day/
> The whirlwinds gathered and came out to meet me/
> Leading clouds and rainbows to give me welcome.

But his search was fruitless, as he was unable to find an opportunity to put his ideals into practice. So he took the advice of Ling Fen the fortune teller and Wu Xian the wizard, and made preparations to leave his home, the Kingdom of Chu. He set off jauntily enough, speeding to the west. But when he suddenly caught a glimpse of his hometown at dawn both his charioteer and horses were seized with nostalgia, and refused to continue:

> But when I had ascended the splendor of the heavens/
> I suddenly caught a glimpse below of my old home/
> The groom's heart was heavy, and the horses for longing/

Arched their heads back and refused to go on/
Enough! I say. There are no true men in the state/
Men who understand me. Why should I cleave/
To the town of my birth? Since no one is worthy/
To join me in building good government/
I will go and join Peng Xian in the place where he abides.

He is saying that he would rather die than leave his homeland. This is the end of this long poem. The "Li Sao" is divided into three major sections. The text before the sentence "My sister Nvxu scolded me" comprises the first section, and that following the sentence constitutes the second. The rest of the text succeeding the discussion of praying for good fortune makes up the third section. These sections form three regular opening and closing parts, and each starts off in hope and ends in despair. Hope and despair weave in and out and form a net which is impossible to untangle – a whirlpool of unfathomable feelings which leaves reverberations in the mind of the reader.

The "Nine" in the title "Nine Songs" represents the number of musical movements that go to make up the tune of each. The "Nine Songs" actually contains 11 pieces, including those used in sacrifices to various deities. Some describe man's adoration and praise of the spirits, and others tell stories of love between deities. They are rich in romantic coloring, and later writers have simply been unable to match them for the implicit beauty of their language and their depth of feeling. Let us take a look at one of them, the "Lesser Wielder of Fate":

Autumn orchids and daphnegenkwa,
Are growing in the entire courtyard.
White flowers amidst green leaves,
They greet me with their fragrance.
People naturally have their children,
But why do you look so melancholy?
The orchids are vibrant and verdant,
With purple stems among the leaves,
The room is full of praying women,
Suddenly greet me with ogling eyes.
Not uttering a word I come and go
Riding a wind and holding a cloud.
Nothing is sadder than parting in life;
A new friend is the best thing to have.
In lotuses attire and sweet-clover band,
I unexpectedly come and abruptly go.
Sleeping on the outskirts of Heaven,
Whom are you expecting in the clouds?
I shampoo with you where the sun sets
And I dry my hair where the sunrises.
The beauty I'm awaiting fails to come;
In the wind I sing with sour bitterness.

Beneath a canopy of peacock feathers,
Riding to the space to stroke the comet.
With a sword and a baby in each hand,
You are the one to take charge for us.[24]

The "Lesser Wielder of Fate" is a female deity who "decides whether man will have successors or not."[25] The entire poem is an incantation by a male shaman who presides at a sacrifice, and expresses his love for and worship of her. She suddenly descends from Heaven and, after glancing at the singer with deep emotion, just as suddenly departs. High up in the clouds, she prepares to mount a carriage in which to soar to Heaven. In one hand she bears a long sword, with the other she embraces a child. This child is the guardian spirit, powerful, kindly, steadfast and gentle, and respected and loved by all mankind.

In summary, it can be said that the *Songs of Chu* are enveloped in an atmosphere of myth, and it is in these poems that we can see how closely the spirit world and the human world are connected. There is great artistic appeal in the way the poems describe communication and love between the two, the human attributes of the spirits, the ways in which friendships are formed between humans and immortals, and even in the mysterious atmosphere of the poems themselves and the customs and landscapes of Chu.

The *Book of Odes* and the *Songs of Chu* are products of different times and different places, and represent two different kinds of beauty. The *Book of Odes* has a pungent odor of life and the soil. Its poems are plain and straightforward, and genuinely moving. The poems in the *Songs of Chu*, on the other hand, have a powerful coloring of the legendary and the heroic. They are fantastic and romantic, and profoundly affecting. The *Songs of Chu* represents a new concept of esthetics which arose during the Warring States Period. This era was one in which philosophers emerged, doubting, probing and thinking. It was an era when commonplace customs and practices and stereotyped formulae increasingly came under scrutiny and rejection. The "hundred schools of thought" which arose at this time encouraged men to make new explorations into the realm of esthetics. And this resulted in refreshingly new individual artistic creations. The appearance of Qu Yuan exactly fitted the criteria of the time.

The *Songs of Chu* and the *Book of Odes* also show clear differences in terms of structure. Most of the poems in the latter consist of four characters to a line. They are short, divided into stanzas and with a repetition between each stanza. The poems in the *Songs of Chu*, with the "Li Sao", "Nine Songs" and "Nine Pieces" as examples, are much longer in terms of both lines and overall length. The "Li Sao," for instance, has 373 lines and over 2,400 characters.

The most characteristic feature of the forms of the poems in the *Songs of Chu* is the use of the word "xi (兮)," which expresses a sort of sigh. In addition, there is the coordinated use of the function words "qi (其)," "yi (以)," "yu (与)," "yu (于)," "er (而)" and others, to balance the meter of the lines. Generally speaking, there are three kinds of poetic lines in the Songs of Chu:

For the first kind, we can quote from "Li Sao", which has the character "xi" at the end of each odd-numbered line, marking a major caesura. In the middle of each line is a function word, marking a minor caesura. Two models of this arrangement follow:

The days and months hurried on, never delaying/
Springs and autumns sped by in endless alternation/
I thought how the trees and flowers were fading and falling/
And feared that my Fairest's beauty would fade too.
And
I watered my dragon steeds at the Pool of Heaven/
And tied the reins to the Fusang tree/
I broke a sprig of the Ruo tree/
To lash the sun with/
I wanted to roam a little at leisure.
This verse pattern can be represented as follows:
○○○×○◎, ○○○×○○ ;
○○○×○◎, ○○○×○○。

"Xi" was equivalent to the modern "Ah", and was a sighing sound, without any concrete meaning. Function words signified grammatical connection, and could be omitted or replaced by another character without affecting the original meaning. For instance:

The days and months hurried on, never delaying/
Springs and autumns sped by in endless alternation/
I thought how the trees and flowers were fading and falling/
And feared that my Fairest's beauty would fade too.

The second version contains the function words "er," "yi," "zhi" and "qi" in verses 1–4 respectively.

This shows how function words can be inserted in certain definite places in the "Li Sao," serving to adjust the overall syllabic rhythm so that the verses are lengthened, slowed and more subtle. "Xi" and the function words also appear in the words of the songs of Yuan Dynasty (1206–1368) drama to balance the verses. If they are underemphasized or dropped altogether, only the bare bones of a five-character verse remain:

I watered my dragon steeds at the Pool of Heaven/
And tied the reins to the Fusang tree/
I broke a sprig of the Ruo tree/
To lash the sun with/
I wanted to roam a little at leisure.

Another pattern in the *Songs of Chu* appears in the "Nine Songs." This pattern does not use concrete function words, but "xi" occurs inside each verse, dividing each into a front part and a back part. For instance:

The princess is coming to the north bank;
In anxiety, I am longing for your arrival.
The autumn breezes are blowing my way,
Rippling the leaf-covered Dongting Lake.
And:
Not uttering a word I come and go
Riding a wind and holding a cloud.
Nothing is sadder than parting in life;
A new friend is the best thing to have.

In the "Nine Songs," "xi" is used where a function word is used in the "Li Sao." Or we could say that the "xi" of the "Li Sao" is moved from the end of the verse to inside the verse. This pattern can be described as follows:

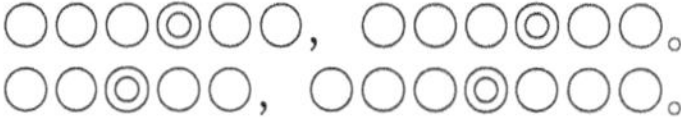

"Xi" sometimes divides a verse into two equal parts of two or three characters each. Sometimes it divides it unequally into parts of three and two characters respectively, and finally it can be under-emphasized and then omitted entirely, leaving a five-character verse.

And so, it could be said that most of the poems in the *Songs of Chu* are characterized by five characters to each verse. But if the latter two-three pattern of verses is taken as the standard, then the poems in the *Songs of Chu* can be regarded as reversed three-two verses. It could also be said that the five-character nature of the poems in the *Songs of Chu*, by introducing this variation, became the source of the later fashionable five-character composition. But, as here we do not intend to discuss the origin of the five-character poems there is no need to discuss whether or not they evolved from the *Songs of Chu*. All I wish to say here is that the poems of the *Songs of Chu* have a basic framework of five-character verses, and this style could well have evolved into the later fashionable five-character poems. A little adjustment was all that was needed, but nobody at that time seems to have made the attempt.

The third pattern used in the *Songs of Chu* appears in the "Summons of the Soul" and the "Great Summons." Here, "xi" is replaced at the end of even-numbered lines by "xie (些)" or "zhi (只)". For example:

There are giants there, a thousand fathoms tall/
Who seek only for souls to catch/
And ten suns that come out together/
Melting metal, dissolving stone. (Summons of the Soul)

This pattern can be represented as follows:
○○○○，○○○○◎。

"Xie" merely represents a sighing sound. If it is under-emphasized or omitted it leaves two four-character lines. This type of line pattern is not a fresh one; a much more important one is the following:

The lovely girls are drunk with wine/
Their faces flushed and red/
With amorous glances and flirting looks/
Their eyes like wavelets sparkle. (Summons of the Soul)
Green Spring receiveth/
he vacant earth/
The white sun shineth/
Spring wind provoketh/
To burst and burgeon/
each sprout and flower.
(Great Summons)
This pattern can be described as follows:
○○○○，○○○◎。

If "xie" and "zhi," which represent sighs, are under-emphasized or omitted, and their lines are run together, they form seven-character verses of four and three characters each, which is exactly the pattern of the later fashionable seven-character poems. Worthy of note too is an irregular pattern which also occurs in the "Summons of the Soul":

On, on the river's waters roll/
Above them grow woods of maple/
The eye travels on a thousand *li*/
And the heart breaks for sorrow.
This pattern can be described as follows:
○○○○◎○○○，○○○○◎○○○。

If the sighing sound "xi" is under-emphasized or omitted, we have a standard seven-character poem divided into four- and three-character verses.

Occasionally seven-character verses are found in the *Book of Odes* too. For instance, the "Xiao Min" in the "Minor Court Hymns" section: "They are like one taking counsel with wayfarers about building a house." This verse has seven characters, but it does not match the later fashion for seven-character poems. In fact, the seven-character verses in the *Songs of Chu*, discussed above are fundamentally different from those of the *Book of Odes*. And so, Zhao Yi of the Qing Dynasty in his *Study of the Works of Gai Yu* and Qian Daxin, also of the Qing Dynasty, in his *Records of Fostering New Things in the Ten-chariots Studio* both emphasize that the new seven-character poem was a rebirth of that of the *Songs of*

Chu in a new form. Liang Qichao in his *Chinese Belles Lettres and their History* and Chen Zhongfan in his *The Literature of the Han, Wei and Six Dynasties* hold up Xiang Yu's "Song of Gaixia," Liu Bang's "Song of the Great Wind" and Zhang Heng's "Poem of Four Sorrows" as evidence of the deterioration of the seven-character poem since the *Songs of Chu*. There is some merit in this argument.

The Music Bureau of the Han Dynasty: origin and development

Another source of poetry and ballads after the *Book of Odes* and the *Songs of Chu* was the Music Bureau of the Han Dynasty. The two former works had a deep and widespread influence on not only the poetry and ballad genre but on Chinese literature as a whole. But the four-character format of the *Book of Odes* soon became ossified, and the formats used in the *Songs of Chu* were not able to sustain the production of a large number of fine works. Four-character poems produced in the Han Dynasty, such as Wei Meng's "Words of Advice" and Sima Xiangru's "Ode for the Mount Tai Sacrifice," and poems written in the same dynasty in *Songs of Chu* styles, such as Dongfang Shuo's "Seven Admonishments" and Wang Bao's "Nine Longings" are only imitations and lack any artistic originality. However, at the same time the government Music Bureau collected and arranged folk ballads, which showed a new charm and a fresh vitality. These works originated among the common people and were later adopted by the literati and displayed an irresistible strength. And it was from the Music Bureau's collection that a new cadence and a new format emerged in the shape of the immortal five-character verse.

The Music Bureau was the name of an office dealing with music set up by the Han Dynasty court. Its duties were to collect songs from among the common people, arrange them, set them to music and perform them. However, a gold-plated bell unearthed in the 1970s and dating from the Qin Dynasty (221–206 BC) bore the characters for "Music Bureau" on the top, so it seems that there was already a Music Bureau before the Han Dynasty.[26] The Han Dynasty Music Bureau seems to have been abolished later, only to be revived and expanded in the time of Han Emperor Wu (140–86 BC). According to the *History of the Han Dynasty * Records of the Rites and Music*, "When Emperor Wu decided to hold the Suburban Sacrifice . . . he set up the Music Bureau, which collected songs and had them sung in the evening. There were songs from Zhao, Dai, Qin and Chu."[27] Later, the folk songs that had been collected, arranged and performed by the Music Bureau were called "Music Bureau Poetry," "The Words of Music Bureau Songs" or simply "Music Bureau" for short. "Collected Poems of the Music Bureau" compiled by Guo Maoqian of the Song Dynasty, in 100 volumes, records songs from the earliest times down to the "New Music Bureau" of the Tang (618–907) and Five Dynasties period (907–960). This is the most comprehensive collection of Music Bureau works. There are more than 40 chapters devoted to Han Dynasty Music Bureau poems and songs, notable of which are the chapters "Xianghe Song Lyrics," "Music for Drums and Flutes" and "Miscellaneous Tunes and Songs."

The special characteristic of the "Xianghe Song Lyrics" was that "stringed and wind instruments were in special harmony, and the singer beat time."[28] The singer beat a percussion instrument called a "jie" or a "jiegu" as accompaniment to the string and wind instruments in the orchestra. This type of singing performance was somewhat like the modern "guci" popular in modern North China, except that "guci" does not have string and wind accompaniment. The various "Xianghe Song Lyrics" nearly all originated in street ballads either without accompaniment or with one singer and three accompanists. The structure of these songs was fairly simple. Most of them had a straightforward tune and "ci" and "sheng." The "ci" were the words of the songs, while the "sheng" were function words used to fill out a line. Volume 26 of the "Collected Poems of the Music Bureau" explains "Xianghe Song Lyrics" as follows: "Every tune has its 'ci' and 'sheng.' The 'ci' are the words of the song, and the 'sheng' are empty fillers, like 'yi' and 'ye'."[29] Referring to the *Records of Ancient and Modern Music*, as part of its "Six Strands of Xianghe," the same volume of the same book says, "All the Xianghe songs had seven kinds of accompanying instruments, viz, the *sheng* (a wind instrument made of bamboo pipes of various lengths), the *di* (flute), the *jiegu* (drum), *qin* (zither), *se* and *pipa* (both types of lute)."[30] Aristocratic banquets during the Han Dynasty usually featured music and dancing, as can be seen from painted tomb bricks of that period excavated in Jiaxiang in Shandong Province and Nanyang in Henan Province. These depictions also help us understand how the Music Bureau items were performed. The "percussion and wind tunes" were folk tunes from Northern China which were adopted in the reign of Emperor Wu as martial music. As for the "Lyrics of the Mixed Melodies" both the words and notes are lost and cannot be recovered.

A characteristic of the Han Dynasty Music Bureau was that the contents of its poems and songs were "Its feeling sprang from sorrowful airs, and it produced a sense of predestined things."[31] This "sense of predestined things" has often been interpreted as merely narrative in nature, but this is not entirely accurate. Narrative is only one aspect of the items in the Han Dynasty Music Bureau's collection. The phrase "sense of predestined things" does not have this exclusive meaning. It refers to singing about certain things felt to be the products of actual life. It means written works springing from feelings, and not feelings springing from written works. The "things" part of the phrase refers to the points at which poetic emotions are sparked off. In poems and songs these "things" can be described or not. "Predestined things" and narrated things are not identical. "Producing a sense of predestined things" is a realistic expression and a condensed one. But when writers of later generations studied the Music Bureau's "producing a sense of predestined things," they did not write empty works. Society and human life which they saw before their very eyes spurred them to take their material from concrete reality with which to record their feelings and ideas, even drawing them to the weighty problems of society and politics, i.e. the national economy and the people's livelihood. This resulted in literary works of practical significance. "Producing a sense of predestined things," as the spirit of the Han Dynasty Music Bureau, was studied and inherited by later literary figures, and became a fine tradition of

Chinese culture. And this is where its importance lies. It is also important because such leading poets as Du Fu, Yuan Jie, Bai Juyi and Pi Rixiu studied the Music Bureau's poems and songs.

The spirit of the Han Dynasty Music Bureau was inherited and developed by literary figures of later generations, and from it was born a new style of poetry marked by five characters to a verse. So its influence on Chinese poetry and ballads should not be underestimated. The typical format of the five-character poetry was two cadences per verse divided into two units of first two syllables and then three syllables. The *Songs of Chu* had five-character verses, but in their case the three-syllable cadence preceded the two-syllable one, and so they can not be considered true five-character poems. In the "Eighteen Tunes for Cymbal Songs," a surviving work dating from the Western Han Dynasty (206 BC–25 AD), most of the pieces are marked by the five-character style of the Music Bureau poems. Let us take a look at "Deep in Thought":

> The one I love lives south of the sea.
> What shall I give him as a keepsake?
> Here's a hairpin made of turtle shell
> Adorned with pearls and jade rings.
> Now that I've learned of his betrayal,
> I am smashing and burning them all,
> And let the wind scatter their ashes.
> From now on I'll never think of him,
> And he won't expect to think of me.
> He and his wife must know our tryst;
> For we may have stirred up their dog.
> Alas, I feel worse in the fall wind,
> I'll tell him everything when it's bright.[32]

This poem has nine verses of five characters each, divided into two cadences of first two characters and then three. Such five-character poems appear frequently in the Music Bureau collection of the Western Han Dynasty. Typical is the ancient-style "South of the River" from the "Harmonizing Songs":

> Plucking lotus blossoms in the land south of the Yangtze River. How fragrant their leaves! Fishes play among the lotus leaves. They play east of the lotus leaves. They play west of the lotus leaves. They play south of the lotus leaves, and they play north of them too.[33]

This ancient poem already has a complete set of five-character verses. It is a poem with a free and natural charm, without a trace of any deliberate attempt at embellishment, and a rare and excellent piece of versifying. Another example of a poem made up completely of five-character verses is "Watering my Horse at a Gap in the Great Wall," which describes the feelings of a man thinking about his wife. It borrows details of real life and is in the form of a letter from a husband far away. Its expression of longing is particularly profound:

> Green grows the grass by the riverside, long the road which leads my thoughts away. A road too long to imagine, at dawn in a dream I see him. I dream I see him standing by me, then I wake and know that he is in some strange place. Some strange place in some strange county, I toss and turn, and he is seen no more. The withered mulberry tree knows the wind, and the sea knows the cold. He enters and we look at each other pleased, but who is willing to exchange words? A guest comes from afar, offering me a pair of carp. I tell the servant to fry them, together with the fish there is a letter. Kneeling, I read it slowly; what does it say? It starts with instructions about the fish dish, and then recounts memories from long ago.[34]

In a dream her husband is standing beside her. But when she wakens she knows that he is on the far frontier. "I dream I see him standing by me, then I wake and know that he is in some strange place." These ten characters in the original very appropriately utilize a common occurrence from everyday life. The wife was hoping to receive news of her husband's return in the letter, but it simply contains details of how to cook the fish and then writes of old memories. The wife's feelings of disappointment are implicit in the poem.

"The Peacock Flies Southeast" is a long narrative poem. It describes the tragic married life of Jiao Zhongqing and Liu Lanzhi. At first they were a very loving couple, but they are separated due to the enmity of Liu Lanzhi's mother-in-law. Her elder brother wants her to marry someone else, and a local official tries to bully her into marrying him. In protest, Liu Lanzhi kills herself. When he hears the news, Jiao Zhongqing also commits suicide. They are buried together on the side of Mount Hua. Thereafter, every night a pair of mandarin ducks is heard calling, perched on a tree growing near the grave. The story is not a complicated one, but there is no shortage of detailed dialogue in the narrative and, intermingled with some lyrical elements, the poem shows some definitely new techniques of expression. Let us look at the section which describes the lovers' parting:

> A governor's clerk drags ahead on horseback,
> Followed by his newly wed wife in the wagon,
> Which rolled along squeaking and screeching,
> Till they came to a stop at a main crossroad.
> Alighting the horse he clambered into the cart,
> Tête-à-tête he murmured into his wife's ear,
> "Ne'er shall we be apart, so go home for now,
> And I'm starting off for the governor's office.
> Before long I'll come back and be with you;
> I swear to heaven that I'll never betray you.
> Said the newlywed wife to her dear husband:

"I'm grateful for your loving commitment.
As you my husband love me so very much,
I expect you to return as soon as you can.
I compare you my darling to a large crag,
While I compare myself to pampas grass.
'Cause pampas grass is tough and tensile,
And a crag stands firm and unshakable.
But as you know I have a brother at home,
Who has as hot a temper as a thunderbolt,
And may not give me freedom for action.
Thinking of this I feel worried to no end."
Then they waved good-bye at each other,
Finding it hard to tear themselves away.[35]

We can see from the poems handed down to us today that five-character-verse poetry has been written since the Han Dynasty. From the Western Han Dynasty we have such poems attributed to Mei Cheng, Li Ling, Su Shi and Ban Jieyu, but their authentication awaits further study. It is commonly accepted that earliest five-character-verse poem extant is "Singing of History" by Ban Gu of the Eastern Han Dynasty (25–220 AD). It tells the story of the filial daughter Tiying of the time of Western Han Dynasty Emperor Wen (179–156 BC), who offered herself as a concubine in order to save her father from punishment. Nineteen ancient poems in the five-character format appeared by unknown authors in the latter part of the Eastern Han Dynasty. They were included in the *Collected Works of Zhao Ming* under the title, "Nineteen Ancient Poems." These works demonstrate the artistic level of the authors of five-character poems of that dynasty. Liu Xie calls them the "crowning glory of the five-character mode." (*Carving a Dragon with a Literary Heart * Explanation of Poetry*). Their themes center on the traveler far from home and thinking of his wife and disappointment while pursuing and official career, sometimes accompanied by lamentation at the shortness of life. For example:

Off you go to a faraway place,
Leaving us separated forever.
Each is at one end of the world,
With ten thousand *li* between us.
Facing the distance and obstacles,
When can we meet once again?
Northern horses like north wind;
Southern birds perch southward.
The longer lasts the separation,
The smaller I look in my clothes.
As drifting clouds shield the sun;
So wanderers forget to miss home.
Thinking of you I'm getting old,
A year's unnoticeably passing by.

All I want to say I put in a wish:
Have good health and appetite.[36]

This poem describes the emotion of a wife missing her husband who has journeyed far from home. It expresses sadness and misgiving: Even barbarian horses and the birds of the deep south miss their homes. But does her husband? Another example is:

Altair, distant Star of the Cowherd,
Vega, brilliant Star of the Weaver.
With her fair-skinned slender hands,
Tsiek, tsiek, she's busy at her loom.
Not a piece of fabric can she make,
All day long her tears fall like rain.
Clear is the Milky Way, the Silver River,
How far apart can the two souls be?
Facing each other across the waters,
They're unable to express their love.[37]

This poem imagines the Cowherd and the Weaving Maid (two stars about which a legend was woven) gazing at each other across the barrier of the Milky Way, unable to exchange a word. In fact, the poem expresses a universal emotion. The lines "A turbulent river in between them, dumbly longing for each other" exude a spirit which indirectly reaches the acme of beauty.

The above discussion has traced three sources of Chinese poetry and ballads – the *Book of Odes*, the *Songs of Chu* and the Han Dynasty Music Bureau. In the two aspects of spirit and form it was the works in the collection of the Han Dynasty Music Bureau that later generations inherited. It was chiefly the spirit of the *Book of Odes* and the *Songs of Chu* that influenced the creation of poetry and ballads of later generations; their forms did not fully develop in the realm of poetry and ballads. Nevertheless, it is interesting to note that the *Book of Odes* and the *Songs of Chu* helped to bring about a different genre – the *fu* style of poetry.

Notes

1 Qiyou, Chen: *Mr. Lv's Spring and Autumn Annals Emended and Translated*, Vol.5, Xuelin Publishing Company, 1984, P. 284.
2 [Han Dynasty] Ye, Zhao: *The Spring and Autumn Annals of the Kingdoms of Wu and Yue*, Vol.9, "Unauthorized Story of King Goujian's Conspiracy," *Collected Writings of the Four Basic Branches of Literature*.
3 Wenlan, Fan: *Carving a Dragon With a Literary Heart Annotated*, Vol.6, People's Literature Publishing House, 1978, P. 519.
4 [Han Dynasty] Gu, Ban: *History of the Han Dynasty*, Vol.24, *Food and Goods*, Zhonghua Book Company, 1962, P. 1123.
5 [Han Dynasty] Gu, Ban: *History of the Han Dynasty*, Vol.30, *Records of Art and Literature*, Zhonghua Book Company, 1962, P. 1708.

6 [Han Dynasty] Qian, Sima: *Records of the Historian*, Vol.47, Zhonghua Book Company, 1959, P. 1936.
7 In "Confucius' Discussion of Poetry" there is a difference in the nomenclature and arrangement of the categories in the *Book of Odes*. Where the latter has "Airs," "Minor Court Hymns," "Major Court Hymns" and "Eulogies," the former has "Song" (Eulogies), "Great Xia," Small Xia" and "Airs of the States." See the *Warring States Bamboo Records* (1) in the collection of the Shanghai Museum, Shanghai Ancient Books Publishing House, 2001.
8 [Qing Dynasty] Yuan, Ruan: *The Yanjing House Collection*, Vol.1, *Rendering Hymns*, Third year of the Daoguang reign period (1823) block print by the Wexuanlou.
9 [Song Dynasty] Xi, Zhu: *A Collection of Poems Handed Down * Zhounan * Geqin*, Annotated, Zhonghua Book Company Shanghai Editorial Section, 1958, P. 3.
10 *Commentary on the Thirteen Classics*, World Bookstore photocopy of the Ruan woodblock print, P. 374.
11 *Commentary on the Thirteen Classics*, World Bookstore photocopy of the Ruan woodblock print, P. 359.
12 *Commentary on the Thirteen Classics*, World Bookstore photocopy of the Ruan woodblock print, P. 377.
13 *The Rites of Zhou*, Vol.23, *Spring Official * Great Master*, Commentary by Zheng Xuan, Explanation by Zheng Zhong, *Commentary on the Thirteen Classics*, World Bookstore photocopy of the Ruan woodblock print, P. 796.
14 Wenlan, Fan: *Carving a Dragon With a Literary Heart Annotated*, People's Literature Publishing House, 1978, P. 601.
15 [Song Dynasty] Yin, Hu: *A Collection of Brilliance*, Vol.18, "Introduction to Li Shuyi," from *The First Collection of the Complete Four Repositories*.
16 *The Orthodox Mao Poems*, Vol.4, *Commentary on the Thirteen Classics*, World Bookstore photocopy of the Ruan woodblock print, P. 342.
17 "Book of Odes * Zhounan * Osprey," *Commentary on the Thirteen Classics*, World Bookstore photocopy of the Ruan woodblock print, PP. 273–274.
18 "Book of Odes * Zhounan * Plantains," *Commentary on the Thirteen Classics*, World Bookstore photocopy of the Ruan woodblock print, P. 281.
19 [Qing Dynasty] Yurun, Fang: *Origins of the Book of Odes*, proofread by Li Xian'geng, Zhonghua Book Company, 1986, P. 85.
20 Guanying, Yu: *Selections From the Book of Odes*, People's Literature Publishing House, 1979, p. 11.
21 *Book of Odes * Airs of Wei * Bo Xi, Commentary on the Thirteen Classics*, World Bookstore photocopy of the Ruan woodblock print, P. 327.
22 *Commentary on the Thirteen Classics*, World Bookstore photocopy of the Ruan woodblock print, P. 2461.
23 *The Orthodox Mao Poems, Commentary on the Thirteen Classics*, World Bookstore photocopy of the Ruan woodblock print, P. 6.
24 [Song Dynasty] Xingzu, Hong: *Additional Commentary on the Songs of Chu*, Vol.2, Zhonghua Book Company, 1983, P. 74.
25 [Qing Dynasty] Fuzhi, Wang: *A Complete Explanation of the Songs of Chu*, Shanghai People's Publishing House, 1975, P. 36.
26 See Xiaoxin, Kou: "An Investigation of the Qin and Han Music Bureau," *Journal of Shaanxi Normal University*, 1978, Issue 1.
27 [Han Dynasty] Gu, Ban: *History of the Han Dynasty*, Vol.22, *Records of the Rites and Music*, Zhonghua Book Company, 1962, P. 1045.

28 [Liang Dynasty] Yue, Shen: *History of the Song Dynasty*, Vol.21, *Records of Music 3*, Zhonghua Book Company, 1974, P. 603.
29 [Song Dynasty] Maoqian, Guo: *Collected Poems of the Music Bureau*, Zhonghua Book Company, 1979, P. 376.
30 [Song Dynasty] Maoqian, Guo: *Collected Poems of the Music Bureau*, Zhonghua Book Company, 1979, P. 377.
31 [Han Dynasty] Gu, Ban: *History of the Han Dynasty*, Vol.30, *Records of Art and Literature * A Short Discussion on Shi and Fu Poetry*, Zhonghua Book Company, 1962, P. 1756.
32 [Song Dynasty] Maoqian, Guo: *Collected Poems of the Music Bureau*, Vol.16, *Words and Music for Drums and Flutes * Eighteen Han Cymbal Tunes*, Zhonghua Book Company, 1979, P. 230.
33 [Song Dynasty] Maoqian, Guo: *Collected Poems of the Music Bureau*, Vol.26, *Harmonizing Songs*, Zhonghua Book Company, 1979, P. 384.
34 [Tang Dynasty] Li Shan, Lv Yanji et al: *Selection of the Major Writings of Six Officials*, Vol.27, *Collected Writings of the Four Basic Branches of Literature*.
35 [Chen Dynasty] Ling, Xu ed: *New Chants From the Jade Terrace*, Vol.1, *Collected Writings of the Four Basic Branches of Literature*.
36 [Tang Dynasty] Shan, Li, Yanji, Lv et al: *Selection of the Major Writings of Six Officials*, Vol.29, *Collected Writings of the Four Basic Branches of Literature*.
37 [Tang Dynasty] Shan, Li, Yanji, Lv et al: *Selection of the Major Writings of Six Officials*, Vol.29, *Collected Writings of the Four Basic Branches of Literature*.

2 The rise and fall of *shi* and *fu* poetry

The rise of the *fu* poetry of the Han Dynasty

The word *fu* (rhapsody or poetic exposition) was originally one of the "Six Formats" of poetry, namely *feng* (airs), *ya* (hymns), *song* (eulogies), *fu* (straightforward), *bi* (simile) and *xing* (with introduction). About this, Ban Gu, in his "Preface to the *Fu* Poetry of Two Capitals": "Some people say that *fu* is a branch of ancient poetry." The same author, in his *History of the Han Dynasty * Records of Art and Literature*, says, "Recitation without chanting is called *fu*." Later it became the custom to distinguish between poetry and *fu*, with the latter specifically a genre for reading aloud. In the *Carving a Dragon with a Literary Heart * Explanation of Fu Poetry* we find, "And so *fu* was given its name by poets, and had its origin in the *Songs of Chu*. It is generally accepted today that *fu* is connected with both the *Book of Odes* and the *Songs of Chu*. But we must also take notice of the fact that in the course of its formation *fu* incorporated some elements of pre-Qin prose. Zhang Xuecheng, in his *Chapter 15 of General Meaning of Proofreading * Shi and Fu Poetry from the Treatise on Literature of the History of the Han Dynasty* says, "The *fu* masters of antiquity entered the ranks of the literary figures of the Warring States Period from the *Book of Odes* and the *Songs of Chu*. For instance, the works of Zhuangzi and Liezi transmit parables; Su Zhang's sweeping style is an example of a broad wielding of power; Han Fei's 'Store of Words' is an example of parallelism leading to harmony; and the significance of classifying *Spring and Autumn Annals of Mr. Lv* lies in verifying its materials and putting them together properly." There are similar and very incisive explanations in the same author's *Comprehensive History of Literature * Poetry Section.*

According to extant materials, Xun Kuang of the State of Zhao in the latter part of the Warring States Period was the first to write poetry in the *fu* style. In the "*Shi* and *Fu* Poetry Section" of *History of the Han Dynasty * Records of Art and Literature*, we find "Ten *fu* poems by Sun Qing." Sun Qing was Xun Kuang, also called Xun Qing. Today in the book called *Xunzi* there are *fu* poems which celebrate the Rites, knowledge, clouds, silkworms and admonition. In addition there is a book called *Complete Xiang Lyrics*, where *xiang* is a type of ancient ballad, showing that Xun Kuang's *fu* poetry was influenced by folk literature. His *fu* works are basically written in four-character style with rhymes ending even lines and express his emotions through describing concrete objects. Another *fu* poet of the latter part of the Warring States Period was Song Yu of the Kingdom of Chu. In the "*Shi* and *Fu* Poetry Section" of *History of the Han Dynasty * Records of Art and Literature*, we find "Sixteen *fu* poems by Song Yu." Only ten *fu* poems attributed to Song Yu exist today, and only four of them which are included in the *Selected Works of Literature* can be accounted authentic. These are the "*Fu* Poem on Wind", "*Fu* Poem on Exalted Tang," "*Fu* Poem on Fairy Lady" and "Dengtu Zi's *Fu* Poem on Lust for Women." In the *Records of the Historian * Biographies of Qu Yuan and Jia Yi*, it says, "After Qu Yuan's death, his disciples Song Yu, Tang Le and Jing Chai – all of the Kingdom of Chu – devoted themselves to literature and expressed themselves in the form of *fu* poetry. Regarding Qu Yuan as their master, they spoke bluntly, using the same relaxed wording that he had used."[1] Four-, five- and seven-line verses can all be found scattered through Song Yu's *fu* works, and the phrasing of the *Songs of Chu* appears in many places. His writing style is lengthy, vigorous and wide-ranging, even tending to exaggeration and wordy elaboration. In all of these traits the influence of the *Songs of Chu* can be identified. In his "*Fu* Poem on Exalted Tang" Song Yu describes how King Huai of Chu encounters in a dream the goddess of Mount Wu, who describes herself as "clouds in the morning and rain in the evening." As narrated by Song Yu, the story goes as follows:

> Once, King Xiang of Chu and Song Yu toured the Yunmengtai (Cloud and Dream Tableland). Looking at the Gaotang Tower in the distance, they spotted a strange cloud hovering above it soaring like a mountain. All of sudden, it began to change its shape, which varied from minute to minute. King Xiang asked Song Yu what that cloud was, and Song answered, "It's the so-called Morning Cloud." The king then asked the reason for the name. Song Yu replied, "During his visit to the Gaotang Tower, an emperor of ancient times became tired and dozed off while it was still light. He dreamed of a fair lady who told him that she lived on Mount Wu and was visiting the Gaotang Tower. Learning that the king was also a visitor, she said she would like to recommend herself to him as his sleeping companion. The king readily consented, and slept with her. Before her departure, she told the king that she lived on the precipitous mountain south of Mount Wu. She said that she took the form of a morning cloud at sunrise and drifting rain at dusk. 'So I'm hanging around the south side of the tower day and night.'" The next morning the king observed that what Song Yu had told him was true. Therefore, he had a temple built and dedicated to the fair lady, and named it "Morning Cloud." He then told Song Yu: "Try and come up with a rhapsody for this spectacle for me." Song Yu agreed.

Where the Gaotang Tower stands, the magnificent view of the locale has no match, not even boundless Mount Wu, with crisscrossing paths meandering up its side. Looking down from its precipitous cliff, a deep pool lies against the vertical slope of great length. Immediately after rain, the water in the myriads of ravines comes together in torrents.[2]

In view of this close relationship between *fu* and the *Songs of Chu*, works by Qu Yuan came to be known as *fu* in the Han Dynasty. (See *History of the Han Dynasty * Records of Art and Literature.*)

In the Han Dynasty *fu* became the most fashionable genre of literature, so that in later ages Han *fu* was ranged alongside Tang poetry, Song *ci* and Yuan drama. Following its rise in popularity during the Han Dynasty, *fu* gained an honored place above traditional poetry and the style of the *Songs of Chu*. This was a very interesting phenomenon. As for the origin of this, the empire unified under the Han Dynasty needed a type of literature which could praise its achievements and virtues, and *fu* prose-poetry fitted this demand neatly, with its special characteristics of expansiveness, lofty diction and exaggerated ostentation. In addition, the flourishing of *fu* had something to do with the common practice during the Han Dynasty of the lords and kings gathering literary men around them, and these literary men in turn submitting resounding poetic creations to their patrons. Mei Cheng, Zou Yang and Yan Ji were all clients of Liu Bi, king of Wu, and Sima Xiangru was once a client of Liu Wu, king Xiao of Liang. This trend is illustrated by the *History of the Han Dynasty * Records of Art and Literature*, which records 82 *fu* poems dedicated to kings south of the Huai River, and 44 dedicated to kings or courtiers in the same area.

Mei Cheng's "Seven Discourses" and Sima Xiangru's "*Fu* Poem on Zixu" and "*Fu* Poem on Shanglin" were the works which pioneered the way for Major *Fu* poetry in the Western Han Dynasty. The contents of the latter two poems are similar to one another. The author puts words in the mouths of three figures – Zi Xu, Wu You and Prince Wang Shi. First, Zi Xu extols the vastness of the Yunmeng region of the Kingdom of Chu and the magnificent spectacle of the hunting expeditions of the king of Chu, then Wu You expatiates on the huge territory of the State of Qi, and finally Prince Wang Shi boasts of the grandeur of the Son of Heaven's Shanglin park, and uses exaggerated techniques to describe the park and the emperor's grand hunting display. Below is a small portion:

> Furthermore, how can things of the Qi and Chu states be commended? Have you never seen the magnificent sight with your own eyes? Have you never heard of the emperor's Shanglin Park? It borders Cangwu on the left and Xiji on the right. The Dan River traverses its southern territory; the Ziyuan, its northern part. While the Ba and Chan rivers linger within its boundaries, the Jing and Wei flow in and out, and the rivers Feng, Hao, Liao, and Yu meander in the park. The eight surging rivers of different shapes rush crisscrossing and gush out of the Jiaoqiu Ravine sandwiched between two high mountains. They pass by the islet formed by accumulated sandstone, through the forest of osmanthus trees, and in the vicinity of the vast prairie. The waters then pick up speed and expand in volume, tumbling down the cliffs towards the narrow mountain pass. As they plunge down to the crags and lash upon the winding sand banks, they rise in tempestuous waves of wrath. Their rapids swell as their waves clash with each other producing thumping reports. Their crosscurrents swirl and swell with audible notes, and their torrents strike the

> rolling banks with loud rumbling, their waves bounce back and forth along the winding riversides resembling curling clouds. With one wave pushing another ahead, the waters swiftly roll over the pebbles towards the abyss. As they break over the rocks and pound the banks, they are unstoppable. Brushing by the islet and tumbling into the valley, the waters are gradually calming down, their uproars giving way to whispers, before they cascade into the pools down in the valley. Sometimes a pool is so deep and vast that the waters bounce back to produce a loud rumbling. Sometimes the waves churn like boiling water in a cauldron bubbling incessantly in white foam. Sometimes the waters accelerate, make a sharp turn, and rush into the distance. Then the boundless glistening body of waters slowly empties into Taihu Lake in the east, filling it up and then overflowing into the surrounding ponds.[3]

The final part of this *fu* tells us that the emperor realizes the extravagance of his outdoor activities, and decides to give up hunting and turn the Shanglin park into farm fields. This is covert advice to the monarch against over-indulgence in luxury, in accordance with the Confucian ideal of governance. Both these *fu* poems begin and end with prose passages, and the middle parts are in verse. This is the typical format of the *fu* genre.

In addition, Ban Gu's "*Fu* Poetry of Two Capitals" and Zhang Heng's work of the same name are representative Major *Fu* poems of the Eastern Han Dynasty.

When the Major *Fu* of the Han Dynasty had experienced a period of glory and a decline had set in for poetry and ballads in the middle part of the Eastern Han Dynasty, the lyrical Minor *Fu* emerged as a lyrical form, with perhaps Zhang Heng's "*Fu* Poem on Returning to the Fields" as the standard work. This poem has a total of 40 verses, celebrating the poet's delight in returning to a life of leisure in the countryside. The individual's lyrical feelings are richly expressed:

> Having been an official in the capital for long, I found that I was running short of astuteness and resourcefulness with which I could help the emperor. If I only knew how to compliment the great taste of fish by the riverside, I was not sure how long I had to wait till the water of the Yellow River became clear. Thinking that Cai Ze failed to realize his aspiration, I had to ask Tang Ju for help to resolve puzzling problems through physiognomy. Being aware of the law of nature's capriciousness, I decided to follow the path of fishermen enjoying themselves on the river to stay away from sordid society and worldly chores forever.
>
> Now it was the second Chinese month, right in the middle of spring, with mild temperature and ample sunshine. On both high and low land, trees were lush and grass exuberant. Cormorants were flying above the water with their wings extended; orioles singing merrily in the trees; mandarin ducks entwining their necks on the river; and flocks of birds circling in the sky, singing their sweet songs. Wandering at leisure in the wilderness in spring, I felt extremely pleasant.

> Therefore I started chanting at the top of my voice by the big lake and on the small hill. I shot an arrow into the sky and cast a fishing hook of silver into the river. The arrow downed a wild goose; the hook caught and lifted a sand-blowing fish from the water.
>
> Soon the sun set and the moon was climbing up. Though having had enough fun, I still felt spirited. Thinking of Laozi's warnings, I returned to my thatched hut on my chariot. Back home, I played beautiful music on the five-stringed zither with my dexterous hands and read some texts from the Confucian classics with profound appreciation. Then, picking up the writing brush, I applied my talent to recounting the exemplifying deeds of the sage emperors of old. So long as I am outside the mundane world, I care neither for glory nor infamy.[4]

The arrangement and impact of this poem mark it as being far from a Major Fu work; it is too short, for one thing. But its blend of scenery and feelings reaches a stage of perfect elegance. This work foreshadows the emergence of the new lyric style of Minor Fu, and, moreover, it gives a wide perspective of such a foreshadowing. In 1996, among a number of wooden slips used for writing on excavated from a Han Dynasty tomb at Lianyungang in Jiangsu Province was a group which contained a fu poem titled "Tale of the Holy Crow."[5] It was probably composed in the latter part of the Western Han period. It is a simple story of a crow told in popular language. Its differences compared with the Han Dynasty Major Fu are worth attention.

The rise of ancient poems

The Major *Fu* genre throve during the Han Dynasty, but with the demise of that dynasty it gave way to a new type of poetry. The Wei (220–265), Jin (265–420) and Southern and Northern Dynasties (386–589) period saw a golden age of five-character ancient-style poetry, with the "Three Caos" (Cao Cao, Cao Pi and Cao Zhi) and the "Seven Writers" (Kong Rong, Chen Lin, Wang Can, Xu Gan, Ruan Yu, Ying Yang and Liu Zhen) as the representative poets. They opened up a new field of literary creation on the basis of studies of the Music Bureau collection by scholars of the Jian'an reign period (196–220) of Han Emperor Xiandi and using five-character verses to produce a new genre featuring new ways of lyricism, diction and narrative. Cao Zhi in particular holds a high position in the history of Chinese poetry, being the representative of the Jian'an school and honored by Zhong Rong in his *Poetical Works* as a writer of "outstanding and lofty spirit, whose words are chosen for their particular ornamentation," and "as precious and rare as phoenix feathers and unicorn horns." In Cao Zhi's poems we can often find images of a "sad wind; for instance, "A sad wind shakes the lofty tree" (from "The Yellow Bird in the Wild"), "How sad the wind on the high terrace," "How sad the wind between the rivers" and "The sad air of the lute" (from "Miscellaneous Poems") and "A sad wind wails around me" (from "Dedicated to Wang

Can"). This image conveys the desolate atmosphere of the Jian'an period (as the downfall of the dynasty drew near). One of Cao Zhi's "Miscellaneous Poems" describes his affection for a bosom friend:

> High tablelands are prone to moaning winds;
> The morning sun shines upon the Sad Forest.
> My friend is ten thousand *li* away from me,
> Separated by rivers and lakes wide and deep.
> How am I going to reach him in this boat?
> The grief of parting is therefore hard to bear.
> A wild goose flying alone towards the south
> Gave a long-winded honk above my house.
> As I looked up, I thought of my friend afar;
> To him a message I'd like the goose to take.
> Now that not a trace of its shadow is visible,
> I can't help but sink deeper into melancholy.[6]

Liu Zhen's upright and noble character is expressed in his poems. The three stanzas of his "Dedicated to My Younger Cousin" respectively use the analogies of an aquatic plant, a pine tree and a phoenix. These are all meant in praise of his younger cousin, but also reflect the poet's own self. The second stanza runs as follows:

> The pine trees stand soaring on the mountain;
> Braving the wind from the valley down below.
> The fierce wind may blow with all its might,
> But to the ground they're firmly holding on.
> Despite the snow and frost falling perennially,
> The pine trees ne'er bend their upright trunks.
> Aren't they suffering from the freezing frost?
> Yes, but by nature they're tolerant of frigidity.[7]

The poems of the Jian'an school all have the characteristics of the era in common. They sing the praises of political ideals, lament the shortness of life, have a fervent and individualistic deep coloring of tragedy. These are summed up as the "Jian'an axis." This "Jian'an axis" soon became a kind of model in itself for later poets to imitate.

Following the Jian'an period of poetry, and through the efforts of poets of the two Jin Dynasties (265–420) and Southern and Northern Dynasties (386–589) such as Ruan Ji, Zuo Si, Tao Yuanming, Bao Zhao, Xie Lingyun and Yu Xin, there was a burst of creativity in the five-character genre, and the whole period of the Wei, Jin and Southern and Northern Dynasties was a golden age for ancient poems in the five-character style.

Ruan Ji lived through the period of the fall of the Wei Dynasty and its replacement by the Jin Dynasty. The 82 stanzas of his "Unburdening My Bosom" reveal his feelings of loneliness and grief at living in a period of degenerate rule. The following is a sample:

Unable to sleep though deep into the night,
I decide to get up to play my mellow zither.
The moon casts its light on my curtain thin,
And a breeze steals in to caress my attire.
A lonely wild goose honks out in the wild,
While birds fly chirping in the Sad Forest.
Flying and circling, what can the birds see?
Nothing but the solitude I'm feeling alone.[8]

Few of Zuo Si's poems survive. In his eight-stanza "Singing of History" he employs ancient personages and ancient things to express his discontent, in common with those of other poor scholars, at the system of patronage by powerful families in his day. He is most indignant when he says:

The brilliant sun rises high in the blue sky,
Upon this Divine Land casting its light.
Replete with houses aligned in good order,
The palace's full of cloud-like flying eaves.
Within the magnificent gate of the building,
Reside all the members of the royal family.
Neither am I a snob nor a social climber,
Why should I loaf around in this place?
I hence stride out in my cotton garment,
To seek the lifestyle of an ancient hermit.
On a hill I shake the dusk off my clothes,
In a river I wash all the dirt from my feet.[9]

In the first half of this poem he waxes eloquent about the prosperity of the capital. In the second half he dwells on his own aspirations, and the ending of the second stanza deals a devastating blow.

The most successful poet of this period was Tao Yuanming, who lived at the end of the Eastern Jin Dynasty (317–420) and the beginning of the Song Dynasty (420–479) of the Southern Dynasties. He was the sole creator of idyllic rural poetry, representative of which is his "Returning to Dwell in the Country." These poems either expounded on the tranquil life of the countryside and the poet's own carefree mood or on the working life of the countryside and the joys and sorrows of its people, or sometimes on the poverty of the villages and the poets own threadbare existence. Whatever, the theme, this was a new and pioneering realm of creativity for poetry. Tao Yuanming wrote many poems which expressed his personal feelings, like "Drinking Wine" and "Miscellaneous Poems." Running through these poems are thoughts like the contradiction between taking up an official post and retiring to obscurity, the sadness of the poet at not being able to realize his ideals, and the exaltation of a noble nature that refused to be sullied in the mainstream of political intrigue. His historical poems sing the praises of figures of ancient times, such as the "Three Worthies," one of whom was the would-be assassin Jing Ke. The poems he wrote when he was wandering from place to place seeking a post express the hardships of such a quest and his yearning to return to his simple country cottage. His "farewell poems" display his true cordial feelings for his friends, and reveal most clearly his real nature. Tao Yuanming's poems achieved a synthesis of the commonplace and the elegant – a unity of mood, scenery and thought. Tao Yuanming extolled Nature, and so his poems are full of the beauties of Nature. His "Returning to Dwell in the Country," in five stanzas, was the first poem he wrote upon abandoning official life and retiring to his farm cottage. In it, he exults in the happiness of the natural freedom he regains after he returns to the countryside. Its first stanza runs as follows:

> While young I was not used to worldly cares/
> And hills became my natural companions/
> But by mistake I fell into mundane snares/
> And thus entangled was for 30 years/
> A caged bird longs for its native wood/
> As do fish in tanks for their home pools/
> I will go back and till my southern fields/
> And take up rustic life once more/
> My plot of ground is but ten acres square/
> My thatched hut has only a few rooms/
> Behind are willows and elms/
> In front peach and plum trees/
> In the far distance a village can be seen/
> Where plumes of smoke waft in the breeze/
> Deep in some alley I hear a dog bark/
> And cocks crowing on mulberry trees/
> But in my courtyard there is no bustle/
> In my bare rooms there is peace and leisure/
> After long years of abject servitude/
> Again in Nature I find homely pleasure.[10]

The poet seems to be welcoming a guest, walking and talking with him while introducing him to his life, his words overflowing with happiness. He describes the atmosphere of village life as "warm," in verses which echo down the ages. There is a ring of truth in Tao Yuanming's philosophical thought that embraces the great questions of the universe, history and human life? Why do the righteous often come to a bad end? What is the value of human life? What is the finest way to live? What is the correct way to regard death and extinction? etc. His thought blends the doctrines of Confucianism and Taoism, and stems from his individual life experience, his unique point of view, and his methods and conclusions; to sum up his thought, it could be said to be a sublimation of his personal practice. In accordance with his delight in a simple life and his reverence for Nature, Tao Yuanming came to two important conclusions about human life, and these became the two pillars of his own life: His thought can be summed up as: By going through the crucible of the sordid world of the "false I" one returns to "true I." Tao Yuanming saw the corruption of the society of his time, but he did not strive to correct it; he merely pursued his own moral perfection. He saw the crises of the society of his time, but he did not seek the true path to its salvation; he merely sought to return to man's original nature.

His "Drinking Wine" has altogether 20 stanzas. The fifth well represents Tao Yuanming's attitude to human life:

> I build my cottage among the haunts of men/
> I hear not the noise of carts and horses/
> If you ask how can this be, I say/
> A secluded heart dwells in a secluded place/
> Picking chrysanthemums below the eastern fence/
> I gaze at the southern mountains far away/
> The mountain air is fresh both day and night/
> I encounter birds on their homeward flight/
> What is the revelation all this brings?/
> I want to utter it, but words fail me.[11]

Although the poet lives among the bustle of crowds he can preserve the tranquility of his life. By relying on "far away," his heart can leave the dusty world and find seclusion. In other words, a man can find seclusion wherever he lives. Seeing the birds returning to the southern hills at dusk, he thinks of returning to his old home in the countryside. He perceives that there is a core of truth in this, and he determines to return and adopt the life of a hermit. Toward life and death, the poet too has an optimistic point of view, and that is, as man originates from the Earth, after death he returns to the Earth: "What road do I take when I expire? I entrust my body to the mountain." In his "Collected Elegies" No.3 he also expresses his attitude toward death: "I abandon myself to the waves of the Great Change/ Neither joyful nor fearful." (Body, Shadow and Spirit)

Tao Yuanming's literary achievement never received recognition either during his lifetime or for a long period after his death. But after the Northern Song Dynasty (960–1127) his prestige grew constantly; his name became a symbol for Chinese literature; and his poems and essays became quoted, taken as models and copied, and continually appeared on paintings, calligraphic works and all kinds of artworks. He was a symbol of uprightness, purity and returning to Nature, of a man who upheld his own individual character and moral integrity unsullied by the mainstream. There have not been many who attained such a lofty position in the history of Chinese literature.

The period of the Wei, Jin and Southern and Northern Dynasties was when the seven-character-verse poetry became established. As discussed above, the embryo of this type of poetry can be found as early as in the *Songs of Chu*. But it was not restricted to the *Songs of Chu*; seven-character verses can be found in folk ballads too, for instance, in the "Going to the Prefecture Song" of the time of Emperor Cheng of the Western Han Dynasty (see *History of the Han Dynasty*, Vol.79, *Biography of Feng Yewang*), "Deep in Thought" in the Han Dynasty's Music Bureau collection and the proverbs quoted in the *History of the Han Dynasty*, Vol.51, *Biography of Lu Wenshu*. Indeed, Mr. Yu Guanying, in his "A Reappraisal of the Origin of Seven-character Verse," claims that this style originated in folk songs.[12] In my view, neither the *Songs of Chu* nor the ancient folk songs can lay claim to being the sole cradle of seven-character verse – both had a hand in its birth. Why do I say this? First of all, because literary figures have always tended to put more emphasis on the *Songs of Chu* than on folk songs as far as degree of maturity and models for emulation are concerned; and secondly we have materials to show conclusively that the earliest seven-character-verse poem was "Poem of Four Sorrows" by Zhang Heng of the Eastern Han Dynasty.[13] Its second stanza goes:

> The girl I love and miss is living on Mount Tai,
> Even a hill below deters my thought of a visit.
> I gazed into the east, tears wetting my clothes.
> My love gave me a knife-shaped coin to keep,
> I'd like to reciprocate her with the best of jade.
> The distance is so far that I can't get it to her,
> And this is the reason why I am in such woe.[14]

This poem preserves traces of the *Songs of Chu*. In another of Zhang Heng's poems "Pondering on a Mystery," his thought comes close to the *Songs of Chu* * Wandering Afar. The winding-up verses of these *fu* poems are of seven characters, and the close relationship between them is convincing evidence that the seven-character poems are connected with the *Songs of Chu*. Of course, if literary men had not had the *Songs of Chu* as models with which to blaze a new trail, they could have transferred their attention to folk songs. But since they were very familiar with this enormously influential work known as the *Songs of Chu*, it only needed slight changes for them to create seven-character verses. And so, they could not neglect the *Songs of Chu*. Once they realized that the five-character verses were no longer adequate for expressing their feelings and thoughts they immediately turned their attention to adapting the *Songs of Chu* and started writing seven-character poems. But why couldn't the *Songs of Chu* evolve smoothly into the seven-character format? Because certain requirements (that of lyricism and that of musical accompaniment) were needed before this could happen. Then why do we say that folk songs were the midwife of seven-character poetry? Because it was folk songs which caused literary men to see that there was another form of verse beyond those of four and five characters. And this form had a new and finer rhythm and tune than the four- and five-character verses, and a new power of expression. And this prompted them to experiment with changes to the *Songs of Chu*. Once this point is realized it is not difficult to explain why the earliest seven-character poem, "Song of the Northern Frontier" by Cao Pi, could be included in the Music

Bureau collection. Moreover, Bao Zhao of the Southern Dynasties, who put great effort into writing seven-character poems and based his seven-character works on the format of those in the Music Bureau collection. Now let us read the second stanza of Cao Pi's "Song of the Northern Frontier," which is particularly fine:

> Rustling autumn wind brings the temperature down,
> Turning the dews on the blades of fallen grass into frost.
> Swallows and wild geese are migrating to the south.
> Living away from home you must be feeling dismal,
> Ill at ease, you must be thinking of returning home.
> Why on earth my darling husband must you stay away,
> Leaving your dear wife behind to live a solitary life?
> Feeling lonely I always think of you my dear.
> Unknowingly, I have wet my clothes with tears.
> Fetching the zither, I start to play a *Qing-shang* tune,
> A short piece I play gently, but it's going on and off.
> Bright Moon, you cast your light on my empty bed;
> Milky Way, as you flow you stretch my restless night.
> Altair and Vega, stars of a loving couple far apart,
> What have you done to deserve such a separation?[15]

This poem contains an exquisitely lyrical description of scenery. Its diction is lucid and elegant. These qualities make it a very successful work of art. In his *History of the Southern Qi Dynasty * A Discussion of Literature*, Xiao Zixian of the Liang Dynasty (502–557) says, "Who composed in seven-character verses before the beautiful works of Wei?"[16] But the above poem has a similar structure and rhyme scheme as the "Poem of Four Sorrows" and "Words Added to 'Pondering on a Mystery'." By the time we come to Bao Zhao of the Song Dynasty of the Southern Dynasties the seven-character format had reached maturity. Let us look at the twelfth stanza of his "Tedious Ways":

> Flowers fill the entire forest in the early spring;
> The hill will be covered with snow next winter.
> Old times are constantly superseded by new,
> But you've been garrisoned in the border region.
> Three years have passed since we bade farewell,
> Recently I've heard little or nothing from you.
> In the morning my sorrow drives me to lament;
> At night, I pine for you till my heart is broken.
> Fragrant as it is, the hair oil I've long ignored.
> My hairdo in a mess I have no mood to primp.
> Dust I allow to fly in the chamber without you.
> One toilet case after another has been wasted.
> What a misfortune to live in this bitter world,
> Where I see no end to my eternal wretchedness.[17]

These lines, thoroughly exposing the feelings of a grieving wife, represent the top level reached by seven-character poems in Bao Zhao's time, but it was not until the Tang Dynasty (618–907) that the full flowering of this genre came about.

When discussing the five- and seven-character ancient poetry produced in the Wei, Jin and Southern and Northern Dynasties periods it is necessary to note their link to the folk songs of the Southern and Northern Dynasties. Like the Han Dynasty, the Southern Dynasties also had a Music Bureau tasked with collecting folk songs and setting them to music. The Southern Dynasties' Music Bureau collected some 500 ballads, most of which belong to the category called *Qing-shang* lyrics, divided into the "Songs of the Kingdom of Wu" and the "Western Tunes." From the time of the Eastern Jin Dynasty there was a great development of the economy and trade in the Yangtze River Basin. Cities flourished, and in the cities singing and dancing thrived.[18] And it was there that the Music Bureau of the Southern Dynasties gathered its material – from the classes of merchants, singing girls and boatmen. Most of them were love songs: "I am as constant as the North Star. Immoveable for a thousand years. I welcome the sun as it rises in the east and sets in the west" ("Song of Midnight"). Characteristic of the folk songs of the Southern Dynasties was their format, which was usually a group of four verses of five characters each, based on a foundation of quatrains. The use of punning words is common, especially in the "Songs of the Kingdom of Wu." The long lyrical poem titled, "The Song of Xizhou," which belongs to the category of *Miscellaneous Tunes and Songs*, seems to have been rearranged by scholars. Its basic content is the lovesick thoughts of a young girl, but inserted in it are descriptions of scenery in the changing seasons. Also, the rhetorical device of calling for the first word or phrase of a verse to be the same as the last word or phrase in the previous one, giving a stopping-and-starting effect. It reaches the pinnacle of artistry of the folk songs of the Southern Dynasties:

> Missing the plum blossoms I'd like to visit Xizhou.
> I want to pick and send some north of the Yangtze.
> The flimsy dress she's donning is as red as an apricot.
> Her hair looks as dark as the feathers of young crows.
> If you ask where's the place known as Xizhou,
> A ferry at its bridge can be reached by boat.
> When the sun sets, the shrikes all fly away,
> Gusts of wind start to caress the candleberry tree.
> Under the candleberry tree is located her abode,
> Whose door ajar reveals the well-adorned lassie.
> Opening it, she sees no sign of her sweetheart,
> So she leaves her abode to pick lotus flowers.
> In the autumn air she's on the Southern Pond;
> There the tall lotuses reach up above her head.
> She amuses herself by popping lotus seeds
> That look as clear and crisp as the rippling pond.
> The ripe seeds assuming a look of crimson red,

She stows them carefully in her sleeve pockets.
How I miss you my love, but you're not with me,
I have to raise my head to gaze at the wild geese.
The sky above Xizhou is full of the flying birds;
To see me, she climbs up to the gray pavilion.
Despite the building's height, she sees me not.
She's leaning against its railings all day long.
Upon the winding railings with twelve curves,
She's hanging her hands as fair as white jade.
Curtains rolled reveal the loftiness of the sky;
The wavy sea shows off its azure for nothing.
The sea waters are as illusory as dreams,
Representing the same worries we share.
Wind from the south knowing my feelings,
Pray thee carry my dream to her in Xizhou.

Most of the songs of the Northern Dynasties were martial ones, and over half were composed from the period of the Northern Wei Dynasty (386–534) onward. These songs steadily trickled south, and became collected in the Music Bureau of the Liang Dynasty, and so became known as "Liang drum, horn and flute tunes." As they originated among various peoples of the north, they bear a distinct flavor of northern scenes and customs. For instance, "The Song of the Chile River" has the following verses: "The Chile River, beneath Mount Yin/The sky like the roof of a yurt/Covers all the steppe beneath it/Across the azure sky and endless plain/The wind bends the grass/Bring to sight cattle and sheep."[19] The Northern Dynasties' Music Bureau contained fewer folk songs than that of the Southern Dynasties – only some 60. The former are characterized by bluntness of feeling and unadorned diction, resulting in a bold and robust style, in contrast to the refined and supple folk songs of the Southern Dynasties. As regards genre, apart from four and five characters to a verse some of these works contain groups of four verses of seven characters each. This was an advance on the seven-character quatrain verse. The finest work of this type is "The Song of Mulan," a folk song of the Northern Dynasties:

Tsiektsiek and again tsiektsiek,
Mulan weaves, facing the door.
You don't hear the shuttle's sound,
You only hear Daughter's sighs.
They ask Daughter who's in her heart,
They ask Daughter who's on her mind.
"No one is in Daughter's heart,
No one is on Daughter's mind.
Last night I saw the draft posters,
The Khan is calling many troops,
The army list is in twelve scrolls,

On every scroll there's Father's name.
Father has no grown-up son,
Mulan has no elder brother.
I want to buy a saddle and horse,
And serve in the army in Father's place."
In the East Market she buys a spirited horse,
In the West Market she buys a saddle,
In the South Market she buys a bridle,
In the North Market she buys a long whip.
At dawn she takes leave of Father and Mother,
In the evening camps on the Yellow River's bank.
She doesn't hear the sound of Father and Mother calling,
She only hears the Yellow River's flowing water cry tsientsien.
At dawn she takes leave of the Yellow River,
In the evening she arrives at Black Mountain.
She doesn't hear the sound of Father and Mother calling,
She only hears Mount Yen's nomad horses cry tsiutsiu.
She goes ten thousand miles on the business of war,
She crosses passes and mountains like flying.
Northern gusts carry the rattle of army pots,
Chilly light shines on iron armor.
Generals die in a hundred battles,
Stout soldiers return after ten years.
On her return she sees the Son of Heaven,
The Son of Heaven sits in the Splendid Hall.
He gives out promotions in twelve ranks
And prizes of a hundred thousand and more.
The Khan asks her what she desires.
"Mulan has no use for a minister's post.
I wish to ride a swift mount
To take me back to my home."
When Father and Mother hear Daughter is coming
They go outside the wall to meet her, leaning on each other.
When Elder Sister hears Younger Sister is coming
She fixes her rouge, facing the door.
When Little Brother hears Elder Sister is coming
He whets the knife, quick quick, for pig and sheep.
"I open the door to my east chamber,
I sit on my couch in the west room,
I take off my wartime gown
And put on my old-time clothes."
Facing the window she fixes her cloud-like hair,
Hanging up a mirror she dabs on yellow flower powder
She goes out the door and sees her comrades.
Her comrades are all amazed and perplexed.

Traveling together for twelve years
They didn't know Mulan was a girl.
"The he-hare's feet go hop and skip,
The she-hare's eyes are muddled and fuddled.
Two hares running side by side close to the ground,
How can they tell if I am he or she?"[20]

This poem is characterized by plain and natural diction, as well as a matchlessly exquisite tempo. In it, the descriptive and lyrical are combined; the descriptive parts are sometimes expansive and sometimes condensed, forming a style in which the delicate and the rough commingle.

The transition from the ancient to the modern style and the emergence of parallelism in *fu* poetry

The three Southern Dynasties (420–589) of Qi, Liang and Chen marked the period of transition from the ancient to the modern style. The new techniques of expression, such as antithesis and rhythm, which marked the modern style, came to maturity during this period.

Antithesis had its origin in an ancient technique of double-matching, and is a rhetorical device characteristic of the Chinese language. Antithesis consists of equal numbers of contrasting words all belonging to the same parts of speech or concepts, forming a beautifully complete whole. The general rule of antithesis is that noun is contrasted with noun, verb with verb, adjective with adjective, function word with function word, etc. Because the number of monosyllables in Chinese is high, even when polysyllabic words are used, the morphemes contained in a piece of verse form a relative independence. In addition, written Chinese is not phonetic but composed of individual characters, and so it is easy to get them to line up in an antithetic way. In fact, antithesis can be found as early as in the poems of the Book of Odes. Poets of later times consciously adopted this rhetorical method, and during the Qi, Liang and Chen dynasties it became universally applied. An example is "Bidding Farewell" by He Xun of the Liang Dynasty:

A stranger here, I have a mixture of feelings;
Roaming alone I'm a thousand *li* from home.
The darkening of the riversides heralds rain,
The whitening of the waves harbingers wind.[21]

In this poem, the last three words of the first part of the first line stand in contrast to the last three words of the second part, and the last three words of the first part of the third line stand in contrast to the last three words of the second part – forming neatly rounded patterns.

The technique of rhythm depends on a knowledge of phonetics. The study of Chinese phonetics commenced in the Southern Dynasties period, when Zhou Yong identified the four tones of Chinese – the level, rising, falling and entering tones – in the Yongming reign period (483–493) of the Qi Dynasty. At the same time, the famous poet Shen Yue studied how sound, rhyme and tone could be combined in poetry, based on the four tones and double rhyming components. He pointed out eight phonetic infelicities to be avoided, called the "eight maladies." The object of this was to "achieve harmony by as diverse means as possible within one poem, and in each two stanzas extremes of weight." [22]

In practical terms, the technique of using the rules of sound incorporates two aspects: rhyme and the combination of level (平) and oblique (仄) tones. Shen Yue and others of the Qi Dynasty used these aspects of phonetics to write their poems. This is known in the history of Chinese literature as the Yongming style, or new poetry style. Let us take a look at Shen Yue's "*Farewell to Fan Ancheng*":

When young, we said goodbye to each other oftentimes.
As we're both aging, parting bears a different meaning.
Don't treat the cups in our hands as vessels of wine only;
For, henceforth, we may ne'er be able to hold them again.
Missing you, I wish I could locate you in my dreamland,
But, alas, each time I try, I lose my bearings halfway.[23]

This is a representative work of the Yongming style. There are eight stanzas altogether. It pays special attention to rhyme and the combination of level and oblique tones makes it especially suitable for reading aloud.

By the early years of the Tang Dynasty poetical composition, phonetic arrangement and rules, and antithesis had progressed to the stage of forming a stylized model and emerged as the established modern poetic form.

As mentioned above, the Major *Fu* form of poetry initially became fashionable in the Han Dynasty, and the lyrical Minor *Fu* poetry, a lyrical form, emerged in the middle part of the Eastern Han Dynasty. The Major *Fu* withered after the Wei and Jin dynasties, while the lyrical Minor *Fu*, with five characters to the verse, greatly flourished. The way that poetry and its *fu* variant advanced and retreated and influenced each other is a regular phenomenon. Concerning this, Lin Geng had something penetrating to say.[24]

"*Fu* Poem on Mounting the Tower" by Wang Can, a poet of the Jian'an reign period of the Eastern Han Dynasty, was composed while he was working in the office of the commanding officer Liu Biao in Jingzhou. It expresses his homesickness: "Though pretty, it is not my homeland,/ What then is worthy of my staying here!"[25] "*Fu* Poem to the Goddess of the Luo River" by Cao Zhi expresses Cao's unrequited longing for the Fairy Maiden of the Luo River, but it also implies his feelings of disappointment at his setbacks in the world of politics. This poem carried an exquisite description of the Fairy Maiden:

Her form is as elegant as a startled swan,
And as graceful as a swimming dragon.
Her face glows like a chrysanthemum,
Her figure is as graceful as a pine in spring.

She flickers like a moon mantled with clouds,
She floats like wind whirling flakes of snow.
From afar, she's like the sun at rosy dawn.
Close, she's like lotus flowers on water.
. . .
Then all the gods and goddesses come over,
Along with their companions and associates.
Some are frolicking in the crystal brooks;
Some are flying over the mystical islets;
Others are collecting luminous pearls;
Still others are gathering kingfishers' feathers.
Followed by the goddesses of the Xiang River,
Holding the Han River nymph by the hand,
The goddess laments the Hugua star's solitude,
And feels sad at the loneliness of Altair.
Sometimes she gazes afar for a long while,
Shielding the sun with her flowing sleeves.
Sometimes she flies airily like a mallard,
Now low, now high in a mysterious way.
She treads the surface of the wavy water,
Her silk stockings kicking up dust-like mists.[26]

In his "*Fu Poem on Leisure*," Tao Yuanming presents a unique description of love, in which the "Ten Wishes" section is perhaps the acme:

I'd like to be the beauty's collar, so I can smell her face's fragrance.
But she may undress herself at night leaving me to lament its endlessness.
I'd like to be the beauty's waistband, so I can hold her by her graceful waist.
But autumn soon will turn cold; she'll switch to new clothes any time.
I'd like to be the beauty's hair oil, so I can moisten her cascading tresses.
But she may wash her hair oftentimes, leaving me tormented in hot water.
I'd like to be the beauty's eye shadow, so I can dance with her twinkling eyes.
But to keep her makeup fresh every day, she applies it from time to time.
I'd like to be the beauty's mat, so she can repose on it for the entire autumn.
But she'll use her fur mattress in winter, and put me to use only next year.
I'd like to be the beauty's embroidered shoes, so I can be close to her feet.
But she'll take a break, slip me off, and stow me away beneath her bed.
I'd like to be the beauty's shadow, so I can follow her wherever she goes.
But she'll eventually come to a tree, making me disappear in its umbrage.
I'd like to be the beauty's candlelight, so I can light up her pretty face.
But the sun will rise in the morning, and then she'll quickly blow me out.
I'd like to be the beauty's bamboo fan, so I can use it to cool her off.
But when frost brings winter back, I will have to quit her sleeve pocket.

> I'd like to be boards of phoenix trees, so I can be made into a zither on her knees.
> But thrown into a bad mood, she may push me away not to touch me anymore.[27]

At the same time as *fu* poetry was emphasizing antithesis and phonetic rhythm, it was also using parallelism. The character used to express this was one which denoted a pair of horses harnessed in tandem, and included the meaning of antithesis. Moreover, in order to achieve roundedness, four to six characters to a verse were used. And level and entering tones were used to emphasize harmony. "*Fu* Poem on Bitterness" and "*Fu* Poem on Farewell" by Jiang Yan of the Liang Dynasty are representative of "parallelism *fu*." Below is the first stanza from "*Fu* Poem on Farewell":

> The most distressing thing is parting, as in the case of the states of Qin and Wu, which were far apart, and the states of Yan and Song, which were a thousand miles away from each other. Parting may happen in early spring, when moss starts to grow or in autumn, when a chilling wind springs up. Therefore, those who travel and live far away from home often cherish a mixture of feelings that make them heartbroken. When a gust of wind whistles, they find the sound strange. When clouds float endlessly, they treat their colors as peculiar. Traveling by boat, they moor it by a river. Traveling on a carriage, they drag along a winding mountain path. How can a hesitant boat move forward? When a horse is sad, it neighs constantly. Holding cups of gold, they find it hard to drink. Having a zither laid out, they are not in a mood to play. Instead the tears they shed wet the carriage. Those who remain at home have to go to sleep sad and longing. They are as disturbed as if they have lost something. As the sun sets behind the wall, it loses its glamour. When the moon climbs up above the windows, it casts a pool of crystal light. On moonlit nights they see peilan flowers covered with dew and catalpa trees mantled with frost. Looking around in a closed mansion, they see no one – just multiple columns. Feeling the silk curtains, they sink into sadness and gloom. Those who travel to or live in faraway places must wander in their dreams, their souls flying towards home.[28]

Yu Xin is a great name in parallelism *fu*. His "Mourning South of the Yangtze River" expresses his grief for his lost homeland as an exile in Northern Zhou. It contains heart-rending descriptions of the transitoriness of all things and the sufferings of the common people who had been taken prisoner. His "*Fu* Poem on Withered Tree" and "*Fu* Poem on Little Courtyard" are also famous works of his. Here is part of the former:

> Birds fly leisurely most of the time, and flowers bloom in accordance with the four seasons. My heart, however, is as listless as the dead wood of Liling;

> and my hair is as disheveled as that found in Suiyang. It is not that the summer sun is unnerving or the autumn weather saddening. Fish grow one or two inches long; bamboos grow in clusters of two or three . . . Fallen leaves are found heaped on half of the bed and flowers are flying throughout the room. It can be called a home for a savage or a ravine for a foolish old man. Only after moments in the cool shade of a thick forest can one appreciate the long-desired lifestyle of a hermit.[29]

The appearance of parallelism *fu* explains how in the Qi, Liang and Chen dynasties both poetry and its *fu* form traveled the same road of standardization of structure, applying the special characteristics of the Chinese language, and demonstrating the formal beauty of that language. The composers of poetry and *fu* of the Southern Dynasties made useful explorations in this respect and made some achievements not to be overlooked; in fact, if it were not for their efforts it is unlikely that the modern poetry of the Tang Dynasty would have taken shape.

Notes

1 [Han Dynasty] Qian, Sima: *Records of the Historian*, Vol.84, Zhonghua Book Company, 1959, P. 2491.
2 [Tang Dynasty] Shan, Li. and Yanji, Lv: *Selection of the Major Writings of Six Officials*, Vol.19, *Collected Writings of the Four Basic Branches of Literature*.
3 [Han Dynasty] Gu, Ban: *History of the Han Dynasty*, Vol.57, *Biography of Sima Xiangru*, Zhonghua Book Company, 1962, PP. 2547–2548.
4 [Tang Dynasty] Shan, Li. and Yanji, Lv: *Selection of the Major Writings of Six Officials*, Vol.15, *Collected Writings of the Four Basic Branches of Literature*.
5 In March 1993 a Han Dynasty tomb was excavated at No.6 Yinwan Village, Donghai County, Lianyungang City, Jiangsu Province. "Excavation Report" in issue No.8, *Cultural Relics*, 1996
6 [Wei Dynasty] Zhi, Cao: *The Collected Works of Cao Zijian*, Vol.5, *Collected Writings of the Four Basic Branches of Literature*.
7 [Tang Dynasty] Shan, Li. and Yanji, Lv: *Selection of the Major Writings of Six Officials*, Vol.23, *Collected Writings of the Four Basic Branches of Literature*.
8 [Tang Dynasty] Shan, Li. and Yanji, Lv: *Selection of the Major Writings of Six Officials*, Vol.23, *Collected Writings of the Four Basic Branches of Literature*.
9 [Tang Dynasty] Shan, Li. and Yanji, Lv: *Selection of the Major Writings of Six Officials*, Vol.21, *Collected Writings of the Four Basic Branches of Literature*.
10 Xingpei, Yuan: *The Collected Works of Tao Yuanming with Commentary*, Zhonghua Book Company, 2003, P. 76.
11 Xingpei, Yuan: *Collected Works of Tao Yuanming Annotated*, Zhonghua Book Company, 2003, P. 247.
12 Guanying, Yu: *Collected Essays on the Poetry of the Han, Wei and Six Dynasties Periods*, Shanghai Classical Literature Publishing House, 1956, P. 144.
13 "The Poems of Bailiangtai," part of the connecting verses of scholars and officials of the time of Emperor Wu of Han (reign: 140–86 BC), although in seven-character verses, seem to be fraudulent. See Gu Yanwu *Records of Daily Knowledge*, Vol.21
14 [Tang Dynasty] Shan, Li and Yanji, Lv: *Selection of the Major Writings of Six Officials*, Vol.29, *Collected Writings of the Four Basic Branches of Literature*.

15 [Tang Dynasty] Shan, Li and Yanji, Lv: *Selection of the Major Writings of Six Officials*, Vol.27, *Collected Writings of the Four Basic Branches of Literature*.

16 [Liang Dynasty] Zixian, Xiao: *History of the Southern Qi Dynasty*, Vol.52, Zhonghua Book Company, 1972, P. 908.

17 Collected Works of Qian Zhonglian Annotated: *The Collected Works of Bao Zhao Annotated*, Vol.4, Shanghai Ancient Books Publishing House, 1980, P. 238.

18 [Tang Dynasty] Yanshou's, Li: *History of the Southern Dynasties * Biography of Five Virtuous Officials* extract: "In every district of 100 households there was a market, bustling with people and with singing and dancing everywhere," Zhonghua Book Company, 1975, P. 1696.

19 [Song Dynasty] Maoqian, Guo: *Collected Poems of the Music Bureau*, Vol.86, *Miscellaneous Songs and Rhymes 4*, Zhonghua Book Company, 1979, P. 1213.

20 [Song Dynasty] Maoqian, Guo: *Collected Poems of the Music Bureau*, Vol.25, *Tunes for the Flute 5*, Zhonghua Book Company, 1979, P. 373.

21 Qinli, Lu ed. and checked: *Poems of the Pre-Qin, Han, Wei, Jin, and Northern and Southern Dynasties*, Zhonghua Book Company, 1983, P. 1710.

22 [Liang Dynasty] Yue, Shen: *History of the Song Dynasty*, Vol.27, *Comments on the Biography of Xie Lingyun*, Zhonghua Book Company, 1974, P. 1779.

23 [Tang Dynasty] Shan, Li. and Yanji, Lv: *Selection of the Major Writings of Six Officials*, Vol.20, *Collected Writings of the Four Basic Branches of Literature*.

24 See "Some Landmarks in the High Tide of the Discussions of Tang Poetry," *Social Science Front*, 1982, Issue 4.

25 [Tang Dynasty] Shan, Li. and Yanji, Lv: *Selection of the Major Writings of Six Officials*, Vol.11, *Collected Writings of the Four Basic Branches of Literature*.

26 *The Collected Works of Cao Zijian*, Vol.3, *Collected Writings of the Four Basic Branches of Literature*.

27 Xingpei, Yuan: *Collected Works of Tao Yuanming Annotated*, Zhonghua Book Company, 2003, P. 499.

28 [Song of the Southern Dynasties] Yan, Jiang: *Collected Works of Jiang Yan of Liang*, Vol.1, *Collected Writings of the Four Basic Branches of Literature*.

29 *Collected Works of Yu Zishan*, Vol.1, *Collected Writings of the Four Basic Branches of Literature*.

3 The peak of poetry

Tang poems

Chinese poetry reached its golden age in the Tang Dynasty. There was no cessation in the composition of *fu* poetry. This type of composition continued to receive close attention from literary men; in fact, it was included as one item in the civil service exams. The *fu* genre was also important on solemn occasions, such as the time when Du Fu presented his "*Fu* Poem on Three Great Ceremonies" to Tang Emperor Xuanzong (reign: 713–756). About the same time, some gems of this kind of composition appeared, including Li Bai's "Great Roc" and Du Fu's "Vulture." Nevertheless, this genre did not keep pace with the ascent to glory of standard poetry. Here again, we can see a phenomenon in which standard poetry progressed while *fu* declined.

As described above, Chinese poetry and ballads had three principle origins: the *Book of Odes*, *Songs of Chu* and the Han Dynasty Music Bureau. The next stage was when the five-character-verse old-style Music Bureau poems were continued and flourished during the period covered by the Wei, Jin and Southern and Northern Dynasties. The poetry of this period can be compared to the water of the Yangtze River at the Three Gorges; one can see the pent-up strength but not the vista of the broad and bold sweep of the river. During the Tang Dynasty it is as if the Yangtze had flowed out of the Three Gorges and were making its way across the flats. Li Bai has a refreshing description of this in his "Farewell to My Hometown as I Pass the Jingzhou Gateway": "The mountain follows the plain and tapers off/ The river enters the desert and meanders on."

One can gauge the level of prosperity of Tang poetry by its sheer volume. One only has to consult the *Complete Tang Poems* compiled in the Kangxi reign period (1662–1723) of the Qing Dynasty (in 900 volumes) to find that it contains over 48,900 works by more than 2,200 poets. This has been greatly increased by the efforts of modern research, which has turned up a number of previously lost Tang poems. It was not just the "giants" such as Li Bai and Du Fu who made Tang poetry so magnificent, lesser poets too, all masters of their craft, contributed. These included Chen Zi'ang, Wang Wei, Meng Haoran, Wang Changling, Gao Shi, Cen Shen, Han Yu, Liu Zongyuan, Liu Yuxi, Bai Juyi, Li He, Li Shangyin and Du Mu. In the Tang Dynasty poetry soared higher than during any other dynasty in Chinese history. Its variety of subject matter and description marks the Tang Dynasty as the peak of poetry in China.

Tang poetry is divided into the four periods of Early, Flourishing, Middle and Late. The first two can be classified together as the Former Period, and the latter two as the Latter Period, the dividing line between them being the "An-Shi Rebellion," which broke out in the fourteenth year of the Tianbao reign period (755).

Ascending the peak

Tang poetry in the first part of the dynasty basically followed the patterns laid down in the preceding Liang and Chen dynasties, although some progress was made in efforts to mingle the southern and northern literary aspects. In the later years of the first part of the Tang Dynasty poetry managed to break free of the restraints of the frivolous and fantastic subject matter of the Liang and Chen dynasties, and initiated a sturdy and robust new poetic style, covering a broad spectrum of social life and dealing with weighty matters of state. The emergence of the "Four Worthies" (Wang Bo, Yang Jiong, Lu Zhaolin and Luo Binwang) marks the turning point here. Yang Jiong's frontier fortress poem "I Would Rather Fight" encapsulates the spirit of this new era:

The beacon fire shines o'er the capital,
My agitated mind can't calm down.
By imperial order we leave the palace hall,
Our armored steeds besiege Dragon Town.
Snow darkens pictures sewn on banners red,
With howling winds are mingled our drumbeats.
I'd rather fight at a hundred men's head,
Than pore over books, eschewing feats.[1]

Chen Zi'ang was a successor to the "Four Worthies," robustly continuing to open up the road of development for Tang poetry. He not only restored to poetry the sturdy tradition of the Han and Wei dynasties, he also strengthened the trend of writing both political and lyrical poetry. This marked a turning point for poetry during the early part of the Tang Dynasty. His representative works are "Upon Mounting Youzhou Tower" and the 38 stanzas of "Disappointment." Let us look at "Upon Mounting Youzhou Tower":

Where are the great men of the past?/
Where are those of future years?/
The sky and earth forever last/
Here and now I alone shed tears.[2]

Casting their eyes over the long flow of history, from ancient times until their own day, poets have acutely felt the brevity of human existence, and burst into tears at the realization that the limitations of life make it impossible for them to fully display their powers. A kind of deep sigh over the tragedy of life and historic emotionalism, together with an unstoppable momentum have moved countless readers of their poems.

Following in the footsteps of the poets of the Southern Dynasties, those of the Early Tang Period used the patterns of the earlier tradition – five or seven characters to the verse and stanzas of eight lines. They also paid great attention to the use of level and oblique tones and antithesis. An example of one of the poems using five characters to a verse is "Eve of the Lantern Festival" by Su Weidao:

> The trees festooned with lanterns seem to be on fire;
> The lamp-decked city bridge gives unchecked access.
> The dust kicked up by horses is rendered invisible;
> People come streaming under the bright moonbeams.
> Courtesans dressed to the teeth mooch around in the streets,
> Singing the hit song "Fallen Plums" as they enjoy the views.
> When the curfew of the night is lifted from this golden city,
> Why are you, silvery hourglass of sand, in such a hurry?[3]

An example of a poem with seven characters to the verse is Shen Quanqi's *An Ancient Poem to Qiao Zhizhi, a Buque Official:*

> There's a young married lady in a tulip-scented chamber,
> On its turtle-shell-decked beam perches a swallow couple.
> The sound of beating clothes shakes off autumn leaves.
> Her man has been at the Liaoyang garrison for a decade.
> No words have ever come from north of the Bailang River.
> She's been left in the capital enduring long autumn nights.
> Who can feel her pain as she suffers from her loneliness?
> Through the curtain the moon shines untimely to add to it.[4]

As we ascend the path to the peak in our study of the poetry of the Former Tang period we must pay particular attention to the special characteristics of the five-character format, which made this genre diffuse and laid the groundwork for the transition of Tang poetry from being one-dimensional to its full richness of content. The Former Tang period saw the emergence of five-character poetry which combined emotion with sensual delight, such as Luo Binwang's "Cicada Ode" and Wang Bo's "Farewell to Prefect Du." But, viewed from an overall way it propelled the era's poetry to its height of prosperity had to await the coming of Wang Wei and Du Fu in the heyday of the Tang Dynasty. The breakthrough that was made in poetry in the Former Tang period was chiefly in the seven-character format, which brought with it a new direction in creativity, performing an important function in pushing Tang poetry in the direction of its summit. The special characteristics of the seven-character poetry of the Former Tang period, the smoothness of its diction, served as a model for later writers in this genre. Representative works in this regard are Lu Zhaolin's "Style of Old Chang'an," Luo Binwang's "A Poem on the

Imperial Capital", "Liu Xiyi's "To Imitate To the Tune of 'The Miserable Gray-haired Old Man'" and Zhang Ruoxu's "Moonlit Night on the Spring River." Luo's poem extols the prosperity of the capital. Liu's poem laments how easily glorious youth slips away: "Year in, year out, the flowers are the same/But with the passing of the years man can't help but change." Once recited, this poem is hard to forget. Zhang's poem describes a night from the rising to the setting of the moon. It combines objective reality with subjective fantasy. The effect is one of haziness:

> In spring the river rises as high as the sea/
> And with the river's rise the moon comes up bright/
> She follows the rolling waves for ten thousand li/
> And where the river flows there overflows her light.
> The river winds around the fragrant isle where/
> The flower blossoms in her light are like snow/
> You cannot tell her beams from hoar frost in the air/
> Nor from white sand upon Farewell Beach below.
> No dust has stained the water blending with the skies/
> A lonely wheel-like moon shines brilliant far and wide/
> Who by the riverside first saw the moon arise?/
> When did the moon first see a man on the riverside?
> Ah, generations have come and passed away/
> From year to year the moon's the same, old and new/
> We do not know tonight for whom she sheds her ray/
> But hear the river say to its water adieu.
> Away, away is sailing a single cloud white/
> On Farewell Beach pine away maples green/
> Where is the boatman sailing his boat tonight?/
> Who, pining away, on the moonlit rails would lean?
> Alas, the moon is lingering over the tower/
> It should have seen the dressing table of the fair/
> She rolls the curtain up to let light into her bower/
> She washes, but can't wash away the moonbeams there.
> She sees the moon but her beloved is out of sight/
> She'd follow it to shine on her loved one's face/
> But message-bearing swans can't flee the moonlight/
> Nor can letter-sending fish leap from their place.
> Last night he dreamed that falling flowers would not stay/
> Alas, he can't go home, although half the spring has gone/
> The running water bearing spring will pass away/
> The moon declining over the pool will sink anon.
> The declining moon sinks into a heavy mist/
> It's far between southern rivers and eastern seas/
> How many can go home by moonlight who are missed?/
> The sinking moon sheds yearning o'er riverside trees.[5]

This poem expresses the writer's nostalgia for the passing of the years of youth and his yearning for a beautiful life, and even his curiosity about the universe. From different perspectives and with different backgrounds he repeatedly describes the moonlight and thereby presents a variety of splendid realms.

To sum up, the Former Tang period, lasting some 100 years, was the longest of the Tang poetry divisions. But it was a time when in both number and quality poems were inferior to those of the other divisions; in the 100 years not a single first-rate poet emerged. Former Tang can be likened to the prologue of a play, the main act of which would only get underway when the poets of the heyday of the Tang Dynasty mounted the stage. The poetry of Former Tang merely prepared the way for the great florescence of poetry in Tang's golden era. This latter was a time when emotion and vigor were united in poetry, and a key time when poetry surpassed the efforts of the previous period and left later periods failing to match it. Nevertheless, the poets of the 100 years of the Former Tang period were important in that they laid the groundwork for the flourishing period of the Tang. We can call Tang poetry the peak of poetical composition in the history of Chinese poetry, even though its starting point was not high. After 100 years of the Tang Dynasty, Emperor Xuanzong came to the throne, and suddenly there was a great outpouring of poetic talent, and then Tang poetry swiftly reached its peak.

The heyday of Tang poetry lasted no more than 50-odd years, but it produced a dozen great poets. This period saw three major genres – political, frontier and landscape poetry. These poems were marked by imposing thrust, enterprising spirit, all-inclusive embrace and wholesome emotions, forming a variegated artistic style. Their allure has served to attract countless readers of later times, and made of this period a pinnacle of poetic artistry never attained before or since.

Wang Wei was an all-round genius. He was not only a poet; he was a musician, painter and calligrapher too. In addition, he was steeped in Buddhist lore. This genius of rounded talents can be held up as a representative of the golden age of Tang poetry. As a devout Buddhist, the concepts of Chan Buddhism are blended in his poems. For instance, "A Deer Park":

> In pathless hills, no man's in sight/
> But I still hear an echoing sound/
> In gloomy forests peeps no light/
> But sunbeams slant on mossy ground.[6]

The first two lines describe the emptiness of the mountain valley; the last two describe the lapse of time. There is boundless charm expressed in a very compressed space. About Wang Wei as a painter, the contemporary poet Su Dongpo said in his "On Wang Wei's Painting of Blue Fields and Misty Rain": "Savoring Mo Jie's poetry, one perceives a painting in it; viewing Mo Jie's painting, one perceives a poem in it." Wang Wei's poetry is like "a river flowing from sky to earth/Hills now appear, now disappear" (A View of the River Han). "The sun goes down, brightening rivers and lakes/ The tidewater comes in, darkening heaven and earth" (Seeing Xing Off to Guizhou), "Gazing at the green moss while sitting/

I feel the color coming on to my clothes" (A Description of What I See). All these quotations are fine poetry with the impact of painting.

Although Wang Wei is noted for his landscape poems, he could write fine poems in other genres too, like his "Remembering My Shandong Brothers at the Double Ninth Festival":

> Alone, a stranger in a foreign land/
> I pine for kinsfolk doubly on a holiday/
> I know my brothers would, with dogwood spray in hand/
> Climb the mountain and think of me so far away.[7]

The poet has a clear reminiscence of his brothers far away, and at the same time as he writes about them he is conscious of the fact that they miss him too and are thinking about him as they climb a height (a traditional custom on the ninth day of the ninth month – the Double Ninth day.) The second line expresses an ordinary sentiment but has all the force of an aphorism.

An example of a frontier poem is *"On Mission to the Frontier":*

> An imperial envoy, I'm on my way to inspect the frontier.
> Traveling with a small entourage, I'm now passing Juyan.
> I'm coming to the border like fleabane blown in the wind,
> And like swans returning to their northern home in spring.
> Beacon smoke on this solitary desert is rising straight up;
> The sun appears like a disk as it sets by the Yellow River.
> A scout on horseback comes to meet me at the Xiao Pass,
> Telling me that the general and his troops are at the front.[8]
> An example of a farewell poem is "A Farewell Song":
> The morning drizzle dampens Wei City's floating dust,
> Freshening the green-roofed tavern and willows around.
> Pray, dear friend, have another drink before you go:
> Beyond the Yang Pass, you'll find no one that you know.[9]
> And "Farewell to Shen Zifu Returning to the East of the Yangtze River":
> The willow-filled ferry crossing sees few travelers.
> The ferryman's rowing his boat to the river's east.
> My feeling of missing you is like the color of spring,
> Following as you go anywhere till you're back home.[10]

"Watching the Hunt" is a poem about abnormal weather, with five characters to the verse:

> Arrows dart out whistling in the howling wind,
> Bow in hand, the general hunts outside Wei City.
> Withered grass blind not the eagles' sharp eyes,
> The horses gallop more easily as snow is gone.
> Before long he's passed through Xinfeng City,

Returning in the end to Xiliu Barracks.
Looking back to where he shot the birds of prey,
He sees only the pasture beneath the dim clouds.[11]

Li Bai's poetry reflected the ambience of the heyday of the Tang Dynasty, a glittering period in Chinese history. At that time China was probably the most prosperous and powerful country in the world. Its capital, Chang'an, was an international metropolis. It was the multi-faceted and open social atmosphere of this great unified empire which produced Li Bai, and Li Bai in turn came to symbolize the Tang heyday. The wide-ranging and lofty nature of his poetry matched this era well. The spirit of his poetry, which can be called transcendental and carefree and yet full of vigor, overpowers the reader. This is especially brought out in his representative works "The Rocky Road to Shu" and "Pray Thee Drink Your Wine." The former describes the difficulties on the way to what is now Sichuan Province. There are many quite different opinions on the theme of this poem; however, all readers gasp in admiration at the broad sweep of his writing brush, which, while describing the hardships of the road to Shu at the same time allures the readers to follow in his footsteps.

O, alas! How dangerously high!
The Sichuan Path is so difficult to tread, and to do so is to clamber to the sky.
Cancong and Yufu, why did you found your states here without much thinking?
For forty-eight thousand years, they've had no contact with the Qin.
Mount Taibai in the east has a pass allowing birds to fly over Mount Emei.
Only after some heroes' deaths in an earthquake did these places get connected via stone paths as high as the sky.
Up above, there's the height that even the sun-dragging dragons have to circumvent;
Down below, there's the waterway where whirling torrents break upon sunken reefs.
Cranes that attempted to fly over failed miserably in their attempt.
Monkeys that wanted to climb over were saddened by frustration.
So zigzagging are the paths towards the summit of Qingni Mountain,
That one has to turn nine times for every hundred steps.
Where I can touch the Shen and Jing constellations, I sit and ask with a long sigh, pressing my hands on my bosom:
"Travelers to the west, when will you return?
Climbing over the crags is so dangerous an undertaking that you'd better stop.
Don't you see the poor birds whining plaintively as they fly around the ancient woods, females following their male partners?
Don't you hear the cuckoos sobbing in the moonlit night, their sadness permeating the solitary mountains?

The Sichuan Path is so difficult to tread, and to do so is to clamber to the sky.
Whoever hears my warning would turn pale.
Rolling peaks are inch-close to the firmament, and withered pines cling to the precipices upside down.
Rapids and cataracts are vying for resonance, and stones turned around and around by the torrents crash thundering.
It's so dangerous, why on earth do you travelers from afar have to take the risk?
The Jiange Pass is so lofty that a single person can obstruct the advance of ten thousand men.
If, however, the person is not a protégée, he could turn into a wolf or a jackal.
Here you have to dodge the ferocious tigers by day and giant serpents at dusk;
Grinding their teeth, they suck people's blood and kill them in droves.
The beautiful Chang'an City is a fun place for sure, but you'd better go back while you can."
The Sichuan Path is so difficult to tread, and to do so is to clamber to the sky.
Turning around, I look into the west and heave a long sigh of resignation.[12]

Li Bai was certainly no stranger to troubles; in fact his poems contain many descriptions of heartaches. But there were also times when his noble spirit overwhelmed such weakness, as his "Pray Thee Drink Your Wine" testifies:

Don't you see that the Yellow River coming from heaven roll into the sea never to return?
Are you alarmed to see in the mirror your white hair that was still black in the morning?
When life is good, you'd better enjoy it to the full,
So don't toast the moon with your gold cup of wine without drinking.
Born gifted, I will eventually be useful and able to earn back all the money I spend.
Let's cook some freshly slaughtered sheep and cattle, and have some fun,
And when we drink, we should take three hundred cups in a single gulp.
Hey, Misters Cen Xun and Yuan Danqiu, please drink without putting your cups down.
Let me sing a song for you and please strain your ears to listen.
A life of jade-like food accompanied by a bell-drum show is more than affordable;
Let us get drunk without waking up from inebriation.
Since ancient times, most sages have lived a lonely life, but only drinkers become known in history;
Prince Chen, for example, threw a party at Pingle Palace indulging in priceless wines.

Dear host, why did you say I'm short of money? Feel free to get more wine and we'll drink to our heart's content.
Here are my streaky horse and expensive fur coat.
Ask your son to trade them for some good wine, so that we can drink away all the worries of our lives.[13]

And his "A Farewell Dinner in Honor of Li Yun, the Official Collator, at the Xietiaolou Restaurant in Xuanzhou":

Many a yesterday that has passed is therefore not to be retained.
Many a today that has perturbed me is filled with added worries.
Wild geese flying in the strong autumn wind, it's high time we drank heartily in the pavilion.
Your writings of vigorous style deserve collecting by a fairy library, while mine, like the Younger Xie's, are also buoyant in spirit.
We are both detached in attitude and lofty in aspiration, having the urge to pick the moon from the sky.
The flowing water, however hard we try to slice it with a knife, is still flowing non-stop.
Our worries, no matter how much we drink, we're not going to drink away.
As life is so unsatisfactory, we might as well quit and enjoy ourselves on a hermit's boat tomorrow.[14]

This is quite different from the despairing sorrow of the Middle and Late Tang poems, and not the same as the idle sorrow of the Song Dynasty *ci* poetry. Li Bai's sorrow is sorrow with strength, sorrow out of the ordinary and sorrow marked by grace. In his poetry he exposes the dark side of society, and at the same time does so with an imposing flourish, thus revealing a robustness of feeling.

A major characteristic of Li Bai is his freedom of spirit, expressed as a pursuit of the realm of liberty and the carving out with the utmost striving of a space for imagination. In this, there is a very close connection with Taoist thought. He was inflexible in the face of power and wealth, absolutely refusing to bow and scrape: "How can I bow to the rich and powerful and make myself unhappy?" (A Poem of My Trip to Mount Tianmu as a Farewell Remark). "By nature, I'm an upright pine or cypress tree/ I disdain coveting favor with the looks of peaches and plums" (The Twelfth of *Ancient Style*). "I'd exchange gold and white jade for fun and entertainment/In my month-long inebriety, I have no respect for nobility" (A Poem of Our Past Travels Together Dedicated to Staff Officer Yuan Yan of Qiao Prefecture). But, toward the suffering common people he was modest and unassuming. In both these aspects we can sense Li Bai's strength of character. An illustration of this can be found in his "Staying Overnight at Old Lady Xun's Home":

Staying overnight beneath Mount Wusong,
All by myself, I found nothing entertaining.

I saw farmers toiling in the autumn fields;
I heard women pounding rice in the cold evenings.
Granny Xun serving me food on her knees,
The moonlit plate of wild rice shone like jade.
The granny was so generous and hospitable,
That I thanked her again and again before eating.[15]

Li Bai's poetry is marked by an untrammeled and bold style. The images conjured up by his writing brush are very individualistic, and often transcend reality. They have a fiercely subjective and fantastic coloring. His strong points are exaggeration, richness of imagery and free flow of language. When his emotion is at its height it even bursts the bonds of poetic convention, so that his verses can have a prosaic feel to them. For instance, "In the cold breeze and under the bright moon free of charge/I drink till I fall as a mound of jade without being pushed" (A Xiangyang Ballad).

Du Fu reflects the social turmoil and sufferings of the people which encompassed the time of the An-Shi Rebellion. He expressed the deep feelings of anguish for the country and the people which were felt at that time, but he never lost his hope for life. The reality of social life during the reigns of emperors Xuanzong, Suzong and Daizong, local conditions and customs, and the lifestyles of the various social classes of his time – from emperors to farmers and fishermen – all found realistic reflection in Du Fu's poems. Particularly worthy of note is the way he reflects social and political themes in a timely fashion, so that his works have been honored as "history in poetry." This is Du Fu's creative contribution. His "Song of the Conscripts," "A Beauty Passes," "Song of Aspiration Written on My Way to Fengxian County from the Capital," "The North Expedition," "Three Officials," "Three Partings," "Grieving over the Dead at Chentao" and "Baidi," etc. are all representative of this aspect of Du Fu the poet. His "Grieving over the Dead at Chentao" recounts how Prime Minister Fang Guan was defeated in battle with the rebel forces in 756. Du Fu was in the capital Chang'an when it fell to the An-Shi attackers, and was overwhelmed with sorrow. This poem is an authentic record of that time:

The soldiers drafted from ordinary families of ten prefectures,
In winter battles at Chentao shed their blood that filled its river.
Today no battle sound is heard on the open fields under the sky,
All the forty thousand soldiers died in action on the same day.
Swarms of rebel combatants returned, their arrows dripping blood,
Singing their tribal songs as they drank in the streets of the capital.
To the north where the emperor took his refuge, citizens lamented,
Day and night, they expect him and his imperial army to return.[16]

The benevolent spirit which is characteristic of Du Fu is a clear manifestation of the influence of Confucian thought. He had empathy with both people and things. The consideration he showed for people's feelings he showed also for animals and plants, as the close affinity he showed for cormorants and pine trees manifests. His "The Officer of Xin'an" illustrates this aspect of his character:

"I am traveling as a stranger on a road in Xin'an;
A commotion I see suggests recruit gathering.
I go up to the conscription officer of Xin'an,
Asking if the county has enough adult men.
"From the office I received last night a decree,
That we draft juveniles for a shortage of grownups."
"Adolescents are children, tender and short,
How can you expect them to guard the capital?"
Mothers are seeing the chubby youths off,
While the haggard are there without company.
The river quietly rolls to the east at dusk;
Below the mountain linger the mothers' sobs.
I go up to them who've just sent their kids away.
To solace them, I ask that they stop wailing.
"Don't cry so badly that your tears may dry up.
You know that heaven and earth are senseless."
The royal army starts to attack Xiang Prefecture,
Hoping that they can take it in a day or two.
Out of poor luck they underestimate the enemy.
And are defeated one regiment after another.
"The young soldiers eat in their old barracks;
Receiving training on the outskirt of the capital.
They dig trenches as shallow as above the water line;
They're given jobs as easy as grazing horses.
Moreover, so accommodating are the elite troops,
That they take good care of these children.
I'm asking you not to cry your heart out;
For the officers are treating them as their own."[17]

In the third month of the year 759, right in the middle of the An-Shi Rebellion, Du Fu passed through Xin'an County. There he saw rapacious officials levying taxes even upon under-age boys. The verses he wrote upon this theme stirred widespread indignation.

Du Fu's style can be described as "gloomy and ponderous," but his grand and expansive artistic realm is combined superbly with a fastidious attention to detail, resulting in a mastery of expression, which is "at hand but extends for a thousand miles." His vocabulary is vigorous and powerful, and his versification is rich in variety. He was skilled at writing in various kinds of poetic styles, especially using regulated verses. An example of the latter, using five characters to the verse is "Spring View":

The land of the country remains, though the capital is sacked,
Though spring, the city is laid waste and filled with weeds tall.

At this, even flowers feel so sad that they can't help sobbing.
The cries of startled birds add to the fear of fleeing residents.
The fire of war has been burning for three months running,
Making family letters as precious as a thousand taels of gold.
With sadness I rub my greying hair often as it keeps falling,
Till it becomes so thin that I find it hard to wear a hairpin.[18]

The first verse breaks on the reader like a thunderbolt. It has a great shock effect. It says that although the country is shattered, the mountains and the rivers continue to exist as before; in the midst of sorrow there is still a faint thread of hope. The poet expresses his lament for both his country and his home. Not only does the spring scenery fail to raise his spirits, the very flowers and birds seem to be sorrowing. In the words concerning the beacon fires he only expresses true human feelings. In the final two verses the poet returns to himself. They are like a mirror which sums up the entire poem.

Du Fu's "Thoughts on Autumn," in eight stanzas, and "Unburdening My Feelings for Ancient Relics," in five stanzas, are representative of his seven-character-verse works. "Baidi" is an excellent representative poem showing Du Fu's style:

Dark clouds are spewing out of the gate of Baidi;
A heavy downpour is taking place below the city.
Between the gorges, the torrent is thundering along;
Ancient pines and vines shield the sun and moon.
Warhorses enjoy less leisure than the farming ones;
Only a hundred out of a thousand households still remain.
Heavy levies are imposed on widows already woeful,
From which village do the wails come in this chilly land?[19]

The former four verses show the effects of the times on the poet: Surging river, precipitous gorges, ancient trees, soaring firmament – all are indicative of restlessness. The latter four descend to the life of the ordinary people. The seven characters in the line "One thousand houses now shelter only one hundred families" form a superb expression of the way the upheavals of war have brought unutterable sorrow to ordinary folk. When officialdom at the same time resorted to every means of extortion, it left the common people with no means to survive.

To sum up, after the hundred-year preparatory phase of the Former Tang period, the heyday of Tang emerged as the historical peak of Chinese poetry. This heyday was marked by the "ambience of the heyday of Tang," the three salient points of which were: orientation to the outside world; the search for and manifestation of new experiences; and the display of wide-ranging vision and structure. Of course, the poets of the Tang heyday did not just stick to one style; in fact they used just about every style, or, as the Chinese expression goes, "One hundred flowers bloomed." But still, these variegated styles melded into the common spirit of the age. Extensive, vigorous, far-reaching, transcending; full of strength, the joy of creation and novel experience; it presents a literary concept surpassing the function of imagination. It creates a new form of beauty through the mingling of emotion and sensual pleasure – All these things were the special features that differentiated the heyday of Tang from the other periods of poetic flowering in China.

Coming down from the peak

The middle part of the Tang Dynasty saw the greatest production of poems, and the greatest number of schools of poetry. The idealism and fervor of the Former Tang period began to wane. Grim and chilly reality forced the poets to adopt an attitude of sober reflection and inquiry. A number of them, represented by Bai Juyi and including Yuan Zhen, Zhang Ji and Wang Jian, applied themselves to the study of the Han Dynasty Music Bureau's collections and used plain language to reveal the sufferings of the common people and the corruption of the government. Bai Juyi advocated "prose written in tune with the times, and poetry written in tune with the essence of reality" (A Letter to Yuan Zhen) and "singing of the people's woes and hoping that Heaven will take note" (A Message Sent to Tang Qu). Some of his satirical poems, like "An Old Charcoal Seller", are scathing comments on the times:

> An old charcoal seller cuts wood and burns it to charcoal on Mt. Zhongnan,
> His face covered with soot, his hair greyed, and his fingers blackened.
> With the money he earns from selling charcoal, he buys clothes and food.
> Though thinly clad, he wishes that the temperature will fall so he can sell more.
> At dawn, he drives his oxcart out on the road iced with last night's snow.
> At noon, he rests in the mud by the market's south gate, hungry and tired.
> Trotting up to him lightly a eunuch dressed in gold and a bailiff in white.
> After reading a decree from the emperor, they lead his oxcart to the north.
> He hates the officials for taking away his precious charcoal, but what can he do?
> They gave him only fifty feet of raw silk and ten feet of satin as payment.[20]

This poem describes how the officials harass the people. Comparing it to "A Chronicle of the Emperor of Shunzong," it is simply a straightforward report of social problems of the time, but this kind of satire on current politics displays the effect such politics had on Du Fu himself. As well as this, Bai Juyi's "The Long Lament" borrows the love tragedy of Tang Emperor Ming and Lady Yang to give expression to his yearning for the heyday of Tang. In this poem a particularly fine passage describes Emperor Ming's return from Shu:

> Back to the capital, he found the pools and gardens remained the same,
> So do the lotuses in the Taiye Lake and the willows by Weiyang Palace.
> The lotus flowers remind him of her face and the willows of her brows;
> Looking at them, who wouldn't be touched and shed sorrowful tears?
> Spring breezes urge peach and plum blossoms to bloom in the evening;

Autumn rain sweeps the leaves of the parasol trees off to the ground.
The Taiji and Xingqing Palaces are infested with autumn weeds;
Red fallen leaves covering all the stair cases without being swept away.
He spotted grey hair on the heads of his court singers and dancers,
And traces of aging on the faces of his female officials and attendants.
In bed he thinks of his beloved while fireflies hover around his palace,
Lamp oil burnt out, he shows no sign of drowsiness in the lonely night,
Finally there comes the sound of bells and drums heralding the dawn.
Looking at the twinkling Milky Way, he feels that the night's too long.[21]

His "Song of the Lute," which is an account of the tragedy suffered by a singing girl, contains a superb description of music:

Lightly plucking in and slowly plucking out, she also strikes the strings in and out,
She plays the Rainbow and Feather Garment tunes afore the Green Waist melody.
Tsiek, tsiek, tsiek, there go the thicker strings that make sounds akin to a storm.
Chirp, chirp, chirp, the thinner strings make murmurs like a woman's whisper.
Tsiek and chirp and chirp and tsiek, she alternates her plucking on strings of both types,
Producing a chord that sounds like big and small pearls dropping onto a plate of jade.
Sometimes it sounds like the singing of jolly orioles gliding beneath blossoms;
Sometimes it labors as if it were a moaning stream gurgling under an ice surface.
The chord drags on and on as if the strings were congealed like the freezing stream.
Since the strings of the *pipa* are frozen as it were, silence reigns momentarily.
There must be suppressed sorrow and hatred that the player has been harboring;
Silence in this particular situation is more significant than when a tune is played.
Then all of a sudden the sound rises as if a silver vase full of water had been toppled,
And as if cavalrymen on the charge engaged their enemies with clashing swords.
Before she finishes, she gives a forceful final strike to the center of the instrument,
Thus creating with four strings a unison that resonates like silk fabric being torn.

All of a sudden, silence befalls this pleasure-boat and other sampans all around;
Nothing seems to be in existence except the brilliant moon reflected on the river.[22]

In the lines "Thinking that we're both strangers cast into this remotest corner of the world/I really appreciate our first encounter, not caring if we have ever met before." the poet's attitude to the singing girl is one of equality, a most admirable position to adopt.

Another group of poets, represented by Han Yu and including Meng Jiao, reflected social problems through their individual misfortunes. They pursued a peculiarly bitter style, traveling a different road from that of Bai Juyi. Han Yu, for instance, in his "Fire on Mount Luhun," says,

Tigers, bears, elks, and boars closely following monkeys and apes,
Lizards, alligators, tortoises, fish and giant soft-shell turtles,
Crows, owls, vultures, eagles, pheasants, gulls and magpie-robins.
Who can escape from being baked, steamed, or cooked on a slow fire?

He uses in this poem a prose method, which had a powerful influence on the later poetry of the Song Dynasty. Li He, who died at the early age of 27, used fantastic images and an extraordinary romantic style to mark out a separate path for Late Tang poetry. An example is his "To the Tune of the Governor of Yanmen Prefecture":

Dark clouds are weighing down as if to crush the city;
Armor glistens in the sun like the scales of gold fish.
In the wind of autumn horns are calling far and wide;
On the frontier blood stains turn purple in the twilight.
The troops are marching by the Yi River, colors flying.
Their battle drums are muffled because of heavy frost.
To repay the kindness bestowed to us by His Majesty,
Wielding our swords, we will fight till our last breath.[23]

Li He's poems thoroughly embody the charm of poetic language, and, transported by this charm, he wrote poems which transcended all the conventions of the craft. He loved to use powerful and colorful words such as "death," "tears" and "blood." His brush was very meticulous when it came to writing details, and as a consequence the overall composition often loses balance. So when we read his poems we can detect some points of convergence with modern schools of poetry.

The representatives of the Later Tang period on the poetic stage are Du Mu and Li Shangyin. They regretted the passing of the golden age of Tang Dynasty poetry, and their works are full of fin-de-siecle nostalgia, to the extent of lamentation. Looking back in helpless sorrow at history, reflecting on experiences and impressions of human life, and the pursuit of pure skill and artistry are the three aspects forming the beauty of Later Tang poetry. A kind of drawing-to-a-close atmosphere settled on the poetic stage, presaging the end of a great era of poetry. This atmosphere is captured in Du Mu's "Moored by the Side of Qinhuai River":

Haze enshrouds the cold water as moonlight veils the sand,
I moor my boat for the night by a tavern on the Qinhuai River.
Courtesans across the river knowing not the kingdom's fall,
Are still singing a song composed by a conquered emperor.[24]

And in Li Shangyin's "The Amusement Mound":

Toward the evening, I fall into a bad mood;
In my carriage, I climb to the ancient mound.
There the setting sun looks impressively beautiful,
But unfortunately darkness will soon prevail.[25]

These two poems reveal the real aspect of their times.

Du Mu's quatrains using seven characters to the line have been much praised for their refreshing and dainty style. A representative example is "Mountain Journey":

The stone path zigzags far into the cold mountain,
I see a few houses lurking in the mists and clouds.
I alight from my carriage for the love of the view:
At dusk, maple leaves look redder than February flowers.[26]

Li Shangyin's poems are marked by an implicit and understated style, rich in multiple meanings. An example is his "A Beautifully-Decorated Zither":

How come you beautiful zither have fifty strings?
Each string and fret reminds me of the good old time.
Like Zhuangzi's butterfly, I can't tell reality from dream;
Like Wangdi's cuckoo, I feel the same pain of lost love.
As in a myth, I resemble a pearl of tears under the moon,
Or a jade stone veiled in beguiling mists on Mt. Lantian.
Why do we now have to remember our past joy and grief?
Weren't we blind and indifferent enough to them at the time?[27]

There are many explanations of the meaning of this poem: some say that it deals with love; some that it has political connotations. There are also different opinions on the love object. But what is perhaps certain is that the basic tenor of the poem is a lament for the loss of a beautiful hope that ought to belong to the poet. His untitled poem, with its lingering, sorrow-laden and obscure cadences, awakens in the reader a plethora of responses. Among these is the difficulty of pinning down the theme, although some people are sure that love is the topic. An example is one of the two stanzas of "Untitled":

> While stars were bright and breezes cool last night,
> East of a painted pavilion and west of a scented house.
> Without phoenix wings we couldn't fly side by side,
> But the magic rhino made us feel affectionate.
> Sitting facing, we drank guessing hook-like tokens;
> In groups we played a drinkers' wager game in candlelight.
> Alas, the morning drum sounded, and I had to go to work,
> I galloped to Lantai like grass whirling in the wind.[28]

This perhaps describes an unfulfilled tryst with a lover. The two sentences begin with "without phoenix wings" have become a much quoted phrase.

A general view of the poetry of the Tang Dynasty leads us to conclude that its most important significance in the history of Chinese literature was its establishment of the norms of poetry. Following the Tang, Chinese poetry followed either of the two roads of following closely or diverging from these standards. The mainstream of Ming Dynasty poetry stuck to these standards, while that of the Song Dynasty diverged from them. In the Qing Dynasty, some poets clove to them while others abandoned them; either way, they all revolve round the poetic tradition laid down in the Tang Dynasty. It was only following the May 4 Movement of 1919 that Chinese poets started to learn from the West, and Chinese poetry started to blaze a new trail. From this point of view, it becomes clear that in the history of Chinese poetry the poetry of the Tang Dynasty occupies a pivotal position.

Notes

1 *Complete Tang Poems*, Vol.50, Zhonghua Book Company, 1960, P. 611.
2 *Complete Tang Poems*, Vol.83, Zhonghua Book Company, 1960, P. 902.
3 *Complete Tang Poems*, Vol.65, Zhonghua Book Company, 1960, P. 752.
4 *Complete Tang Poems*, Vol.96, Zhonghua Book Company, 1960, P. 1043.
5 *Complete Tang Poems*, Vol.117, Zhonghua Book Company, 1960, P. 1183.
6 *Complete Tang Poems*, Vol.128, Zhonghua Book Company, 1960, P. 1300.
7 *Complete Tang Poems*, Vol.128, Zhonghua Book Company, 1960, P. 1306.
8 *Complete Tang Poems*, Vol.126, Zhonghua Book Company, 1960, P. 1279.
9 *Complete Tang Poems*, Vol.128, Zhonghua Book Company, 1960, P. 1306.
10 *Complete Tang Poems*, Vol.125, Zhonghua Book Company, 1960, P. 1307.
11 *Complete Tang Poems*, Vol.126, Zhonghua Book Company, 1960, P. 1278.
12 *Complete Tang Poems*, Vol.162, Zhonghua Book Company, 1960, P. 1680.
13 *Complete Tang Poems*, Vol.162, Zhonghua Book Company, 1960, P. 1682.
14 *Complete Tang Poems*, Vol.177, Zhonghua Book Company, 1960, P. 1809.
15 *Complete Tang Poems*, Vol.181, Zhonghua Book Company, 1960, P. 1844.
16 *Complete Tang Poems*, Vol.216, Zhonghua Book Company, 1960, P. 2267.
17 *Complete Tang Poems*, Vol.217, Zhonghua Book Company, 1960, P. 2282.
18 *Complete Tang Poems*, Vol.224, Zhonghua Book Company, 1960, P. 2404.

19 *Complete Tang Poems*, Vol.229, Zhonghua Book Company, 1960, P. 2505.
20 *Complete Tang Poems*, Vol.427, Zhonghua Book Company, 1960, P. 4704.
21 *Complete Tang Poems*, Vol.435, Zhonghua Book Company, 1960, P. 4819.
22 *Complete Tang Poems*, Vol.435, Zhonghua Book Company, 1960, P. 4821.
23 [Qing Dynasty] Qi, Wang: *The Collected Poems of Li Changji with Commentary*, Vol.1, Shanghai Ancient Books Publishing House, 1978, P. 52.
24 *Complete Tang Poems*, Vol.523, Zhonghua Book Company, 1960, P. 5980.
25 *Complete Tang Poems*, Vol.539, Zhonghua Book Company, 1960, P. 6148.
26 *Complete Tang Poems*, Vol.524, Zhonghua Book Company, 1960, P. 5999.
27 *Complete Tang Poems*, Vol.539, Zhonghua Book Company, 1960, P. 6144.
28 *Complete Tang Poems*, Vol.539, Zhonghua Book Company, 1960, P. 6163.

4 The new direction of Song Dynasty poetry and the flourishing of poetry studies

The new direction of Song Dynasty poetry

The Tang poets excelled in wide-ranging imagery, gracious charm, broadness of conception and elegance of style. They would cultivate the spirit of a poem before setting writing brush to paper. Or one could say that they only wrote about things which had attained the height of being worthy to be expressed in poetry. Then they exerted themselves to express the fine inner nature of the thing, pursuing the concept of beauty. The beauty of Tang poetry was an evanescent beauty, like that of flowers in a mirror or the moon reflected in water; it shimmers before the eyes and cannot be anchored. The beauty of Tang poetry is a robust beauty, healthy and vigorous and devoid of pretension. It is a kind of internal beauty, the allure of which lies in its ability to express the richness and colorfulness of life. Its essence is in its innocence and naturalness, and not in its ornate turns of phrase.

By the Tang Dynasty a complete set of poetic genres had developed, and each genre had a full power of expression. All styles had been tried by the poets, and the poets themselves came from every social stratum. Hu Yinglin hit the nail on the head when he said,

> Indeed, poetry saw its heyday during the Tang dynasty. In terms of genres, Tang poetry has it all, such as poems with three, four, five, six, or seven characters to a line; rhapsodies, *yuefu* (Music Bureau folk songs), *gexing* (poems to a tune), *jintishi* (modern-form poems), and *jueju* (poems with broken-off lines). In terms of genres, it can describe almost everything – high and low, far and near, thick and thin, deep and shallow, big and small, sketchy and detailed, exquisite and clumsy, and strong and weak. In terms of styles, it covers all, including grace, vigor, profoundness, magnificence, beauty, leisure, novelty and vulgarity. In terms of characters, it covers emperors and kings, generals and ministers, court officials, commoners, children, women, Buddhist monks and nuns, as well as shamans and supernatural beings.[1]

This led Lu Xun to say, "In my opinion, all the good poems were composed by the Tang Dynasty. Since then, it has been totally unnecessary for one who doesn't possess the superpower of somersaulting out of the Buddha's palm, like the 'Monkey King' to try his hand."[2] Wen Yiduo said,

> In most of our histories of literature from the Western Zhou Dynasty to the Song Dynasty there is only one history of poetry, and it seems that the development of poetry stopped with the Northern Song Dynasty. We feel that the poetic movements and debates of Ming and Qing dynasties were a last-ditch battle not even worth mentioning. Every defeat in such a battle gives us fresh proof that the effort was not worthwhile. The two millennia from the Western Zhou to the Northern Song was plenty of time for all types of melodies to have been sung. . . . After that came the eras of the novel and the drama.[3]

Wen Yiduo may be a little extreme here; nevertheless, he points out a basically authentic trend.

The literature of the Song Dynasty was more extensive than that of the preceding Tang Dynasty, and the number of writers was greater also, assisted by the wide application of advances made in the art of printing. The number of literary collections handed down from Song times is much bigger than that of the Tang – and about double the number of poems. According to the *Complete Song Poems*, in 72 volumes, published by the Peking University Press, there were nearly 10,000 Song Dynasty poets, who produced over 250,000 works. This is indeed a huge legacy. But the creativity of the Song poets, facing the challenge of the heyday of the Tang, refused to follow in the footsteps of its glorious predecessors, and followed a new road. They did not seek their way in poetry pure and simple, but used other genres for reference, even applying prose techniques to the writing of poetry; by pursuing prose literature to create poetry, they made poetry out of prose. They seemed to say: "Wasn't the acme of poetry reached by you Tang poets? It was, but I have made non-poetry into poetry." And there should be a reference to the quote. All the elements that went to make up poetry from the Han Dynasty to the Tang Dynasty – richness of structure, exquisiteness of form – were steadily reinforced. But the Song poets reversed this trend: They pulled poetry down from its summit, and made it non-poetry. Taking into account the efforts of the Song writers, we can praise the new direction they took, or we can criticize it. Nevertheless, we cannot but recognize their new efforts at creativity, and find them praiseworthy. In this regard, Zhu Ziqing said, "The topics covered by the Song poets were many, but they were consistently covered. They used common words mostly, and eschewed grandiose rhythms. Those who extol Song poetry maintain that everything on Earth is lacking and needs changing; only when it is changed can it function properly. And the situation is exactly the same with poetry. Change is renewal, expansion and progress. Without willingness to change, one is left with a stereotype or even plagiarism. Such 'drama actors' and even plaster casts are not worth talking about."[4] Qian Zhongshu says, "Taking Tang poetry as their model was the great good fortune of the Song poets, and their great misfortune as well. The good aspect of this model was that the Song poets learned how to constantly improve their use of words and technique. But at the same time they tended to be lazy, simply copying the patterns. It has been said by a Ming Dynasty critic that Song poets who studied Tang poems ended up writing poems that read just like Tang poems. For instance, see 'On Reading *Quintessential Records*' in the 26th volume of *The Collected Works of He Jingming*. Reviewers of Huang Tingjian's collected poems since the Song dynasty have all compared his poetry to that of Du Fu. These verses are not bad, but it is impossible to detect any Song creativity or sense of values in them. The Ming Dynasty poets who studied Tang poetry did so not in a complete way: They are like Tang poems and yet not like Tang poems. However, they lack individuality and new concepts, and so earned the epithets "blind imitation of Tang poetry", "fake ancient poems" and "drama actors" (See Vol.11 of Yu Shenxing's *Collected Writings of the Gucheng Mountain Hall* [Preface to the Poems of Feng Zongbo]; Like a painting master, he reproduces what is seen . . . Nothing that is not like . . . But in the end there is no meaning . . . There is likeness, but the reality is lost.' Again, in the 'Preface to the Collected Works of Zhu Guanglu,' we find, 'Overall, they copy the format of previous works, while plagiarizing words and phrases. They are long on form and short on substance. These are the words of a passer-by who once was under the influence of the Seven Writers."[5]

The chief characteristic of Song poetry can be summed up in Yan Yu's words: "The dynasty's literature was in its poetry, its learning was in its poetry, and its topics were in its poetry."[6] Qian Zhongshu goes a step further when he points out, from the angle of esthetics: "Tang poetry is superior when it comes to exalted sentiments, but it yields to Song poetry in the matter of solid thought."[7] Song poetry arose at a time when there were no people of poetic feeling or poetic inspiration to point the way to becoming a poet, and scholars had to make themselves poets. The concrete way they did it was to wrest their own poetic creations from those of the ancients, using the ancients' materials and words in a makeshift way, and transforming them and patching them up to make their own poetry. So anyone who was well read and well acquainted with classical quotations, and could express ideas in depth (either by inferential methods or implying them by means of images) and could turn apt phrases would be considered an outstanding genius. Huang Tingjian, the leader of the Jiangxi school, himself said, "When Du Fu wrote poetry he divorced himself completely from prose. Not a single word came from that source. They were not as well read as their successors, and so it was said of Han and Du that their words were their own. The ancient writers were able to mold everything to the shape they themselves desired, when later writers used their writing brushes and ink on words and phrases culled from the ancients, it acted like a magic elixir, turning base iron into gold."[8] But the successful Song poets were not satisfied with such an approach; they sought the materials for their poetry from real life, paying special attention to the daily life around them and making efforts to dig out the connotations of such life activities. But what they called daily life was mainly the life of literary men, and so the Song poets tended to exude a literary flavor. The poets of the Tang Dynasty, especially those of the Tang heyday, placed emphasis on dealing with and representing images from

Nature, whereas those of the Song Dynasty tended to place their emphasis on literary men for their material. This is the major difference between the Tang and Song poets.

The above is just a general description which discusses the creative tendency of the Song poets, with the objective of pointing out the characteristics which marked Song poetry off from that of the Tang. On the one hand, I have affirmed the spirit and efforts of the Song poets in their search for innovation; on the other, I have pointed out their shortcomings. However, each of the Song poets had his strong points, and if we want to get a clearer picture of Song poetry we need a more concrete discussion of the history of development of Song poetry.

The representative poets of the early part of the Northern Song Dynasty could be said to be Mei Yaochen and Ouyang Xiu. The former's style is a pedestrian one, while the latter's is "plain and with the use of pithy words."[9] But their imagery is lacking in richness and literary grace. Artistically, they are far from successful. Following them came Wang Anshi, a man of profound knowledge, who claimed that he had "read all the works of the philosophers, and all the novels, even the *Yellow Emperor's Canon of 81 Difficult Questions*, *Basic Questions*, and *The Compendium of Materia Medica*."[10] In his poems he liked to show off his erudition with quotations from the classics and express his opinions. At the same time he paid great attention to ornate diction. There is a famous example of this. In his "Mooring My Boat at Guazhou," there are the lines:

> Guazhou faces Jingkou across the Yangtze River/
> My home Mount Zhong lies a few ranges beyond/
> The spring breeze is painting the river's south green/
> When will the moon take me back to my home?

The word ""green" started off as "arrive," and then went through "pass," "enter" and "full" before finally becoming "green."[11]

Su Shi was the most accomplished figure on the literary stage of the Northern Song Dynasty. Over 4,000 of his poems are extant. He had a bold imaginative spirit, and his thoughts gushed onto the paper as naturally as floating clouds or flowing water. His strong point was the application of rich and apt metaphors – so incisive as to take the reader's breath away. Examples are "Black clouds gather, but fail to cloak the mountain/White rain is beating on the boat like pearls dropping" (One of the Five-Character Poems Composed in Inebriety on the Lake-Watching Tower on June the 27th). "I compare the West Lake to the famed beauty Xishi/Who looks gorgeous with light or heavy makeup" (Drinking the Water of the Rain Soon after It Stops over the Lake). "I sweep the floor, burn incense and sleep after closing the temple/On my bamboo mat of wavy patterns and in my mosquito net of misty veils" (The fifth of the five South House poems). These are all very good examples. Su Shi was not only good at describing natural phenomena and daily life, he was also able to elevate these ordinary descriptions to comments on the philosophy of human life. For instance "Inscription on the Wall of Xilin Temple":

> It's a peak when looked at from the front and a range from the side.
> The mountain's form changes when viewed at varying distances.
> I find it hard to figure out what the true features of Mount Lu are,
> Simply because I'm looking at everything in the mountain itself.[12]

In the Later Northern Song period Huang Tingjian put forward some new theories of poetic and ballad creativity, and, with the support of Chen Shidao and others, founded the Jiangxi School of poetry. In his "*Ying Kui Lv Sui (Essence of Lvshi Poetry in Honor of the Eighteen Scholars Climbing Mount Yingzhou on an Auspicious Night When Five Planets Lined Up in the Sky)*," Fang Hui states that this school has one patriarch and three ancestors: The patriarch was Du Fu, and the three ancestors were Huang Tingjian, Chen Shidao and ChenYuyi. The Jiangxi school's doctrines can be roughly divided into two: One was "Not one word without an origin" (Huang Tingjian's "A Letter in Reply to Hong Jufu"), stressing comprehensive reading and seeking verbal excellence from scholarship; and the other was "smelt iron into gold" (ibid.) and "reject the covering and seek the substance." By the first, the poets of this school meant elaborating on the verbal arrangements of the ancients, and make them into a brand-new vocabulary; and as for the latter, Huang Tingjian said, "The artistic conception of poetry is infinite, while a person's creativeness is finite. To seek the infinite with the finite requires even more than the talent of Tao Yuanming or Du Fu. To create words without changing the conception is but "being reborn with a different skeleton." To comprehend the conception and describe it with words is "being reborn with a new embryo."[13] The first principle stresses the aspect of words, the second the aspect of poetic meaning. Both are types of creative effort. For instance, Huang Tingjian says in his "A Poem Written on High-Quality Rice Paper in Reply to Wang Bingzhi Using His Rhyme Sequence": "Lord Wang's beard resembles the bamboos growing along the mountainside/The poem chanted from his shielded mouth is like wind blowing in a hollow valley."[14] Here he uses the description by Wang Bao in his "An Agreement with Servants" of the whiskers on a servant as like "bamboos on a verdant hillside" in a fresh form of words. However, if these poets were to put their efforts into making something new out of the ancients' poems and ballads how were they to express their own feelings and interests without stepping down into a secondary position? If their artistic level was to be gauged by their skill in innovation, it would be like taking somebody else's old woolen overcoat and reshaping it to fit oneself; although this would be a type of creativity, it would still look shabby.

The patriotic Southern Song poet Lu You wrote nearly 10,000 poems. He started by studying the Jiangxi school, and then in middle age, after joining the army, he cast off this influence. He then achieved great success. The poets of the Jiangxi school adopted the subject matter and flowery language of the ancients, and added touches of their own to form a new type of poetry. Lu You studied the methods of the ancients, but sought his inspiration in real life and forged his own grandiose diction. He said, "What a piece of writing should avoid above all is the garments of the Hundred Schools" [of ancient philosophers] (A Poem Written Using the Same Rhyme Sequence and Words as the One Composed by Yang Bozi) and "What is acquired from books is always shallow" (Demonstrating to My Son Yu When I Was Reading One Winter Night). He also said, "I can recognize the fine parts of your poems, just as if I were traveling by mountains and streams" (Inscription on the Back Cover of a Poem Collection by a Scholar Named Xiao Yanyu from Luling). These are all barbed references to the malpractices of the Jiangxi school. Lu You's poetry followed the great tradition of Tao Yuanming, Li Bai, Du Fu, Cen Shen and Bai Juyi. But it was rooted in his own life experience. He created his own unique style. Although his writing is smooth and clear, it still manages to present a grandiose and vigorous spirit. His poems express a fierce feeling of patriotism. Representative of this is the second part of his Thoughts Arising from Going out of the Fence Gate to Cool off One Autumn Night poems:

> The Yangtze of three-thousand miles rolls to the east sea,
> The mountains of five thousand feet reach to the blue sky.
> Tears of the survivors are dried up by the conquerors' war dust.
> For another year, they're expecting their royal army to return.[15]

And "Written on the Rainy and Windy Fourth Day of the 11th Month":

> Lying stiff and cold in a lonely village, I'm not pitying myself.
> I'm thinking of defending the Luntai frontier instead.
> Hearing a sputtering rainstorm late at night,
> I dream of armored horses galloping on frozen rivers.[16]

The poems in which he describes everyday life are also full of interest, like (A Trip to a Village West of the Mountain):

> Don't laugh at the farmers when they offer you their home-made wine;
> In a good year, they have enough chickens and pork to treat their guests.
> Mountain after mountain and river after river, I doubt if there's a way;
> Beyond a shady willow forest, I see a village amidst brilliant blossoms.
> As the New Year is close at hand, I hear flutes and drums wherever I go;
> Clad in plain clothing and headgear, they adhere to their ancient custom.
> If I were allowed to return for more leisure trips under bright moonlight;
> I would surely come on my walking stick to knock at your doors any night.[17]

Like Lu You, the equally famous Yang Wanli also started out by studying the poetry of the Jiangxi school, and later created his own style. In his *Canglang's Remarks on Poetry*, Yan Yu called it the "Yang Chengzhai Style." So we can see how influential Yang was at that time. In his "Introduction to Chengzhai's

Jianghu Collections," Yang Wanli says, "When I was young I wrote over a thousand poems, but during the Shaoxing reign period I burned them all. They were probably Jiangxi school works."[18] In his "Introduction to Chengzhai's Jingxi Collections" he says that he sought poetic joy in Nature: "Walking in the back garden, climbing ancient city walls, picking wolfberries and chrysanthemum flowers, and pulling down and plucking flowers and breaking bamboos – everything in nature can be manifested in and used as source materials for poetry. Then the muse cannot be checked: New poems are eager to pop up from your mind before you finish proofreading the ones you have just finished. Thus you'll never find it difficult to write poems."[19] Yang Wanli's poems have a "lively method" to them, which is described by Qian Zhongshu as follows; "He puts his effort into objects, especially those of the natural world, recreating the real flesh-and-blood relationship between mother and son. He seeks to restore the simple and natural impressions of sight and sound. He does not allow restless objects to become the sacrificial vessels of moribund writings. He tears down the film that gathers over one's eyes from reading too many ancient books, and with his lively and nimble writing brush he brings to life scenes which are difficult or even impossible to describe in words. And so Jiang Kui praised him in these words; 'Everywhere the mountains and the streams fear to see the master.' In fact, they fear to fall under his gaze, and become portrayed down to the smallest detail in one of his poems."[20] Representative poems by Yang Wanli are "Waking up from Napping at a Leisurely Early Summer Noon":

> The *yangmei* berries are so sour that they set my teeth on edge;
> The palms' green color is reflected upon the screen windows.
> Days becoming longer than nights, I get up late with boredom;
> Having nothing to do, I watch children catching willow catkins.[21]

And "Preparing Breakfast at Qigongdian after Crossing Songyuan":

> Don't expect the trip to become easier down the hill,
> You travelers might celebrate your triumph too early;
> For after you enter the labyrinth of a thousand ranges,
> One after another the mountains will block your way.[22]

These two poems contain real-life discoveries of his own. They are lively, brisk and pleasing.

Fan Chengda ranks with Yang Wanli as a poet. His rustic poems are all taken from real life, and have a thick flavor of that life. An example is No.44 from his "Miscellaneous Joys of the Four Seasons in the Country":

> On the ground just leveled as smooth as a mirror,
> Every family is busy threshing while it's frost-free.
> Laughter and singing rise like gentle thunder,
> There's the sound of flailing throughout the night.[23]

In the Late Southern Song period there emerged the poetic schools of The Four Spirits of Yongjia (the name of a reign period – 307–313 – of Emperor Huai of the Jin Dynasty) and The Rivers and Lakes. The former were four poets from the region once ruled over by Emperor Huai – Xu Zhao, Xu Ji, Zhao Shixiu and Weng Juan. All four were poor itinerants who took Jia Dao and Yao He as their predecessors, resolutely turning their backs on the Jiangxi school and continually coming up with innovations. They did not travel the same road as the poets of the Late Tang; theirs was a narrow and cramped road, and did not allow any great achievement. The other school was also dissatisfied with the Jiangxi school. Seeking another path, it followed that of the Four Spirits of Yongjia. Its representative and most famous member was Liu Kezhuang.

From the above account it can be seen that the Jiangxi poetic school occupied center stage starting in the Northern Song Dynasty, and the evolution of Song poetry was basically connected with the development of this school.

The flourishing of poetry studies

The peak of the development of the theory of poetry in ancient China came in the Song Dynasty. In the categorized statistics in the *Great Dictionary of Chinese Poetic Studies*, edited by Fu Xuancong et al., there are over 200 theses on the various kinds of poetic genres.[24] And these only cover the special topics of "type," "language," "style," "narrative," etc. If we include the prefaces and postscripts of collections of poems, discussions of poetry in books and letters, and in scientific and historical accounts, and literary works, as well as in anthologies and works of criticism, we find that the field of poetic theory was a rich one indeed. The contents of this field covered the five main topics of creativity, origins, appreciation, authors and functions.

The *Ouyang Xiu's Notes on Poems* by Ouyang Xiu of the Northern Song Dynasty was the first work of poetry criticism that had such a title. The high tide of Chinese poetry studies was the period from the appearance of this book to that of the *Canglang's Remarks on Poetry* by Yan Yu of the Southern Song Dynasty. In this period poetic studies developed in both breadth and depth, and this form, with an ultimate degree of flexible Chinese characteristics, was widely applied. And it was from these "poetry notes" that "*ci* poetry notes" emerged. The core of the *Ouyang Xiu's Notes on Poems* was "new ideas and precision in words" and "meaning outside the words." These ideas can be traced to a conversation between Ouyang Xiu and Mei Shengyu. In practical terms, what they are advocating is:

> Mei Xiaochen often says to me, "A poet always acts at his own will and finds it difficult to get the right words. However, if he is creative and skillful in language and acquires the way that previous poets failed to, then it will be all fine with him. He will certainly be able to describe what is hard to do as if it were right before his eyes and convey the inexplicable thoughts beyond words. Then he will become perfect . . ." I reply, "This is exactly what we call an expert."[25]

"New ideas and precision in words" stresses verbal creativity, while "meaning outside the words" stresses inspiration drawn from words. It is well worth noting that this latter entails a search for the manifold meanings a single word can have. Following this came Su Shi's poetic studies, the core of which is his worship of Nature. This is the theoretical basis for the esteem he held Tao Yuanming in. The core of Huang Tingjian's poetic theory is "no word without an origin," "forging iron into gold" and "reject the covering and seek the substance." Under the influence of Huang Tingjian, concentration on the source (of a quotation, et.) became a trend. And in the Southern Song Dynasty, Yang Wanli's "method of life" became the new focus of attention. Lu You poured all his attention into linking practical life with poetic connotations.

Certain Song Dynasty philosophers, such as Shao Yong, Zhu Xi and Lu Jiuyuan, also had their own theories of poetry. But as they tended to stress doctrine at the expense of literature the effect of the entry of philosophy into poetry was a tempestuous one.

Especially worthy of attention in this regard is Yan Yu's *Canglang's Remarks on Poetry*. This book extols the poems of the Han, Wei and Jin dynasties, and those of the heyday of the Tang Dynasty. It highly praises their ambience and diction. This was a new and very meaningful achievement in the field of poetic theory:

> Discussing poetry is like discussing Zen. Poems of the Han, Wei, Jin, and the Glorious Age of the Tang dynasty are the most Zen-significant . . . Only when they are comprehended in Zen terms can their true nature or intrinsic quality be revealed.[26]

Yan Yu pays great attention to the special characteristics of poetry. He points out that poetic and scholarly writing are different. As for the connection between the two, the following is important:

> Poets must have special talents, which have nothing to do with book reading. Poems possess a special artistic charm beyond reasoning. But paradoxically, poetry cannot be perfect without poets reading more widely and reasoning more thoroughly. The best poet is one who does not fall into the trap of reasoning and word-mincing. A poet is a singer of disposition. The poets of the Glorious Age of the Tang dynasty put poetic art first; therefore their unconventional works showed no trace of human efforts. The beauty of their poems lies in that they were exquisite craft instead of sloppy patchwork. They were like the music in heaven, matter in appearance, the moon on water, and the image in a mirror. Therefore they were profoundly meaningful with limited words.[27]

Yan Yu's personal contribution was to find a new position for poetry and ballads. He stressed their characteristics of being different from scholarship as such, and being unconnected with reasoning. At that time, this was a very penetrating thesis which had a profound influence on later generations.

The tandem prosperity and decline of *fu* and *shi* poetry

During the high tide of poetic and ballad creativity in the Tang Dynasty, and in the conditions of striving for a new direction for poetry and ballads in the Song Dynasty, *fu* poetry continued to thrive.

In the Tang Dynasty the writing of *fu* poetry was widespread, and many writers of that time have left such works. This probably has something to do with the fact that, beginning in the later part of the reign of Emperor Gaozong (650–684), the writing of *fu* poems was included in the national civil service examinations. However, this and the attention paid to *fu* creativity probably interacted with each other to boost the popularity of this genre.

The outstanding works of Tang *fu* poems are Wang Bo's "Winter Pine at the Bottom of a Gorge," Li Bai's "Great Roc," Du Fu's "Vulture," Han Yu's "The Sentiments of Two Birds," Bai Juyi's "Long Painful Journey," Liu Yuxi's "Autumn Sounds" and Du Mu's "Epang Palace." Here we will give a brief introduction to Li Bai's "Great Roc" and Du Mu's "Epang Palace."

"Great Roc" borrows its image from the legendary bird mentioned by the philosopher Zhuangzi. This bird is of such mettle that "neither anger nor courage can induce it to engage in strife." It is free to "soar into the empyrean or plunge to the lowest depths." Zhuangzi contrasts it to petty birds such as parrots, while Li Bai uses it as a metaphor for his own spirit of seeking freedom by breaking the bonds of convention. In his "Epang Palace," Du Mu uses the story of the destruction by fire of this luxurious palace built by the First Emperor of Qin (reign: 246–209 BC) as a warning to the ruling circles of the Tang Dynasty. The final part of the poem goes:

> Alas, what conquered the six states was not Qin, but the six states themselves. What brought about the downfall of Qin was not its people, but its government. Alas, if the sovereigns of the six states had loved their people, their states could have had the resources to resist Qin. By the same token, if Qin had demonstrated its benevolence to the people of the six states, its sovereign throne could have been passed on to the third and even ten-thousandth generations. Who then could vanquish it? The people of Qin did not even have the time to lament, leaving that to later generations. Nevertheless, if the later generations only lament without learning a lesson from history, they in turn will be lamented by their posterity.[28]

The outstanding *fu* poems of the Song Dynasty are Ouyang Xiu's "Autumn Sounds" and Su Shi's "Verses on the Red Cliff." The former, by skillfully capturing the sounds and aspects of autumn, laments the worries and toils of human life. It draws on the artistic characteristics of the prose works of Han Yu and Liu

Zongyuan. Its use of parallelism and phonetic harmony is somewhat free. It is a representative work of the "literary *fu*" type.

> Master Ouyang was reading one evening, when he heard a sound coming from the southwest. Startled, he listened. "Strange!" he thought. At first, it sounded like the pattering of light rain sweeping up. Then suddenly it turned into a rushing and a banging sound, like the pounding of waves in the night or the beating of a storm. Everything it touched clanged like iron or the clash of arms on a battlefield. As if men were rushing to war gagged so as not to alarm the enemy, no orders were heard, but there were definitely the sounds of men and horses. He called his servant, and asked, "What is that noise? Go out and have a look." The servant reported, "The stars and the moon are clear and bright. The Milky Way is shining in the heavens. There is no human sound anywhere. The noise is in the trees."[29]

Su Shi's "Verses on the Red Cliff" and "Sequel to the Verses on the Red Cliff" have very much a prose format. The former deals with the principle of the changes and non-changes in the interconnection between human life and the universe, and the compatibility between what ought to be and actual creation. The latter contains a superb description of the scenery at the Red Cliff in winter, and concludes with an account of a Taoist monk who sprouts wings in a dream and becomes an immortal crane. "Verses on the Red Cliff," in its entirety, is as follows:

> On July 16, 1082, I took a boat tour with some friends to the place right beneath the Red Cliffs. Flurries of cool breezes came without disturbing the tranquility of the river. I then invited my guests to drink and recite the "Modest retiring, and virtuous young lady" poem from the "Rising Moon" section of the "Odes of Chen" chapter of the *Book of Odes*. Before long, the moon appeared from behind Xishan Mountain and started to linger between the Dipper (Sagittarius) and the Ox (Capricornus) constellations. A white veil of mist mantled the surface of the Yangtze, the glistening light of its waves being connected to the starry sky. We let the sampans float freely on the vast, misty river, which rolled endlessly as if it were flying up and away in the wind, to stop at no one knows where. How graceful! It was just like a celestial being sailing out of this world up to Paradise.
>
> As we enjoyed drinking, we began to sing, beating on the sides of the boat with our hands. The lyric said, "Poles of cherry bay wood and oars of magnolia/splitting the clear river water/The boat greets the oncoming glistening light of waves/How profound, my feelings!/O, I look to my love in the faraway place." Among the guests, someone started to play his vertical bamboo flute. We then sang to its accompaniment. The flute whimpered as if to express bitterness or lovesickness, sounding like sobs or murmurs bent on pouring out one's heart. Long after it came to a stop, the music lingered like a thread of silk unwinding endlessly. The music could make the flood dragon

> lurking in depths of the water emerge and dance, and cause a widow on the boat to shed her tears. I could not help feeling sorrowful. Tidying my clothes and sitting straight up, I asked, "Why so?" The guest replied, " 'The moon is bright and stars scarce/Magpies are flying southward.' Isn't this a sentence from a poem by Cao Mengde? If you look to the west, you see Xiakou; to the east, Wuchang. In between the water meanders around the mountains covered with a wild profusion of vegetation. Isn't this where Cao Mengde was besieged by Zhou Yu? After taking Jingzhou, he captured Jiangling. When he went down towards the east on the Yangtze River, his warships stretched out for a thousand miles, banners and flags blotting out the sky. Presiding over a memorial ceremony involving the sprinkling of wine into the river, he held a long spear horizontally in his hands, and chanted poems and verses. How heroic he was! But, alas, where is he now? The less-important people like us, while toasting one another on a lonely boat, catching fish, cutting wood, taking fish and shrimps as our companions, and making friends with elks, we are but mayflies living a parasitic life in this world, as insignificant as a tiny grain of rice dropped into the vast sea. We are grieving over our ephemeral life and envious of the eternity of the Yangtze. We wish we could roam with celestial beings and like them become as immortal as the brilliant moon. I know this is not always possible to realize, so we have but to entrust the lingering music to the sadly cool autumn wind."
>
> I said, "Where the river water and the moon are concerned, the water flows constantly but never disappear. The moon wanes and waxes but never gets more or less. Speaking of their transformation, everything under the sun changes in an instant. In terms of their eternity, everything including us will exist forever. Why do we have to envy them? Besides, all things on earth have their specific owners. We'll never get what we are not to claim. Only the cool breeze over the Yangtze River, the bright moon between the mountains, the sound we hear, and the colors we see, we can possess without any one's hindrance. As Mother Nature's inexhaustible treasures, use them, and I will share them with you."
>
> After hearing this, the guests broke into joyful laughter. Washing out the cups, we started to drink again, until we finished the good food and fruit, leaving behind a messy array of empty utensils. We fell asleep, lying upon or close to one another. Before we realized it, daylight had already broken in the east.[30]

From the Yuan Dynasty on, there was some continuance of creativity in the *fu* genre, but not much, and a trend of degeneration made its appearance. Some of the better *fu* works of this period are Yuan Haowen's "Gazing at the Autumn," Liu Ji's "A Rhapsody to Castigate a Parasitic Lifestyle," Zong Chen's "Angling Terrace," Huang Zongyi's "Seaside Market," Fang Bao's "Double Seventh" and Yuan Mei's "A Rhapsody of Derision."

The writing style of "A Rhapsody of Derision" is broad and vigorous. The first part mocks misers, muddle-headed officials, foolish people who believe in superstition and witchcraft, and inveterate gamblers. The second part satirizes various distasteful phenomena common in Confucian circles. Its barbs aimed at cloddish officials are particularly telling:

> And there are others that are willing to leave their land of comfort and happiness to seek officialdom, thereby climbing up to the dangerous top, as it were, of an acrobat's bamboo pole. This only wins them one man's favor from the top but complaints from many down below. However, some may not end up getting what they are craving after all, so that they may find themselves laughing too early. The higher they climb, the harder they may crash to the ground. The further they are into the sea, the worse disaster they may encounter. Are they crazy if, in that situation, they still miss the cranes' pleasant singing and the flavored water-shield soup at home?[31]

Notes

1 [Ming Dynasty] Yinglin, Hu: *Garland of Poetry*, Extra edition, Vol.3, Shanghai Ancient Books Publishing House, 1979, P. 163.

2 *The Collected Works and Letters of Lu Xun*, Part 2, People's Literature Publishing House, 1976, P. 699.

3 "Historical Trends in Literature," *The Complete Works of Wen Yiduo*, Part 1, *Myths and Poems*, Ancient Literature Publishing House, 1957, P. 203.

4 Ziqing, Zhu: *Talks on the Classics * Poetry No.12*, Sanlian Bookshop, 1980.

5 Zhongshu, Qian: *Song Poems Selected and Annotated * Preface*, People's Literature Publishing House, 1958, P. 14.

6 *Canglang's Remarks on Poetry * Discussing Poems*, Collated and Translated by Guo Shaoyu, People's Literature Publishing House, 1961, P. 24.

7 Zhongshu, Qian: *Records of Discussions of Art*, Zhonghua Book Company, 1984, P. 2.

8 [Song Dynasty] Tingjian, Huang: "A Letter in Reply to Hong Jufu," *The Collected Works of Huang Tingjian*, Vol.19, *Collected Writings of the Four Basic Branches of Literature*.

9 [Song Dynasty] Shaoyun, Ye: *Discussion of the Poems of Shilin*, First Part, [Qing Dynasty] Wenhuan's, He: *Talks on the Poetry of Successive Dynasties*, Zhonghua Book Company, 1981, P. 407.

10 [Song Dynasty] Anshi, Wang: *The Collected Works of Mr. Linchuan*, Vol.73, "Reply to Zeng Zigu's Letter," *Collected Writings of the Four Basic Branches of Literature*.

11 [Song Dynasty] Mai, Hong: *Sequel Essays From Rongzhai*, Vol.8, Shanghai Ancient Books Publishing House, 1978, P. 317.

12 Xuancong, Fu et al. eds. *Complete Song Poems*, Vol.806, Peking University Press, 1991, P. 9339.

13 [Song Dynasty] Hong, Hui: *Night Words of the Cold Studio*, Vol.1, *Collected Literary Works*.

14 Xuancong, Fu et al. eds. *Complete Song Poems*, Vol.986, Peking University Press, 1991, P. 11370.

15 *Lu You's Collected Works * The Jian Nan Poetic Manuscripts*, Vol.25, Zhonghua Book Company, 1976, P. 686.

16 *Lu You's Collected Works * The Jian Nan Poetic Manuscripts*, Vol.26, Zhonghua Book Company, 1976, P. 710.
17 *Lu You's Collected Works * The Jian Nan Poetic Manuscripts*, Vol.1, Zhonghua Book Company, 1976, P. 710.
18 [Song Dynasty] Wanli, Yang: *The Chengzhai Collection*, Vol.80, *Collected Writings of the Four Basic Branches of Literature*.
19 [Song Dynasty] Wanli, Yang: *The Chengzhai Collection*, Vol.80, *Collected Writings of the Four Basic Branches of Literature*.
20 Zhongshu, Qian: *Song Poems Selected and Annotated*, People's Literature Publishing House, 1958, P. 180.
21 [Song Dynasty] Wanli, Yang: *The Chengzhai Collection*, Vol.3, *Collected Writings of the Four Basic Branches of Literature*.
22 [Song Dynasty] Wanli, Yang: *The Chengzhai Collection*, Vol.35, *Collected Writings of the Four Basic Branches of Literature*.
23 [Song Dynasty] Chengda, Fan: *The Collected Poems of the Hermit of Stone Lake*, Vol.27, *Collected Writings of the Four Basic Branches of Literature*.
24 See Xuancong, Fu et al. eds: *Great Dictionary of Chinese Poetic Studies*, Zhejiang Education Publishing House, 1999.
25 [Qing Dynasty] Wenhuan, He ed: *Talks on the Poetry of Successive Dynasties*, First Part, Zhonghua Book Company, 1981, P. 267.
26 *Canglang's Remarks on Poetry * Discussing Poems*, Collated and Translated by Guo Shaoyu, People's Literature Publishing House, 1961, P. 11.
27 *Canglang's Remarks on Poetry * Discussing Poems*, Collated and Translated by Guo Shaoyu, People's Literature Publishing House, 1961, P. 26.
28 [Tang Dynasty] Mu, Du: *The Fanchuan Collection*, Vol.1, *Collected Writings of the Four Basic Branches of Literature*.
29 [Song Dynasty] Xiu, Ouyang: *Collected Literary Works of Ouyang Xiu*, Vol.15, *Collected Writings of the Four Basic Branches of Literature*.
30 [Song Dynasty] Shi, Su: *The Collected Works of Su Dongpo*, Vol.33, *The Complete Four Repositories*, Pavilion of the Imperial Library
31 [Qing Dynasty] Mei, Yuan: *The Collected Poems of the Cottage on Mt. Xiaocang*, Vol.25, *Shanghai Zhonghua Book Company's Essentials of the Four Treasures*, 1936.

5 The ebb tide of poetry

The Yuan, Ming and Qing Dynasties

The Tang and Song models

The poetry of the Yuan Dynasty presents a dreary picture with occasional flashes of brilliance. The dynasty's most celebrated poets were Liu Yin, Wang Mian and the "Four Yuan Masters" – Yu Ji, Yang Zai, Fan Peng and Jie Xisi. The structure of Liu Yin's poems was as lively as that of Yang Wanli. For instance, here is Liu Yin's "By the Stream":

> Sitting long on a mossy stone I felt cold seeping into my body,
> With my walking stick, I shuffled into the shade along a stream.
> Tired, the soughing of the wind in the pines was dying down;
> Drifting rapidly, the clouds were darkening the mountains.[1]

Wang Mian was also a noted artist, and the signature poems he inscribed on his paintings are replete with lofty sentiments. For instance, his "A Plum Tree Painted with Ink":

> This is the plum tree by our ink stone-washing pool:
> Each of its blossoms bloom with ink marks subtle.
> Not seeking to covet praise for its pretty colors,
> It's bent on leaving its fragrance to the universe.[2]

During the Ming Dynasty there developed a controversy in poetry circles over whether to adopt the Tang or Song style as a model. The most influential voice in the Ming Dynasty was that of the Former and Later Seven Writers schools, which favored the Tang. The leaders of the Former Seven Writers were Li Mengyang and He Jingming, who were active in the Hong Zhi (1488–1506) and Zheng De (1506–1522) reign periods of emperors Xiaozong and Wuzong, respectively. The *History of the Ming Dynasty * Literary Biography* says, Li Mengyang is intrepid and possesses great imaginative power. He arrogantly considers himself to be an advocate of returning to the ancients. During the reign of the Hongzhi Emperor, Prime Minister Li Dongyang was in charge of evaluating and selecting successful imperial examinees. All the people of his time respected him. Li Mengyang, being an exception, ridiculed the former as being weak, while he insisted that prose composition must return to the ages of the Qin and Han dynasties poetry making, to the Glorious Age of the Tang Dynasty. Otherwise, it would be against the way of literature.[3] It also says that, according to Li Mengyang, in poetry there are seven difficulties to surmount: "keeping to the style of the ancients," "flexibility," "smoothness," "significance of verse units," "roundness of sound," "immediacy of thought" and "sincerity." He considered that the Song poets did not conform to these standards, and so "produced no poetry."[4] In addition, he said, "By the Tang Dynasty, the ancient rhythms had been lost, and so the best that the Tang poets could do was write for orchestral accompaniment. The Song poets stressed texture over rhythm, and so even the Tang rhythms were lost . . . But has there ever been poetry without texture? So even if you concentrate your efforts on the texture alone, what you write must be poetry, mustn't it?"[5] According to He Jingming, "The *Book of Odes* was superseded by the *sao*-style poetry of Qu Yuan, which in turn was superseded by the *fu* poetry, which then yielded to *shi* poetry. In the Qin Dynasty there was no *Book of Odes*; in the Han Dynasty there was no *Li Sao*; in the Tang Dynasty there was no *fu;* and in the Song Dynasty there was no *shi*."[6] The Later and Former Seven Writers of the Jiajing Reign Period (1522–1567) of the Ming Dynasty drew their inspiration from the Tang Dynasty, while ignoring the poetry of the Song Dynasty. They were somewhat more meticulous than their Tang predecessors, and nevertheless had some tolerance for the Song poets. Their leading lights were Li Panlong, Wang Shizhen and Xie Zhen. Li Panlong made a compilation of poems from previous dynasties, which did not include a single Song or Yuan poem. Wang Shizhen took the poems of the heyday of the Tang as his standard, having nothing to do with poems from the mid-Tang onward.[7] He once said, "The era cannot do without the man; the man cannot do without the composition; and the composition cannot do without the wording."[8] By this he meant that he did not deny the Song poets altogether. Xie Zhen's pen name was "Man of Mount Siming," and his *Siming's Poetic Discussions* was widely circulated and very influential. In it, he tends to extol the Tang at the expense of the Song. Hu Yinglin, who was not a member of the Later Seven Writers, also promoted the Tang in his *Garland of Poetry*. He says, "Tang poems are like the hibiscus when it first sprouts; it is naturally lovable. But reading Song poems is like panning for gold; much labor for little reward."[9] The criticism of Song poetry by the Former and Later Seven Writers no doubt hit the nail on the head when it concluded that the achievements of the Song poets could not match those of the Tang poets. But the Song poets after all did make some explorations and contribute some creativity, and it cannot be denied that they produced some fine works. Although on the whole it is fair to say that the Tang era was superior to that of the Song, we cannot say the same about all the individual poets of the two periods. Poetic creativity following the Tang Dynasty, since it could not match the excellence of the heyday of the Tang, was forced to find a new direction. And so even the Former and Later Seven Writers, who favored the Tang, had no choice in their poetic compositions but to follow the new trail blazed by the Song poets. The Seven Writers soon found themselves at loggerheads with the "Three Yuans of Gong'an" (Yuan Boxiu, Yuan

Zhonglang and Yuan Xiaoxiu). Yuan Zhonglang was the most talented of the trio. He said, "The spirit of poetry diminishes with every era; in ancient times it was robust, but now it is only a shadow of its former self. But the exquisite craft in poetry is inexhaustible. It increases with every era. In ancient times it had unfathomable spirit, and now it exceeds the ability of man to fully describe it. So how can you call the compositions of ancient times exalted, and those of modern times base?"[10] He even said that he himself had been "excessive" in saying that "there was no poetry in Tang times."[11] Whereas the Seven Writers honored Du Fu, Yuan Zhonglang put great effort into promoting Ouyang Xiu and Su Shi. He comments that Ouyang Xiu's poetry "is like a storm able to overturn the sea. Therefore he is almost as good as Du Fu."[12] He further observes, "Not a single word in Su Shi's poems is poorly chosen. Li Bai was good at fantasy, while Du Fu, reality. Being good at fantasy only, Li Bai left us many a miraculous image; being exclusively an expert at reality, Du Fu could only compose poems to describe mortals instead of celestials and nature instead of fairyland. Su Shi's poems can be both worldly and spiritual. Whether the language is coarse or refined, they are all profound. They may sound ecstatic, but they are not without realistic expression. That is because he is extremely talented, and his scholarly attainments well exceed those of Li Bai and Du Fu. His works therefore can be eternally exceptional. As for the popular conviction that his poems are not as vigorous as Du Fu's or as bold as Li Bai's, it is not because he lacks talent, but because of his fate."[13] However, both the partisanship of the Tang by the Seven Writers and that of the "Three Yuans" on behalf of the Song eventually faded away, and these views were succeeded by the more balanced one of Zhong Xing and Tan Yuanchun in their book *A Retrospective on Tang Poetry*. As they were both from Jingling, they are known to literary history as the "Jingling School." In the preface to the book, Zhong Xing criticizes both the Seven Writers and the Yuans. Zhong and Tan tried to patch up the gap in the concept of Tang poetry of the Seven Writers, which had come to nothing, with visions of peaceful places amid lonely mountains, resulting in what they called "real poetry." In the "Preface" it says, "Real poems are products of the spirit, perceiving solitary feelings, independent conduct, and tranquil hopes amidst the hustle and bustle of the world. They can therefore transcend this world to roam quietly by themselves without effort or distraction of the mind."[14] For a time, the influence of Zhong and Tan eclipsed that of the Three Yuans. Mr. Qi Zhiping presents an incisive analysis of this phenomenon in his book *A Brief Account of the Tang-Song Poetry Controversy*.

To sum up: Throughout the Ming Dynasty the creative mainstream took Tang poetry as its model. Ming poets studied the achievements of their Tang predecessors. We cannot do better here than quote Li Mengyang's "Zheng Sheng Returns from Mount Tai":

> Looking down, one fails to see the land of Qi and Lu;
> Gazing to the east, one finds the sea sitting like a cup.
> Standing upon the summit of the precipitous Mount Tai,
> One's uncertain if there're any other peaks around.

One sees the sun jump off from the tree where it rests;
The horizon recedes to reveal a famed mountain inland.
Long after the First Emperor of Qin paid his visit here,
A spectacle still is the monument he left then and here.[15]

The style and diction of this poem have clearly been learned from Du Fu's "Gazing at Mount Tai." It is certainly not lacking in verve, but in the final analysis it does not have the richness of Du Fu's poetry, and it seems to just fade away.

The Qing Dynasty: a riot of poetry schools

The period from the start of the Qing Dynasty until the mid-Qing was one of creative brilliance. The poets of this time were divided roughly into those who took the Tang poets as their models and those who favored the Song poets, with the former being the mainstream, represented by Gu Yanwu, Zhu Yizun, Wang Shizhen, Wang Fuzhi and Mao Qiling. To the latter school belonged Huang Zongyi, Lv Liuliang and Wu Zhizhen (Lv and Wu jointly edited the *Transcriptions of Song Poetry*). Particularly worthy of note is Wang Shizhen, the most famous of the Qing poets. His appreciation of poetry basically went through three phases: In his early years he admired the Tang; in middle age he became an enthusiast for the Song; and in his later years he returned to the Tang. See the "Preface to Discussions of Yu Yang's Poems," by his disciple Yu Zhaocheng. The "Synopsis of the *General Catalog of the Complete Four Repositories*" is not far wrong when it says, "He took the heyday of the Tang as his model," and "made romantic charm his master."[16] The two characters meaning "romantic charm" first appear in "Records of Ancient Paintings" by Xie He of the Qi Dynasty, one of the Southern Dynasties. In a critique of Gu Jun's paintings, Xie He says, "In romantic charm and vigor, he does not match up to the old masters, but in subtlety and attention to detail he surpasses the philosophers." By "subtlety and attention to detail" the writer is referring to the positive and meticulous way the painter represents his figures; by "romantic charm" he is clearly referring to something outside the figures themselves. This expression "romantic charm" was constantly quoted afterwards, but only to Wang Shizhen was it applied as a term of special praise. See *Three Glimpses of Tang Masters*, *Discussions of Yu Yang's Poems* and *Discussions of the Poems of Daijing Hall* edited by Wang's disciple Zhang Zongnan. In the case of Wang Shizhen, "romantic charm" implies some spiritual force beyond the actual words. He recognized that writing a poem did not simply entail forcefully bringing to the gaze some concrete thing or stubbornly sticking to stark reality, pursuing form at the expense of the inner truth. Much more important was to use enlightening language lavishly to express a spirit of the unity of the viewer with the object viewed. The same thing is expressed by the phrases "A wealth of meaning coming from mere words" and "While the words are limited, the meaning they express is boundless." Another way of putting it is to say that reality emerges from emptiness. Representative poems of Wang Shizhen are "Four Stanzas on Autumn Willows" and "Random Poems about the Qinhuai River." Part of the latter goes:

For months I've been feeling sad on the boat around Nanjing,
Skeins of sorrow winding around pavilions by the Qinhuai River.
Wispy strands of rain have been drifting for the past ten days;
Like a late autumn season feels the misty thick air of spring.[17]

"Passing Loujin Shrine Again" is also full of "romantic charm."

The ornamental headwear and earrings remain the same,
Green are the clouded lake and misty trees by the temple.
Travelers are mooring their boats for the night at moonset.
Outside, virtuous white lotus flowers bloom in the wind.[18]

Loujin Shrine is in Gaoyou County, Jiangsu Province. The story goes that a girl once spent the night in the open there. It was the height of summer, and mosquitoes were swarming. There was a plowman's hut nearby, but she would not seek shelter there to be sure of preserving her chastity. As a result, she was eaten alive by the mosquitoes. Only her bones, drenched with dew, were found in the morning. The local people erected a shrine there to commemorate her uprightness. The final two verses of this poem are reflected in the poem "White Lotus" by Lu Guimeng: "You're about to wither in the bright moonlight and cool breeze. Can anyone with bitterness but no mercy understand you?" in which the white lotus refers to the girl. In his "Stele at Loujin Shrine," Mi Fu of the Song Dynasty says, "The girl's surname was Xiao, and her given name was Luohua (falling blossom)." Therefore it would not be too far-fetched to say that white lotus refers to this girl.

During the Qianlong (1736–1795) and Jiaqing (1795–1821) reign periods the Tang-Song controversy came to a head, with each side clearly stating its position. Shen Deqian came down heavily in favor of Tang, with his exaltation of style. The books *Sources of Ancient Poetry* and *A Collection of Tang Poems of Different Genres*, for which he selected the poems, became very influential. Yuan Mei accentuated mood, insisting that the composition of a poem reveal the freshness and feelings of an individual, and not be bound by ancient fetters. He said, "It is often said that poems are different in terms of good or bad craftsmanship but not in time changes. As for the poets' temperament and life experience, each is different from the other. Therefore, contemporaries cannot imitate the ancients and be like the ancients, or fear them and be limited by them."[19] What he meant by mood was the poet's genuine feeling at the moment of creativity, a sort of magical empathy between him and the reader. This proposal of Yuan Mei had a tendency to harmonize the views of the pro-Tang and pro-Song camps. Nevertheless, Yuan Mei's own poetry had its own individuality. An example is his "Moss," using the five-character format:

Where the sun never shines,
Its frail life reaches its prime,
Flowers as tiny as millet grains,
It tries to bloom as peonies do.[20]

The feelings and the words are both fresh, and they are also both his own. Weng Fanggang pays great attention to the texture of the poem, striving to fill the gaps in the "romantic charm" with scholarly references, and including some of the flavor of the Song poems. Shen, Yuan and Weng all had their own ideas, but the pro-Song tendency predominated. This was closely connected with the scholarly enthusiasm for textual research and the Tongcheng school of ancient literature which arose during the Qianlong and Jiaqing reign periods. In addition to the above three, there was Huang Jingren, who wrote about his poverty-stricken and downtrodden life, and in doing so strove to produce something novel. Such as; "Unnoticed, I stand on a bridge in the market/Gazing long at a star as if it were the moon" (One of the "Poems Written by Chance on the New Year's Eve of 1773"). "All the family members are exposed to the wind/Heavier clothes are not yet tailored in September" (Thoughts in Autumn at the Capital's Gate). His poems, which are full of resentment, contain lines such as: "Nine out of ten people suffer contemptuous looks/A scholar is one who's ninety-nine percent useless" (Random Thoughts). "Random Feelings" were highly appraised in his day.

Following the Opium Wars, there came a turnaround in poetic creativity. Gong Zizhen, troubled about the fate of his country, with his great literary endowments issued an epoch-making call. Two lines of his "Miscellaneous Poems of Ji Hai" illustrate this:

> Grief of parting surges as the sun sets in the west,
> Whip in hand, I gallop to the far end of the world.
> Red flowers falling are not necessarily senseless;
> Tending as mud to blossoms of the coming spring.
> Full of vigor, China should release a raging storm,
> But it's sad to find the warhorses kept quiet.
> I pray thee, Ruler of Heaven, pull yourself together;
> Breaking all your rules, the best talents you find us![21]

During the Tongzhi (1862–1875) and Guangxu (1875–1911) reign periods the so-called Tong-Guang style of poetry flourished. Its representatives were Chen Sanli, Chen Yan and Shen Zengzhi. They modeled themselves on the Jiangxi school. Each had noticeable accomplishments, their influence was very strong, and it could be said that they surpassed the Song poets. But in this genre anything could serve as the subject of a poem, whether it had any poetic spirit or significance or not. As a result, poetry writing became a tool for showing off the writer's scholarship, and although some fine pieces emerged, most of the corpus of this era developed in the direction of not being poetry at all, and ended up in a worthless dead end.

In these circumstances, Huang Zunxian started a revolutionary new trend for poetry. As a diplomat, Huang had traveled to Japan, England, the United States and Singapore, and these experiences had widened his horizons and given him new ideas and new subject matter, ranging from steam ships, trains, the telegraph, London fog and the Eiffel Tower in Paris – They could all be used as subjects of poems. Following this, Liang Qichao raised the slogan of a "revolution in the poetic world," and a group of progressive poets put a lot of energy into creating a new realm of poetry. However, their achievements were limited.

The new poetry movement which started with the May 4 Movement of 1919 looked to Western models and used colloquial language, thereby creating a brand-new face for Chinese poetry.

Notes

1 [Yuan Dynasty] Yin, Liu: *The Collected Works of Mr. Jingxiu*, Vol.12, *Collected Writings of the Four Basic Branches of Literature*.

2 [Yuan Dynasty] Mian, Wang: *The Zhuzhai Collection * Continuation, The Complete Four Repositories*, Pavilion of the Imperial Library.

3 [Qing Dynasty] Tingyu, Zhang et al: *History of the Ming Dynasty*, Vol.286, *Literary Biography*, Zhonghua Book Company, 1974, P. 7348.

4 [Ming Dynasty] Mengyang, Li: *The Kongtong Collection*, Vol.48, *Reminiscences of the Man of Mount Qianqiu, The Complete Four Repositories*, Pavilion of the Imperial Library.

5 [Ming Dynasty] Mengyang, Li: *The Kongtong Collection*, Vol.52, *A Preface to the Sound of Fou, The Complete Four Repositories*, Pavilion of the Imperial Library

6 [Ming Dynasty] Jingming, He: *The He Dafu Collection*, Vol.38, *Miscellaneous Words, The Complete Four Repositories*, Pavilion of the Imperial Library.

7 [Ming Dynasty] Shizhen, Wang: *Four Types of Literature in Manuscript From the Man of Mount Yanzhou*, Vol.65, *Preface to the Collected Works of Xu Rusi*, Ming Chongzhen block print.

8 [Ming Dynasty] Shizhen, Wang: *Continued Manuscripts of the Man of Mount Yanzhou*, Vol.41, *Preface to a Selection of Song Poems by Shen Meng*, Ming Chongzhen block print.

9 [Ming Dynasty] Yinglin, Hu: *Garland of Poetry*, Extra Edition, Vol.6, Shanghai Ancient Books Publishing House, 1974, P. 234.

10 [Ming Dynasty] Hongdao, Yuan: "A Letter to Qiu Changru," *The Collected Poems of Yuan Hongdao Annotated*, Vol.6, *The Brocade Sail Collection*, No.4, Shanghai Ancient Books Publishing House, 1981, P. 284.

11 [Ming Dynasty] Hongdao, Yuan: *The Collected Poems of Yuan Hongdao Annotated*, Vol.11, *A Collection of Vimoksha or Emancipation*, No.4 "A Letter to Zhang Youyu": "Most People Like the Tang, but I Say the Tang Dynasty Produced no Poetry . . . Most People Disdain the Poetry of Both the Song and Yuan Dynasties, but I Say that the Great Poets Were Those of the Song and Yuan Dynasties," Shanghai Ancient Books Publishing House, 1981, P. 501.

12 [Ming Dynasty] Hongdao, Yuan: "Letter to Li Longhu," *The Collected Poems of Yuan Hongdao Annotated*, Vol.23, Shanghai Ancient Books Publishing House, 1981.

13 [Ming Dynasty] Hongdao, Yuan: "Reply to Mei Kesheng," *The Collected Poems of Yuan Hongdao Annotated*, Vol.21, *Flower Vase Studio Collection*, No.9, Shanghai Ancient Books Publishing House, 1981, P. 734.

14 Xing, Zhong: "Preface to Tang Poems Retrospect," *Hidden Splendor Studio Collection * Collection of Wen Ze*, Ming Tianqi block print.

15 [Ming Dynasty] Mengyang, Li: *The Kongtong Collection*, Vol.23, *The Complete Four Repositories*, Pavilion of the Imperial Library.

16 *General Catalog of the Complete Four Repositories*, Vol.196, Critiques of Poetry Collections, Category 2, synopsis of *The Record of Teachers' and Friends' Commentaries on Classics of Poetry*.
17 [Qing Dynasty] Shizhen, Wang: *Quintessental Records*, Vol.5, *The Complete Four Repositories*, Pavilion of the Imperial Library.
18 [Qing Dynasty] Shizhen, Wang: *Quintessental Records*, Vol.5, *The Complete Four Repositories*, Pavilion of the Imperial Library.
19 [Qing Dynasty] Mei, Yuan: *The Collected Poems of the Cottage on Mt. Xiaocang*, Vol.17, *Reply to Shen Dazong on his Discussion of Poetry*, Qing Qianlong block print.
20 [Qing Dynasty] Mei, Yuan: *The Collected Poems of the Cottage on Mt. Xiaocang*, Vol.18, Qing Qianlong block print.
21 [Qing Dynasty] Zizhen, Gong: *Collected Works of Gong Zizhen, Collected Writings of the Four Basic Branches of Literature*.

6 The structure and style of *shi* and *fu* poetry

Above, I have discussed the origin and evolution of *shi* and *fu* poetry, sketching their structure and style characteristics in the sequence: Ancient, *sao*, *shi and fu*. In the process, I have touched on the origins of the five-character and seven-character *shi* poems. However, these questions have not been explained clearly, and neither have the topics of the origin and evolution of *shi* and *fu* poetry. There is no need to go over this ground again; here, I will just first discuss the forms of the ancient poems, and then, in more detail, discuss those of the more modern poems. Finally I will cover the characteristic features of the *shi* and *fu* poetry.

The structure of the ancient poems

"Ancient poems" were defined as such after the Tang Dynasty, and preceded recent poems. They differ mainly in the fact that the latter came after the former, hence the designations. Nevertheless, even after the recent poems started to be written there were still lots of people writing in the ancient style. So the two differ in pattern. The typical patterns of the ancient-style poems are as follows:

1 There was no limit to the number of verses – they could be many or few. A long one, "The Peacock Flies Southeast," has 357 verses; a short one like "Song of the Great Wind" has only three.
2 Each character could have either a level or oblique tone, with no restriction, and so the composition of such poems came close to that of prose. In that respect, the ancient-style poems were not like those of the modern style, in which the arrangement of level and oblique tones affects the order of words.
3 Antithesis replaces rules.
4 Rhyme is necessary. Level and oblique tones may rhyme, generally on alternative lines but also in a series of lines. Also, every line in a poem may rhyme (When a seven-character-verse poem contains the same rhyme throughout, it is called the "Bailiang style"), or they may alternate. The demands of the ancient-style poetry were fairly broad as regards rhyme – unlike the tight restrictions of modern poetry – and could also be based on colloquial or dialectal rhymes. An example is No.5 of the "Nineteen Ancient Poems":

Xi bei you gao lou, shang yu fu yun qi.
(In the northwest there's a pavilion so tall that it touches the clouds),
Jiao shu jie qi chuang, e ge san chong jie.
(Tree-storied, it has decorative windows of crisscrossing lattice work),
Shang you xian ge sheng, yin xiang yi he bei.
(Upon it there comes sad singing to the accompaniment of strings).
Shui neng wei ci qu, wu nai Qi liang qi.
(Who other than the grieved wife of Qiliang could make this music?)
Qing shang sui feng fa, zhong qu zheng pai huai.
(The Qing-shang tune carried in the wind sounds hesitant halfway);
Yi tan zai san tan, kang kai you yu ai.
(Sighing three times with each plucking, the player sounds sorrowful.)
Bu xi ge zhe ku, dan shang zhi yin xi.
(Lack of appreciative listeners is more piteous than the player's plight.)
Yuan wei shuang hong hu, fen chi qi gao fei.
(She wishes that she and her love were as inseparable as a swan couple.)[1]

This poem follows a system where rhyme takes place every other sentence. During the Han dynasty, the Chinese characters "qi," "jie," "bei," "qi," "huai," "ai," "xi" and "fei" belonged to the same rhyme category found in the Pingshui system created by Liu Yuan of Pingshui. Later, however, the system broke into several subcategories such as "Qi," "Jia," "Zhi," "Hui" and "Wei." It is obvious that poems of the Han Dynasty could not possibly have a rhyme system that emerged at a later time. Even later writers of "ancient-style" poetry were not bound by the Han Dynasty scheme, providing more freedom for composers of such poems.

As ancient-style poems did not have tight phonetic restrictions, nor did they have strict demands on antithesis. Rhyming was fairly relaxed. We could say that ancient-style poems were ones which approached freedom of composition, or at least were half-free in this respect.

Ancient-style poems could have four, five or seven characters to the verse, or a mixture. The latter, which had different numbers of characters to the verse, appeared in poems with unmatching verses.

Some people include the *Songs of Chu* and the Music Bureau collection in the category of ancient poems; others do not agree.

The structure of modern-style poetry

Modern-style poetry is a type of poetry which took shape in the early Tang Dynasty. It evolved from ancient-style poetry, and can be divided into the two categories of regulated verse and quatrains. The first can have five or seven characters to the line (A long poem of this sort may have five characters to the verse and more than eight verses, which, all except the first and last lines, form antitheses.) Quatrains may have five or seven characters to the verse.

Except for the long poems, regulated-verse poems all have eight verses and a rhyme scheme. The third and fourth verses and the fifth and sixth verses must each form an antithesis, and there is a set pattern of level (平) and oblique (仄) tones for the characters in every verse.

The first thing to be explained is the matter of rhyme. Prior to the Tang Dynasty, rhyme was based completely on colloquial speech; following the Tang it was necessary to consult rhyme books. Sun Mian of the Tang Dynasty published his *Tang Rhymes* based on a book called *Rhymes Explained.* The former became the standard book of rhymes. In the Song Dynasty, Chen Pengnian and others brought out the *A Comprehensive Book of Rhymes*. This book's phonetic system was based on that of *Tang Rhymes*. With a total of 206 rhyming characters divided into four tonal categories, this work is somewhat cluttered, but since near-rhymes are included, the number of proper rhymes is only 112. Wang Wenyu of the Jin Dynasty edited a book called *A New Edition of the Brief Rhymes of the Bureau of Rites*, meant for civil service examination candidates. Its 206 entries are paired into 106 rhymes. This book was used throughout the Yuan, Ming and Qing dynasties, and is still in use today.

Next, we must discuss antithesis. There are two major demands on antithesis:

1. The positioning and type of words in a pair of antithetical verses had to correspond – noun to noun, adjective to adjective, verb to verb, function word to function word, etc. If the words used to correspond with each other belonged to the same sub-category (for instance, two astronomical nouns) or if two opposites were used to correspond (for instance "up" and "down") then the antithesis was considered particularly neat.
   二、
2. The phraseology of the two antithetical verses had to correspond; for instance, a subject with a subject, and an object with an object.

Below are some examples of antithesis:

The mountain follows the plain and tapers off/The river enters the desert and meanders on (Li Bai: Farewell to My Hometown as I Pass the Jingzhou Gateway).

All wild paths are dark/Only river boats are lit (Du Fu: Happy to See Rain Fall on a Spring Night).

I hear the cock crow in the thatched cottage under the moon/I see footprints on the frost-covered plank bridge (Wen Tingyun: A Morning Stroll on Mount Shang).

The Hanyang trees are clearly seen in the bright sunlight/The Yingwu Shoal is lushly covered with green verdure (Cui Hao: Yellow Crane Tower).

Warships with upper decks triumphed at the Guazhou Fork in the midnight snow/Warhorses with iron armor prevailed at the Dasan Pass in the autumn wind (Lu You: Writing of Indignation).

A conquered country is like a catkin blown by the wind/A vicissitudinary life is like duckweed thrashed by the rain (Wen Tianxiang: Crossing the Lingding Sea).

In an antithetical couplet the level and oblique tones had to correspond, too, to achieve a double artistic effect.

Third, it is necessary to explain the system of level and oblique tones. There are basically six rules for the placement of the tones in regulated and quatrain verse.

Two level tones and two oblique tones forming a basic unit ad a robust effect.

Within a verse, two level tones can alternate each with two oblique tones, as can pairs of such tones.

Pairs of verses – first and second, third and fourth, fifth and sixth and seventh and eighth – can have alternate level and oblique tones.

The end of the top verse of a lower couplet can match that of the bottom verse of a higher couplet with the same level or oblique tone.

A verse cannot end in either three level tones or three oblique tones.

If even verses end in level tones, the first verse may or may not rhyme. Apart from internal level-tone rhymes, a verse must have at least two level-tone characters (to avoid isolated level tones).

Summing up the above six patterns, we can say that there is only one principle, and that is that the changes must be made in an orderly way. These six patterns can be condensed into the following major structures (The brackets enclose the rhymes).

The first shows a five-character verse pattern in which a level tone starts and ends the first and ends the second verse.

平平仄仄[平]，仄仄仄平[平]。
仄仄平平仄，平平仄仄[平]。
平平平仄仄，仄仄仄平[平]。
仄仄平平仄，平平仄仄[平]。

A five-character verse pattern in which level tones are followed by oblique tones and vice versa:

平平平仄仄，仄仄仄平[平]。
仄仄平平仄，平平仄仄[平]。
平平平仄仄，仄仄仄平[平]。
仄仄平平仄，平平仄仄[平]。

A five-character verse pattern in which oblique tones are followed by level tones:

仄仄仄平[平]，平平仄仄[平]。
平平平仄仄，仄仄仄平[平]。
仄仄平平仄，平平仄仄[平]。
平平平仄仄，仄仄仄平[平]。

A five-character pattern in which oblique tones start and finish the first verse:

仄仄平平仄，平平仄仄[平]。
平平平仄仄，仄仄仄平[平]。

仄仄平平仄，平平仄仄平。
平平平仄仄，仄仄仄平平。

A seven-character pattern in which the first verse begins and ends with a level tone:

平平仄仄仄平平，仄仄平平仄仄平。
仄仄平平平仄仄，平平仄仄仄平平。
平平仄仄平平仄，仄仄平平仄仄平。
仄仄平平平仄仄，平平仄仄仄平平。

A seven-character pattern in which a level tone starts the first verse, while an oblique tone ends it:

平平仄仄平平仄，仄仄平平仄仄平。
仄仄平平平仄仄，平平仄仄仄平平。
平平仄仄平平仄，仄仄平平仄仄平。
仄仄平平平仄仄，平平仄仄仄平平。

A seven-character pattern in which an oblique tone starts the first verse, while a level tone ends it:

仄仄平平仄仄平，平平仄仄仄平平。
平平仄仄平平仄，仄仄平平仄仄平。
仄仄平平平仄仄，平平仄仄仄平平。
平平仄仄平平仄，仄仄平平仄仄平。

A seven-character pattern in which the first verse is started and ended with an oblique tone:

仄仄平平平仄仄，平平仄仄仄平平。
平平仄仄平平仄，仄仄平平仄仄平。
仄仄平平平仄仄，平平仄仄仄平平。
平平仄仄平平仄，仄仄平平仄仄平。

As examples of the above, we can quote a seven-character and a five-character poem. The five-character one is “Parting with My Half-brother Whom I Have Just Met Happily” by Li Yi:

We’ve been separated for a decade due to fires of war,
Now grown up, we’re able to see each other again.
We exchanged our names and tried to recall our old faces.
As we chatted on, we found that a lot had transpired.
Before we stopped talking, morning bells were striking.

"Tomorrow we have to say goodbye on the Baling road,
Ahead of you lies many a mountain of gloomy autumn."[2]

The seven-character one is "Untitled" by Li Shangyin:

Reunion is hard but more difficulties parting,
Which is like flowers withered by the wind.
Silkworms exhaust their silk ere their death;
Candles drain their tears after they burn away.
At dawn my hair appears grayed in the mirror;
Last night's moonlight felt chilly as I chanted.
Your hometown Pengshan is not at all distant,
I wish a fairy bird could be our messenger diligent.[3]

There is a definite rule for the arrangement of level and oblique tones in the first four verses of regulated verse.

An example of five-character regulated verse in which the first verse begins and ends with a level tone:

平平仄仄平，仄仄仄平平。
仄仄平平仄，平平仄仄平。

An example of five-character regulated verse in which the first verse starts with a level tone and ends with an oblique one:

平平平仄仄，仄仄仄平平。
仄仄平平仄，平平仄仄平。

An example of five-character regulated verse in which the first verse starts with an oblique tone and ends with a level one:

仄仄仄平平，平平仄仄平。
平平平仄仄，仄仄仄平平。

An example of five-character regulated verse in which the first verse starts and ends with an oblique tone:

仄仄平平仄，平平仄仄平。
平平平仄仄，仄仄仄平平。

An example of seven-character regulated verse in which the first verse starts and ends with a level tone:

平平仄仄仄平平，仄仄平平仄仄平。
仄仄平平平仄仄，平平仄仄仄平平。

An example of seven-character regulated verse in which the first verse starts with a level tone and ends with an oblique one:

平平仄仄平平仄，仄仄平平仄仄[平]。
仄仄平平平仄仄，平平仄仄仄平[平]。

An example of seven-character regulated verse in which the first verse starts with an oblique tone and ends with a level one:

仄仄平平仄仄[平]，平平仄仄仄平[平]。
平平仄仄平平仄，仄仄平平仄仄[平]。

An example of seven-character regulated verse in which the first verse starts and ends with an oblique tone:

仄仄平平平仄仄，平平仄仄仄平[平]。
平平仄仄平平仄，仄仄平平仄仄[平]。

Wang Zhihuan's "Ascending the Stork Tower" uses the five-character format:

The bright sun sets against the hill;
The Yellow River flows into the sea.
One more story you have to ascend
To gaze as far as your eyes can see.[4]

An example of a poem that uses the seven-character format is the third part of Wang Changling's "Odes to Autumn at the Changxin Palace":

I swept the golden palace as soon as it opened its gate at dawn.
Now with a moon-shaped fan, to kill time I pace up and down.
With a face as white as mutton fat jade, I'm no match for a crow:
It can fly into the Palace and return with the monarch's shadow.[5]

The stylistic characteristics of *shi* and *fu* poetry

What is meant by stylistic characteristics? It means the use of words in accordance with different rules, variation and the frequent application of such rules to create emphasis. In some styles of writing variation and stress are the chief characteristics.

The earliest poet to discuss the word styles of *shi* and *fu* poetry was Cao Pi. In his *Dissertation on Scholarship * On Literature*, he divides all styles into four categories. He picks out the word "beauty" in describing the important trait of *shi* and *fu* poetry. This is in contrast to the styles used in the other three categories – memorials to the throne, expository writing and inscriptions. Lu Ji, in his "Rhapsody on Literature" divides literary style into ten categories. He differentiates between *shi* and *fu* by saying, "*Shi* deals with the emotions and the obscure, while *fu* deals with concrete things and clarity." The two expressions "emotions" and "concrete things" apply to the internal contents of the two types of poetry, while "the obscure" and "clarity" respectively apply to their use of words. With respect to "the obscure," Li Shan, in his *Literary Selections Annotated*, says, "exquisite words." By this, he means the choice of words rich in literary grace beauty and precision. As for "clarity," Li Shan has this to say: "It refers to brightness," meaning the clearness of the words used. From Lu Ji's perspective, *shi* springs from the feelings, and so the words used to express them are of necessity opaque; *fu* springs from an examination of concrete things, and therefore the words used to describe them are of necessity clear. Lu Ji's analysis is more precise than that of Cao Pi, but his theory concerning the styles of *shi* and *fu* poetry is still somewhat sweeping. Liu Xie, in his *Carving a Dragon with a Literary Heart * The Established Literary Form*, says "*Fu*, Eulogies, Songs and *Shi* Poetry are all wings which enable clarity and beauty to soar." Here he quite obviously chimes in with Lu Ji's two lines about *shi* and *fu* poetry. Liu Xie, in his discussion of literary style, pays attention to the different types of writing. In his *Explanation of Poetry* he says, "In the orthodox poems with four characters to the verse, elegance and gloss are the basis; in the case of the ones with five characters to the verse, clearness and beauty reign supreme." In his *Explanation of Fu Poetry*, he says, "*Fu* means spreading out. It is by spreading out the subject matter and examining it that its essence can be expressed in words." And "If concrete things are made to come alive by means of the writer's feelings, then the words must be clear and elegant; and if things are to be perceived through the emotions, then the words used must be fine ones." Liu Xie, in his discussion of *shi* poetry, makes a distinction between the styles of poems which use four characters to the verse and those which use five. In his discussion of *fu* poetry he pays attention to the two aspects of "meaning" and "diction." In this respect, he is much more meticulous than Cao Pi and Lu Ji.

After this, debate about the styles of *shi* and *fu* poetry, especially about the former, became too many to count, and were often bogged down in petty details, lacking much in the way of general guidance. While recognizing that *shi* and *fu* poetry have a close affinity, I feel that their verbal styles can be described as follows: *Shi* is anchored in the emotions, and *fu* is anchored in concrete objects; *shi* does not avoid brevity, and *fu* does not eschew prolixity; the beauty of *shi* lies in its implications, and that of *fu* in what it presents openly; *shi* is used to transmit subtle feelings, and *fu* to transmit dazzling impressions.

Shi poetry can have four, five or seven characters to the verse, and is divided into ancient and modern styles. These differences also imply differences of style.

The verbal style of the four-character poems is plain and simple, marked by ancient classical elegance and like a piece of fine jade that has not yet been carved or a piece of old porcelain which has only the vestiges of painted decoration on it. They exude a kind of pure honesty from the sound in their lines. This style emerges from "short verses and concise cadence."[6] A four-character verse does not leave much room for ornamentation, and so its expression is of necessity brief. Also, its two-by-two arrangement does not allow for much variety of sounds.

Moreover, since the four-character poems arose at an early date, its vocabulary and verse arrangements stick closely to the conventions of the Han Dynasty, and continued to hobble all later composers of this genre. Some poets, in their pursuit of plainness and simplicity, and ancient classical elegance, deliberately choose the four-character style, especially when they want to compose a work with a paean-like effect. We do not have far to look to find a masterpiece of this kind of poem: Tao Yuanming's "Alternating Seasons" will suffice:

> Four seasons alternate nonstop; warm is the morning of spring.
> Clad in my spring garment, I saunter in the eastern suburbs.
> Mists are dissipating on the mountain; a rainbow spans the sky.
> Wind blowing from the south will help the young plants grow.
> The water's tranquil and vast, where we can cleanse ourselves.
> The rolling scene in the distance gratifies my eyes and mind.
> Living a good life as we do, we find happiness easy to define.
> Hold your cups up and high, let's drink to our heart's content.
> Surveying the midstream, I recall a legend of the Qingyi River.
> After class, Zeng Xi swam in it, and sang his way back home.
> I like his gentle personality, thinking of joining him all the time.
> But apart in different times, we cannot be together at all.
> After an outing all day long, I head homeward,
> Rows of flowers passing by together with trees and bamboos.
> The zither still lies on my bed, close to the half bottle of wine.
> Gone are our ancestors' glories, for which I lament with a sigh.[7]

Wang Fuzhi's critical comment is: "This is no tear in the Heavenly garment." (*Critical Selections of Ancient Poetry*, Vol.2). This is another way of underlining the importance of plainness and simplicity, and ancient classical elegance.

The five-character ancient-style poetry was not only characterized by solid simplicity, the changes of cadence marked by every new word showed a remarkable likeness to the original ancient poetry. In his *Preface to Poetical Works*, Zhong Rong observes, "Poetry with four-character *lvshi* poses a difficulty for poets, who are troubled by looking for more words to end up expressing less meaning. Consequently very few people prefer the craft. Playing the most important role in poetic literary history, the five-character *lvshi is* the most interesting verse form, and hence popular among average poets. Is it not the perfect literary form that creates images out of occurrences and depicts objects by exhausting emotions?" *Garland of Poetry* thus comments, "Only the five-character regulated verse can strike a balance between complexity and simplicity, and make the best use of flowery and plain languages."[8] Take some of the beautiful lines from the five-character ancient poems of the Han Dynasty for example: "Xiang qu ri yi yuan/Yi dai ri yi huan/Fu yun bi bai ri/You zi bu gu fan (He's left me so long/And my clothes have become loose/Drifting clouds shield the white sun/Travelers don't want to return.)" (Nineteen Ancient Poems); "He han qing qie qian/Xiang qu fu ji xu/Ying ying yi shui jian/Mo mo bu de yu (The Milky Way's clear and shallow/How far away is it?/A clear river between them/They gaze blushing without words) (Nineteen Ancient Poems); and "Bai chuan dong dao hai/He shi fu xi gui?/Shao zhuang bu nu li/Lao da tu shang bei (Many rivers flow to sea/When are they coming back?/Not working hard when young/One would regret when old. (A Long Poem to a Tune)." Describing scenery, writing of feelings or recording events, the shallower the writing, the deeper it is; the nearer, the further away; rhymes come with the words, and interest comes from the rhymes. Ancient but not abstruse, packed with meaning but not sluggish, and plain but not insipid. All this is evidence that the five-character poetry has a force of expression that the four-character variety does not. Let us look at an ancient poem from the Han Dynasty:

I'm walking out of the east city gate,
Gazing at the road across the Yangtze.
In the snowstorm the day before last,
My old friend left taking this path.
I want to cross the river to join him,
But the deep river has no bridge.
Swans I wish we both could become,
Flying high we'd go home together.[9]

Using plain and simple words, this poem describes a deeply hidden artistic mood, providing a glimpse of the force of expression of the five-character poetry.

The seven-character ancient-style poetry includes ballads written using seven characters to the verse. Such ballads are the most spirited of the ancient Chinese classical forms and the genre with the most fluent verbal composition. They can be long or short, but generally they contain now fewer than eight verses. Their rhyme scheme is fairly loose, using either level or oblique tones, but not mixing them. While most of them appear in seven-character format, this could vary internally. They could take the shape of regulated verse or prose, and utilize a comparatively large number of shades of expression. The seven-character ancient poems are marked by a freedom of composition with rapid changes of pace. It sometimes seems as if there are no rules – now charming, now grand, now transcendental, now firm and forceful. But the basic tenor running through them all is a sense of fluidity; any poverty of expression or hint of cramped style is studiously avoided. Let us look at Du Fu's "Lamenting by the Qujiang River":

An old country man from Shaoling with muffled sobs,
Stole into the depth of the Qujiang River area in spring.
A thousand doors of the palaces closed along Qujiang,
Where are the owners of the willows and sedge plants?
Back then the royal banners came to the South Garden,
Where everything seemed to be shrouded in brilliance.
The most favored royal consort of the Zhaoyang Palace,
Came sharing the seat with the emperor in his carriage.
Armed with bows and arrows, maids walked in front;

White horses following were harnessed with gear of gold.
One maid bent over and shot her arrow up into the sky,
With a single strike, she downed a couple of flying swans.
Where are the consort's clear eyes and sparkling teeth?
Her blood-stained roaming ghost finds no royal home.
The Wei River by which she died is far from his past refuge,
The dead and the living are not able to communicate.
Who with emotion would not shed sympathetic tears?
The plants along the Qujiang River will never perish.
At sunset, dust is kicked up by the rebels' horses again,
His home on the city's south side, he looks north instead.[10]

Five-character regulated verse is either filled with classical elegance, free and easy or vigorous and bold; in any case it is always "well conceived." This is probably the most rule-ordered genre in ancient Chinese poetry. And so the writing of five-character regulated verse became the basic training for Chinese poets. This genre always consisted of eight verses, and the usual format was "first part introduction, last part resolution, four middle verses, two words for background and two for mood."[11] It could be said that the "head" and "tail" of the poem are its mainstays, while the four verses in the middle are merely "filler." An example is Du Fu's "Ascending the Yueyang Tower":

I've heard about the Dongting Lake before;
Finally I'm up here at Yueyang Tower today.
Wu and Chu are in the south and east across,
Sharing the same heavenly bodies above them.
Not a word can be heard from kin or friends,
Sick and old I lead a wandering life on a boat.
War erupts at the northern border once again,
Looking out the window, I'm full of tears.[12]

The skill in composing a five-character regulated poem lies in its strict organization and structure, which presents a rich and multi-colored effect, different thoughts and emotions. In fact, freedom can be found within the bounds of a framework. As regards the antitheses in the middle of each poem, many and varied studies have been made, but an antithesis is not a good one when it is forced, and is a good one when it adds color. Excellent examples of apt antitheses are Wang Wei's "In a boundless desert lonely smoke rises straight up; Over the endless river the round sun sinks" (On Mission to the Frontier), Meng Haoran's "Wind ruffles the leaves on both sides of the river/The moon casts its gleam upon the solitary boat" (Remembrance of a Previous Trip to Guangling While Lodging by the Tonglu River), and Lu You's "Pieces of chess lie in the bare and empty hall/Fragrance of tea lingers in the small cups" (A Visit to Suoxiao Pavilion Late on a Cloudless Day).

As for seven-character regulated verse, in his *Garland of Poetry* Hu Yinglin made a remarkable comment on the seven-character regulated verse, saying, "Seven-character regulated verse came earlier than that with five characters to a line. Limited by set rules and rigid standards, the five-character ancient poems are difficult to write. The seven-character ancient poems, however, are elastic and well proportioned, rising and falling in cadence when chanted. They are therefore the crème de la crème of all genres of ancient poems. Where the five-character regulated verse is concerned, its *gong* (first) and *shang* (second) notes on the (ancient Chinese) pentatonic scale are barely coordinated, and its beats are far from smooth. Fluent, melodious, relaxed and roundabout, the seven-character *lvshi* is the most beautiful of *jintishi* (modern poetry)."[13] In this type of poem there are seven characters to the verse, and the cadence should be rich and varied. The structure, meanwhile, should be tight. Combining these two is a difficult task, as the *Garland of Poetry* also says, "The seven-character poetry is different from the five-character one in that it is more difficult to compose. Why so? Because its images are so confusing that only those who are very accomplished in the craft can handle it. The seven-character ancient poems, nevertheless, are coherent in style and can be handled by people of average poetic talent. The five-character poetry is solemn and rigid in scale. People with not much training in the craft of poetry would find it easy to deal with its structure. The language of seven-character *lvshi* poems are comparatively complicated and flashy, and requires even the very talented to weigh the words with great care. If written without antithetically parallel sentences, a seven-character *lvshi* poem would become very boring; vice versa, it would become too rigid. The best antithetical couplets must be exceedingly accurate, natural, fluent, refined, classically elegant and neatly structured. Nevertheless, the two sentences complement each other in theory but contradict each other in practice. That is why poets of both ancient and contemporary times have had difficulty writing them."[14] During the Tang Dynasty, Du Fu was the supreme master of the seven-character regulated poem, and Lu You during the Song Dynasty. Examples from Du Fu are "The boundless crop of autumn leaves/ Are rustling ceaselessly down/The endless streams of the Long River/Are rolling forever on" (Ascending a Height) and Waves raging in the gorges seem to billow into the sky/Windy clouds above the frontiers appear to crash on to the ground" (One of the *Thoughts on Autumn* poems), and from Lu You are "Anywhere I die, my body can be buried on a mountain green/Though aging and white-haired, I'm still too shy to ask for help" (Written by Chance as I Went out of the West Gate Drunk). "Mountain after mountain and river after river, I doubt if there's a way/ Beyond a shady willow forest, I see a village amidst brilliant blossoms" (A Trip to a Village West of the Mountain). These all reach the criteria of Hu Yinglin, cited above.

Five-character regulated verse is the shortest of the modern-style poem a ballad genre. At 20 words crammed into four verses, it is limited in structure and has little room for maneuver. It cannot give free rein to its expressions and feelings. So the style of the five-character regulated verse is necessarily one of few words but concise meanings, enabling the reader to see afar within a few steps and get a broad view from a little glimpse, the so-called "power to advance a mile with a short step." The composer of a five-character regulated poem needs to have five words of a lofty classical character; he also needs the pleasing flexibility of the modern poetic genre in order to portray flashes of feeling, broad sweeps of scenery in miniature, using pithy and exquisite expressions, almost like maxims, to arouse in the reader infinite appreciation. Wang Wei was the leading Tang Dynasty master of this genre. Here is his "Birds Singing in a Stream-Traversed Valley":

People are scarce, and osmanthus flowers fall;
Quiet night befalls the spring mountain vacant.
Birds are startled by the rise of the bright moon,
Twittering in the spring ravine now and again.[15]

There are other poems which are fine examples of this genre, such as Wang Zhihuan's "Ascending the Stork Tower," Liu Zongyuan's "Fishing in Snow," Bai Juyi's "A Question for Liu Shijiu" and Li Shangyin's "The Amusement Mound."

There are marked differences between the five-character and seven-character regulated verses. The *Garland of Poetry* says, "Characteristic of vivacity, five-character eight-line *jueju* poetry attaches more importance to simplicity than linguistic ornamentation. Seven-character eight-line *jueju*, on the other hand, features elegance and flamboyance, and therefore does the opposite."[16] But the characteristics of the seven-character poems do not stop here. This genre has four verses and 28 characters, and so it can roam more freely while keeping its expressions pithy and full of meaning. It can have the advantages of being both elegant like the *shi* poems and colloquial like the short lyrics. Tang masters of this genre were Li Bai, Wang Changling and Du Mu. Examples are Li Bai's "To Wang Lun":

Aboard the boat, I, Li Bai, am about to set off,
Then I hear someone come singing on the bank.
It's Wang Lun who's trotting over to see me off;
His friendship is deeper than a bottomless pool.[17]

Wang Changling's "On the Frontier":

The moon of Qin and the pass of Han remain the same,
But soldiers a thousand miles away have not returned.
Were the gallant General Li from the capital here still,
The barbarian warhorses wouldn't have come over Yinshan.[18]

And Du Mu's "Autumn Night":

In autumn, candles cast their silvery light upon the painted screen scold,
Dainty fans of soft silk are used to catch fireflies buzzing around.
The night flooding the stone steps in the open feels like cold water.
Sitting, we're gazing out at the constellations of lovers forced apart.[19]

Interim summary

Here we will make a preliminary summary of what has gone before. The section on *shi* and *fu* poetry concentrated mainly on the former, with the latter as a subsidiary topic. The developments and changes in the two forms of poetry were traced in accordance with their time sequence. Prior to the heyday of the Tang Dynasty, emphasis was placed on the formation of the various types of poetry, especially on an explanation of how poetry and ballad creativity reached a high tide. From the Song Dynasty on, the emphasis was on the evolution the various schools of poetry and ballads, and controversies that erupted among them, especially the pro-Tang and pro-Song schools. This will suffice as a simple outline of the origin and evolution of *shi* and *fu* poetry.

In this regard, I have touched upon the path of florescence and decline of these types of poetry, but only in a desultory way. Now I will add more discussion.

1. As far as *shi* and *fu* poetry are concerned, the rules are much the same, and since they share a close affinity we would expect them to develop and flourish in tandem. However, this was not so. As Mr. Lin Geng says: "Han *fu* and Tang *shi*, each represents the heyday of its respective dynasty, but they also present aspects as incompatible as fire and water. The Han Dynasty had *fu* poets but no *shi* poets, while in the Tang Dynasty it was the opposite way around."[20] Of course, *shi* and *fu* had another aspect to them, one in which they drew from each other. Mr. Lin Geng points out that in the Wei and Jin periods of the Southern Dynasties the original Major *Fu* drew very close to *shi* composition, producing the lyrical Minor *Fu*, and lyricism is a characteristic of *shi* poetry. In much the same way, Liang Chen's palace-style *shi* grew close to *fu*, highlighting elaborate decoration and describing concrete objects, which are characteristic of *fu* poetry.[21]

2. *Shi* and *fu* poetry and prose essays are the three main types of ancient China's orthodox literature. But the language of the essays itself was based on that of *shi* and *fu* poetry. And so the rise and decay of the two types of poetry depended to a great extent on their connection with prose writing.

The adoption of prose vocabulary was one road for *shi* poetry to follow; but it was also a dead end. In the period when the perfection of *shi* poetry was enthusiastically sought in its own special features, the influence of prose was thrust to one side. But once that stage was reached, there came a need for a new direction, and *shi* poetry turned to rely once more on prose and to draw the inspiration needed for a new burst of creativity. But eventually this reached such a pitch that *shi* almost lost its nature as poetry. While prose helped ornament the style of *shi* poetry, at the same time it was an element which contributed to the decay of the essence of this poetic genre. One history of Chinese poetry calls the relationship between *shi* and prose a "history of separation and reunion."

In its initial stage, *fu* poetry absorbed much of the elements of prose vocabulary. This has already been discussed above. Moreover, prose elements infiltrated and had such an influence on *fu* that it even decided the latter's direction of change. Casting our eyes on the aspect of diction, we find that *fu* presents five types, which emerged in sequence: *Sao Fu*, Han Dynasty irregular Major *Fu*, Parallel *Fu* of the Six Dynasties, Tang Dynasty Regulated *Fu* and Song Dynasty Prose

Fu. Of these, the Han Dynasty irregular Major *Fu* (with rhyme and blank verse interspersed, hypothetical question-and-answer, extensive length and a preface, and represented by Sima Xiangru's "*Fu* Poem on Zixu" and Ban Gu's "*Fu* Poetry of Two Capitals") and the Song Dynasty prose *fu* (represented by Ouyang Xiu's "Autumn Sounds" and Su Shi's "Verses on the Red Cliff" in two parts) show the profound influence of prose writings. The sequence of the appearance of the above five phases shows a historical trend of prose-poetry-prose again. And this trajectory of separation and reunion is an inevitable one.

3. One important reason for the long-term vigor of Chinese poetry and ballad-making was its flexibility, its ability to constantly change its diction. From the four- to the five- to the seven-character format, in step with the developments and changes in the Chinese language, new cadences were constantly appearing. One of the earliest forms of poetry was the one using four characters to the verse, and a caesura between the pairs of characters. This format stopped developing and became ossified during the time the *Book of Odes* was compiled. After this, there were not many poems of quality written in the four-character format, an exception being Cao Cao's "A Short Poem to a Tune." The major format of Chinese poetry then became the ones that used the five-character format, with a caesura between the second and third characters, and the seven-character format, with a caesura between the fourth and third characters. The four-character format, with the cadence divided evenly into two and two, was found to be too rigid; the five- and seven-character formats, with flexible syllables and change within regularity, were considered much more lively. As a result, the five- and seven-character poems replaced the four-character ones as the main form of Chinese poetry. Why did the seven-character format not develop into something even longer? I think the answer is that seven syllables were about as long as a reader could cover in one breath. Anything longer would have caused a quickening of the breathing, and such poems would have been difficult to write.

Along with the change in syllables, the rules of composition gradually became stricter. Chinese poetry evolved from a semi-free format (ancient poetry) to a rule-based format (modern-style verse). Nevertheless, even after the predominance of the latter, semi-free ancient-style poems continued to be written, side by side with the modern-style ones, each having its own strong points. Some poets were good at using the strong points of the ancient style, and some were good at using the strong points of the modern style. But the two were skilled in both, and never formed separate schools; in fact, they tended to complement each other in promoting the prosperity and development of Chinese poetry.

A deeper examination shows us that the development of Chinese poetry resulted from the mutual interaction of the two factors of temperament and style. The first change in Chinese poetry was from strength of temperament to strength of style. This change took place in the period spanning the Jin and Song dynasties, and that is from about the time of Tao Yuanming to that of Xie Lingyun. This period saw emergence of awareness and application of the various techniques of modern-style poetry. Lu Shiyong of the Ming Dynasty said, "The Song Dynasty saw the end of the ancient-style poetry and the beginning of the regulated style. The format of poetry changed, and style fully unfolded. Xie Lingyun was so skillful that what he did that it seemed to have been done by the secret workings of nature."[22] In concrete terms, this change was manifested mainly in two aspects – from emphasis on meaning to emphasis on imagery, and from inspired words to realistic words. *Carving a Dragon with a Literary Heart * Explanation of Poetry* describes the change as follows: "Poets work hard to show their craft of structuring antithetical parallel sentences throughout a poem and skill at creating novelty in each sentence. In terms of content, they make particular efforts to depict scenery in a true-to-life manner. Where language is concerned, they do their best to be new and original. This is the goal that modern poets have been vying to achieve."[23] The change in Chinese poetry from Tao Yuanming's time to that of Xie Lingyun reflects the change of poetic style between the two dynasties. As Shen Deqian says, "With the coming of the Song Dynasty, feelings started to take a back seat, while style started to come to the fore, and diction became more restricted." [24] (*First Words on Poetry*) The stage at which style started to be emphasized began in the Song Dynasty of the Southern Dynasties, and from there spread to the early Tang Dynasty. On the one hand, it enriched poetry's techniques of expression, and on the other it erected a firm structure for poetry. By the heyday of the Tang Dynasty feelings and style had blended into a perfect whole, and there followed a high tide of poetic composition.

However, this perfect blending of feelings and style could not endure for long; following the half-century of the heyday of the Tang, the two began to drift apart again. There was both too much feeling and not enough style, or vice versa. It was not that no poets managed to combine the two properly, it was just that no era emerged in which this was consistently done. The overall aspect of the history of Chinese poetry is a brilliant one, but its summit was reached in the heyday of the Tang Dynasty, and lasted no longer than half a century.

Notes

1 [Tang Dynasty] Shan, Li, and Yanji, Lv: *Selection of the Major Writings of Six Officials*, Vol.29, *Collected Writings of the Four Basic Branches of Literature*.
2 *Complete Tang Poems*, Vol.283, Zhonghua Book Company, 1960, P. 3217.
3 [Qing Dynasty] Hao, Feng: *The Poems of Li Shangyin Annotated*, Vol.2, Shanghai Ancient Books Publishing House, 1979.
4 *Complete Tang Poems*, Vol.253, Zhonghua Book Company, 1960, P. 2849.
5 *Complete Tang Poems*, Vol.143, Zhonghua Book Company 1960, P. 1445.
6 [Ming Dynasty] Yinglin, Hu: *Garland of Poetry*, First Part,Vol.2, Shanghai Ancient Books Publishing House, 1979, P. 22.
7 Xingpei, Yuan: *Collected Works of Tao Yuanming Annotated*, Zhonghua Book Company, 2003, P. 8.
8 [Ming Dynasty]: *Garland of Poetry*, First Part Vol.2, Shanghai Ancient Books Publishing House, 1979, P. 22.
9 [Ming Dynasty] Weina, Feng: *Records of Ancient Poetry*, Vol.20, *The Complete Four Repositories*, Pavilion of the Imperial Library.
10 *The Poems of Du Fu Divided into Sections and Annotated*, Vol.3, *Collected Writings of the Four Basic Branches of Literature*.

11 [Ming Dynasty] Yinglin, Hu: *Garland of Poetry*, First Part Vol.2, Shanghai Ancient Books Publishing House, 1979, P. 63.
12 [Qing Dynasty] Zhao'ao, Qiu: *Du Fu's Poems With Detailed Commentary*, Vol.22, Zhonghua Book Company, 1979, P. 1946.
13 [Ming Dynasty] Yinglin, Hu: *Garland of Poetry*, First Part Vol.5, Shanghai Ancient Books Publishing House, 1979, P. 81.
14 [Ming Dynasty] Yinglin, Hu: *Garland of Poetry*, First Part Vol.5, Shanghai Ancient Books Publishing House, 1979, P. 83.
15 *Complete Tang Poems*, Vol.128, Zhonghua Book Company, 1960, P. 1302.
16 [Ming Dynasty] Yinglin, Hu: *Garland of Poetry*, First Part Vol.6, Shanghai Ancient Books Publishing House, 1979, P. 111.
17 *Complete Tang Poems*, Vol.171, Zhonghua Book Company 1960, P. 1765.
18 *Complete Tang Poems*, Vol.143, Zhonghua Book Company, 1960, P. 1444.
19 *Complete Tang Poems*, Vol.524, Zhonghua Book Company, 1960, P. 6002.
20 Geng, Lin: "Remarks and Guidelines to the High Tide of Tang Poetry," *A Summing Up of Tang Poetry*, People's Literature Publishing House, 1978, P. 52.
21 Geng, Lin: "Remarks and Guidelines to the High Tide of Tang Poetry," *A Summing up of Tang Poetry*, People's Literature Publishing House, 1978, P. 52.
22 [Ming Dynasty] Shiyong, Lu: *General Discussion of the Mirror of Poetry, Continued Edition of Poetry Talks Down the Ages*, Zhonghua Book Company, 1983, P. 1406.
23 Wenlan, Fan: *Carving a Dragon With a Literary Heart Annotated*, Vol.2, People's Literature Publishing House, 1978, P. 67.
24 [Qing Dynasty] Deqian, Shen: *First Words on Poetry, Talks on Qing Dynasty Poetry*, Shanghai Ancient Books Publishing House, 1978, P. 533.

Part 2

Ci poems and *qu* verses

I wish to discuss *ci* poems and *qu* verses together because they were both created on the basis of sound; first the melody was composed, and then the words were fitted to it to form a song. Song Xiangfeng of the Qing Dynasty (1644–1911) says in his *Random Discussions on the Music Bureau*: "*Ci* and *qu* emerged together in the period that saw the Yuan Dynasty (1206–1368) replace that of the Song."

The major stages of the evolution of *ci* and *qu* were Song *Ci*, Yuan *Qu* (including *sanqu* and *zaju*), Song-Yuan Southern Opera and Ming-Qing *Chuanqi* Opera.

7 The rise and evolution of *ci* poetry

The rise of *ci* poetry and literati experiments

Ci is short for "*quzi ci*" or words of songs. It is a type of poetry fitted to music and used for songs. In his *Random Discussions on the Music Bureau*, Song Xiangfeng says, "*Ci* is the written words, and *qu* is the regulated sounds." The musical strain that the *ci* is fitted to is called the *Yan* music (There are three different characters for *Yan*, one of which means a feast), and indicated a kind of musical performance given to accompany an entertainment. Its roots can be traced back to folk music from the northwest which infiltrated western China from the Northern Zhou (557–581, one of the Northern Dynasties) and Sui (AD 581–618) dynasties onward. The *pipa* or zither was the main accompanying instrument.

We cannot trace with any certainty the origin of *ci*, as it underwent a fairly long course of development. However, since *ci* accompanied *Yan* music, and the latter gained popularity in the Sui Dynasty, the origin of *ci* can probably be traced back to that period. Wang Zhuo of the Song Dynasty (960–1279) says, in his *Random Notes of the Jade Chicken*: "It was roughly around the period of the Sui Dynasty that what we today call *qu* poetry began to flourish, and it gained some popularity in the following Tang Dynasty (618–907)."[1] Zhang Yan, also of the Song Dynasty, in his *The Wellspring of Ci Poetry*, says, "It was in the Sui and Tang dynasties that poetry began to appear in long and short verses."[2] Both these authors recognize that the Sui Dynasty gave birth to *ci*. Tunes such as "Tale of the River" and "To the Willow," written in the *ci* style, were composed in the Sui Dynasty, according to the records. The most reliable guess is that *ci* originated no later than the heyday of the Tang Dynasty; in fact, over 160 tunes with *ci* verses fitted to them have been discovered in the Dunhuang Grottoes in Gansu Province, many of them works dating from that period.[3] An example is "Pusaman":

> We've vowed a thousand times by the pillow/
> Expect us to break up?/
> Not till the mountains crumble/
> Or till an iron weight floats/
> Upon the Yellow River completely dry/
> Or till the sundered stars are seen together/

And the Big Dipper appears in the south./
None can set us apart/
Unless the sun rises at night.[4]

This *ci* poem describes a girl's unchanging adherence to love and constancy. Textual research identifies it as a work of the Tang heyday.

Literati of the Middle Tang period studied folk *ci*, and by doing so made a breakthrough contribution to the *ci* corpus. Zhang Zhihe, Wei Yingwu, Wang Jian, Bai Juyi and Liu Yuxi all wrote successful pieces in this vein. In the following *ci* poem, "Song of Flirtation," Wei Yingwu describes the scenery of the borderlands in a very straightforward way:

Oh horse, horse of the north/
Left far beneath Mount Yanzhi/
You gallop neighing in the sand and snow/
Looking east and west and all around/
You seem at a loss as to where to go/
On the endless frontier grassland at dusk.[5]

Following is the first of the three stanzas of Bai Juyi's "Fair South Recalled":

South of the Yangtze the land is great/
I've seen its beauty long before/
Redder than fire is the sun over the wavy Yangtze/
Greener than blue is its water in the spring breeze/
How can I ever forget the land in the south?[6]

This is a mature *ci* poem. Its words flow freely and its artistic conception is complete.

In the late Tang and Five Dynasties (907–960) periods scholarly *ci* poems made great strides. Our first discussion should be of the "Huajian (Among the Flowers)" poets, represented by Wen Tingyun. "Among the Flowers" is the name of an anthology of *ci* poems. Zhao Chongzuo of the Later Shu state during the Five Dynasties period compiled a ten-volume anthology named the *Collected Ci Poems Among the Flowers*, which included 500 *ci* poems by Wen Tingyun and Wei Zhuang, as well as16 other poets. The former's poems mainly deal with women's charms, and their style is mostly marked by fineness and elegance. His *ci* artistry has the following characteristics: First, it is highly ornamental, with elegant phrasing. It is often focused on a girl's features and ornaments, and the fittings of her boudoir. In addition, the structure of the poems is finely conceived. Second, he is good at using the technique of suggestion to create an effect of covert meaning. Third, his images are stark, and prompt the reader's imagination to form the connections between them. Fourth, he uses precise description to convey human emotions, putting great weight on exaggerated details, even to the extent of losing the overall balance because of a plethora of details. Let us glance at the first part of "Pusaman":

> The golden color painted on my eyebrows fades partly/
> The curling locks cascade upon my snow-white cheeks/
> I rise languidly to repaint my eyebrows/
> To wash and do my makeup and my hair/
> In two mirrors, I look at myself from front and back/
> Two faces adding radiance and beauty to each other/
> I put on my silk blouse adorned with a new appliqué/
> Embroidered with a pair of golden partridges.[7]

Wei Zhuang and Wen Tingyun are celebrated together as "Wen and Wei." If Wen's *ci* poems can be called "understated," with the poet hiding behind his heroines and allowing their words to state his own sorrows, then Wei's *ci* poems can be called "explicit," as he pours out his heart, telling the reader quite straightforwardly of his romantic notions. If Wen's *ci* poems can be described as "heavily made up," then Wei's *ci* poems can be described as "lightly made up." Wen's poems have a feminine texture, while those of Wei have a touch of masculine affection. Let us take a look at Wei Zhuang's "Pusaman":

> Everyone speaks well of the land south of the Yangtze/
> This is where people away from home should grow old/
> In spring, the water here looks bluer than the sky/
> A drizzle lulls one to sleep on a decorated barge/
> The girl wine-seller is as beautiful as the moon/
> Her bare wrists look to me as white as snow/
> Return not to your homeland until you're old/
> Or you'll be regretful and sorrowful.[8]

Another central thread of the *ci* poetry was that of the Southern Tang Dynasty of the Five Dynasties period, represented by Feng Yansi, Li Jing and Li Yu. The latter was the last ruler of the Southern Tang Dynasty. He met his death by poison three years after surrendering to the Song Dynasty. He wrote *ci* poems to express his profound grief at losing his country. An example is his "Beauty Yu":

> When will the time of spring flowers and autumn moon come to end?/
> How much of the good old days do I remember still?/
> Last night, spring breezes visited me again upon the pavilion/
> In the moonlight, I couldn't bear to recall my past royal days/
> The carved beams and jade staircases of my palace may survive/
> But the people I knew must have lost the vigor of their lives/
> If asked how sorrowful I'm feeling, my answer would certainly be/
> My sorrow is like the Yangtze River flowing to the east in spring.[9]

Wang Guowei, in his *Comments on Ci Poetry*, says, "It was Last Emperor Li who opened the world's eyes to *ci* poetry. This genre's ability to express deep emotions and switch protagonists made it ideal for gentlemen-scholars."[10] This remark aptly sums up Last Emperor Li's position in the history of *ci* poetry.

In our discussion of the Tang and Five Dynasties period there is a particular phenomenon which must not be overlooked, and that is the interaction between the *shi* and *ci* genres of poetry. From the Tang and Five Dynasties period to that of the Song Dynasty, the development paths of the two showed an intersecting trend. To fully investigate the impact *shi* and *ci* poetry had on each other it is not enough to concentrate on *ci* alone; that way one only manages to study the history of *ci* poems in depth. Unfortunately, scholars specializing in the study of the history of *ci* have neglected this point. In addition, we must pay attention not only to the special features of the forms of *ci*; we must also pay attention to the quintessence of this genre. And in this I include the following overall aspects: *Ci* is a literature of urban entertainment; it is a literature of feminine softness; it is a literature with a fine lyric texture; and finally, it is a literature of tangled sentiments. Of course, here we are only talking about the original aspects of *ci*. The poems of Li He of the mid-Tang period belong of course to the *shi* genre and not that of the *ci*. Nevertheless, a fairly large number of his poems differ from the *shi* tradition in their emotional appeal, taste and atmosphere. In fact, they present a completely new aspect, incorporating the special features of the *ci*, and forming what might be called *ci* poetry within *shi* poetry. Li Shangyin's poems too display some of these aspects. The fact also must not be overlooked that Li He influenced the late Tang-Five Dynasties poet Wen Tingyun and the *ci* poets of the Song Dynasty. Moreover, one important reason why Wen Tingyun, Wei Zhuang, Feng Yansi and Li Yu could form a generation of *ci* poets different from the earlier group of poets who dabbled in *ci* poetry – people like Zhang Zhihe, Wei Yingwu, Bai Juyi and Liu Yuxi – was that not only did they, at roughly the same time, fix the characteristics of the *ci* format, they gave the internal essence of *ci* its rich contents, and in doing so they established the special artistic pattern of *ci*. Concerning this question, let me quote from a work of my own "The Inherent Nature of Li Changji's Chanted and Ci Poems," which contains a detailed discussion.[11]

Ci poetry of the Northern Song Dynasty: refined and popular

The Northern Song Dynasty (960–1127) in the main inherited the musical tradition of the Southern Tang Dynasty, but at the same time transformed it somewhat. In the *History of the Song Dynasty * Records of Music* it says, "The Music Instruction Institute was established at the beginning of the Song Dynasty. It inherited the music from the south of the Yangtze River that had already eliminated the *zuobu* (performing while sitting) part of it. Since the establishment of the institute, new melodies have been created to substitute for the old music and hence become smoother and more beautiful."[12] In the early part of the dynasty *ci* poetry basically continued the style of the Southern Tang. Yan Su and Ouyang

Xiu were the heirs of Feng Yansi, so much so that the *ci* poems of the three are difficult to tell apart.

The major turning point in Northern Song *ci* poetry started with Liu Yong. Liu Yong frequented the pleasure quarters, associating with singing girls and musicians, and taking no thought to an official career. He called himself "White-clad Liu Xiang." One of his sayings was, "I would exchange a cup of wine and a song any day for an empty title." When someone recommended him to Emperor Renzong (reign: 1023–1064), the emperor said, "Let him have his cup of wine and song. He doesn't need any empty title I can give him."[13] In the first year of the Jingyou reign period (1034) of Emperor Renzong, Liu Yong passed the highest imperial examination. But he found that official life did not suit him, and so he gave it up to become a gentleman farmer, calling himself "Squire Liu." Liu Yong's contributions to the history of *ci* poetry are twofold:

1 Before Liu Yong's time *ci* poetry tended to be short and staccato; Liu Yong's *ci* poems were longer and more lingering. Some 70 or 80 percent of his 200-odd *ci* poems preserved in the *Collection of Musical Pieces* are of this type.
2 In fact, Liu Yong introduced colloquialisms into *ci* poetry. Liu Yong was an exponent of the tastes of the common people, and from them his ci poems drew much upon the common speech, couching them in a language easy for the ordinary townspeople to appreciate. Liu Yong's *ci* poems have no abstruse contents, nor have they any reticence or hidden meanings. What they express is the raw emotions of life and love.

Liu Yong's *ci* poems often deal with the lives, thoughts and feelings of singing girls, and of his own connections with them. They form the themes of Wen Tingyun's *ci* compositions too, but his singing girls are no more than incarnations of flawed literary figures. Wei Zhuang's *ci* poems deal mainly with himself, a literary figure who had close connections with singing girls. His description of his love affairs with singing girls was done in a fashionably romantic vein. In them, he appears as a young man-about-town: "The young girls in the houses in the lanes are thinking of nothing but romance" ("Reverie on the Heavenly Palace" Second Part); "As I ride over the Slanting Bridge, red sleeves wave at me from all the houses" ("Pusaman" Part Three). It is himself he is talking about; in fact it seems that reminiscing about love affairs is a particular delight with him. Liu Yong, on the other hand, blames his relations with singing girls for his loss of an opportunity to rise in the world and the prejudice against him on the part of the upper classes of society. He regarded this as a high price to pay for his youthful flings. But he treated his amorous partners as equals, understood them and respected them. From his writing brush, Liu Yong's singing girls emerge as they actually appeared to the poet, while Liu Yong himself acts as a sort of spokesman, expressing the complicated thoughts and emotions of their innermost hearts. Liu Yong brought to the *ci* poetry arena new breath, new vigor, new interest and new beauty. Of course, he also brought to the world of refined literature the down-to-earth manners and language of the street, and in this he foreshadowed the direction of development of *ci* poetry to *qu* verse. Let us take a look at his representative poem "Calming the Wind and the Waves":

Since spring sets in,
Plants and flowers look cheerless/
My tender heart is feeling listless/
Though the sun is over the treetops/
Birds among the willows fly and hop/
I'm still lying in my fragrant bed/
My skin losing its glow/
My hair is falling loose/
So wan that I care for nothing/
How helpless I am!/
I hate that my lover's gone forever/
Never thinking of sending me a letter.
I'm feeling extremely regretful/
If I had known he was unfaithful/
I could have locked his stable/
He would then stay in the study/
Doing nothing but writing and chanting/
Without being a step away from me/
Following him closely every day/
Not having to dodge him/
I would do my needlework by his side/
Together with him/
I need not squander my youthful days.[14]

The content of this poem and that of Wen Tingyun's "Pusaman" are very similar. Both describe a weary young woman's early-morning toilet preparations. But the styles are vastly different: One uses elegant phraseology, while the other uses common expressions. If "Pusaman," were rewritten in the sort of language used for "Calming the Wind and the Waves" the subtle feelings hard to describe in words which are lurking in the characters and lines used by Wen Tingyun could be expressed straightforwardly in Liu Yong's blunt speech, saturated in plain statement.

Liu Yong also wrote some elegant *ci* poetry. However, this was kept within the boundary in which it could be appreciated by the common townsfolk: Blunt expressions were mingled with elegant ones, and each complemented the other. His elegant *ci* too have lovesickness as the main theme. Let us look at his "Bells Ringing in the Rain":

Cicadas sang sadly in the late autumn/
Facing He Pavilion, I saw the sunset/

Soon after came a rainstorm/
As we drank moodily by the capital gate/
Word from the boat said it could not wait/
Hand in hand, we gazed tearfully at each other/
Words we had many, but none we could utter/
Just think, after each to the other goodbye says/
There would be nothing but the vastness/
Of mist-covered waters and evening haze/
Departures always hurt the sentimental/
Particularly on autumn days so dismal/
Where will I find myself as I become sober?/
By the riverside lined with willow tree/s
The lune lingering in a morning breeze/
Not being able to meet in years to come/
Fine days and scenes are but phantasms/
Though I'm filled with fond affection/
A person to divulge it I find none.[15]

Liu Yong's *ci* poetry captivated the majority of its readers with the novelty of its format and its intonation. Xu Du, in Part 2 of his "*Essays on Living in Complete Seclusion*," says, "His *ci* poems, although exquisite, have an admixture of vulgar terms, and so particularly circulate among the common people."[16] In Part 2 of Ye Mengde's *Records of Escaping the Summer Heat*, an official returning to the court from Xixia say, "Around every local well there are people who can recite Liu Yong's *ci* poems."[17] From these remarks we can tell how widespread the *ci* poems of Liu Yong were.

In another aspect, Su Shi effected a change in the Northern Song poetic style. As noted above, the style prevalent in the Five Dynasties period spilled over into the first part of the Northern Song Dynasty. Poets knew no other style of composition than the elegant prettiness and subtle understatement of the previous era. Even Ouyang Xiu, who was reckoned the leading reformer in this field with his "filling-in" *ci* poems, merely followed in the wake of the Five Dynasties poets. In fact, there was no innovation until the time of Su Shi, who produced the "gaudy style" of *ci* poetry and thereby gave this genre an entirely new look. Su Shi changed the traditional way of looking at ci poems – they were no longer regarded as a pleasant pastime and an accompaniment to drinking games. Su Shi applied themes traditional to *shi* poetry to the *ci* style, thereby widening the scope of themes of the latter and raising *ci* to a status on a par with *shi*. *Ci* then became a vehicle capable of expressing feelings and moods, investigating the meaning of human life and stating scientific and philosophical thoughts. Su Shi encapsulated the strengths of *shi* in his *ci* poems to form the natural unified style of the two genres, incorporating into *ci* the solemn, expansive and straightforward aspects of *shi*. Worthy of special notice are his expansive *ci* poems. There are not many of them, but they fully indicate the new direction and had a far-reaching influence. For instance, his "Remembering a Beauty * Memories of the Past at Red Cliff":

> To the east the Yangtze River constantly flows/
> Bringing with its waves many an ancient hero/
> West of the fortresses are said to be the site/
> Where Zhou Yu undid Cao Cao at the Red Cliff fight/
> There precipices soar to the sky/
> Battering surf raises heaps of snowy crests/
> A land so beautiful did many a hero glorify!
> Do you recall Zhou Yu of that time/
> A bridegroom to Xiaoqiao, his bride?/
> Then he was right in his heroic prime/
> Holding a feather fan and donning sashes/
> In a matter of talking and laughing/
> He turned Cao Cao's fleet to ashes/
> As if the fiery battle itself I beheld/
> I should laugh at my sentimentality/
> Which has turned my hair unduly gray/
> Life is nothing but a passing dream/
> So, holding a cup, I make a toast/
> To the moon above the Yangtze stream.[18]

Again, his "Prelude to Water Melody" (On the evening of the Mid-Autumn Festival in 1076 I drank merrily till the next morning, when I got inebriated. I then composed this poem as an expression of my longing for my brother Su Zhe):

> When did the bright moon come about?"/
> Holding a wine cup, I ask the sky/
> I'm wondering, up in the Celestial Palace,/
> In which year is tonight?/
> I meant to return to Heaven with the wind/
> But I fear that I could not bear the freezing cold/
> Up high in the buildings of beautiful jade/
> Dancing with my moonlit shadow on the Earth/
> I find it better than ascending to the moon!/
> Rounding the crimson buildings/
> It hangs over the ornamental windows/
> Casting its light upon the sleepless/
> Oh, Moon, you may not hate us/
> But why are you always at your full before we part?/
> Man has grief at separation and joy at reunion;
> The moon wanes and waxes alternately/
> Which has been a fact since antiquity/

May all we humans be blessed with longevity!/
So, though far apart, we can share the moon's beauty.[19]

One of Su Shi's *ci* poems noted for its subtlety is "Water Dragon Chant * To the Rhymes of Zhang Zhifu's Ci Poem about Willow Catkins":

Not flowers, they look like flowers/
No-one cares as they fall by the roadside/
Lifeless, but upon second thoughts/
They look as if they are preoccupied/
And saddened by lonesome longing/
Struggling to keep their sleepy eyes open/
Like in a dreamland a woman forsaken/
Seeking her better half's whereabouts/
But startled awake by orioles' singing/
I hate not that the catkins have all fallen/
I do resent the West Garden, however/
Once fallen there, they return to the trees never/
By the early morning the rain has stopped/
But where are the traces of the flowers?/
They have been swept into the ponds/
Broken like duckweeds by raindrops/
The catkins are seen as three parts/
Two are turned into dirt and dust/
The third is floating in the water/
As I look at them more closely/
They're not willow catkins any longer/
But tears shed by people wandering afar.[20]

Qin Guan, who was a follower of Su Shi's school, wrote *ci* poems in a style far different from that of Su Shi himself. He was called the doyen of the "school of subtlety." Su Shi criticized Qin Guan's sentence "To be enthralled, this is just the time" in his *ci* poem "A Courtyard Filled with Flowers," dismissing it as "Liu Yong's chatter."[21] Further comparing him to Liu Yong, he said that the elegance and lucidity of his *ci* poems with their meticulous emotion-filled wording had a skillfully crafted beauty. An example is "The Magpie Bridge Fairy":

Silky clouds appear in beautiful patterns/
Fleeting meteors convey their affection/
The endless Silver River the place of their tryst/
A rendezvous in the golden autumn is worth/
Many a meeting down in the mundane world.
Their love is as tender as flowing water/
Their rendezvous is as brief as a dream/

It hurts to look back at the Magpie Bridge/
As long as their love for each other lasts/
So what if they can't be together every day?[22]

Zhou Bangyan was the last great *ci* poet of the Northern Song Dynasty. The special features of his works are that he wrote *fu* poetry in *ci* style and used a method of elaborate description. It was actually Liu Yong who was the first to experiment with writing *fu* in *ci* style, but Zhou Bangyan developed this by adding an elaborate angle and level. His *ci* poems are like a symphony combining different instruments and sounds, in which the various instruments are harmonized and the various movements echo each other, while within each movement there are multi-level fluctuations. Liu Yong's *ci* poems are simple and straightforward, whereas those of Zhou Bangyan tend to wind back and forth, ranging between the past and the present and the near and the far. He often uses a system of writing which has a definite beginning and end, an opening and a closing. In this respect, Chen Tingzhuo has this apposite remark in Vol.2 of his "Talks on the *Ci* Poems of White Rain Studio": "There is no technique in all of *ci* poetry that is purer than this."[23] Let us take a look at Zhou Bangyan's representative work "Auspicious Dragon Ode":

On the Zhangtai Road,
Withered plums have lost their perfume/
Peach trees are already in full bloom/
The whole neighborhood is still at rest/
Swallows return to their own nests/
Standing still I gazed in pensiveness/
Thinking of that girl, young and artless/
Peeping out, she stood on the doorstep/
Revealing yellow makeup on her forehead/
Shielding herself from the breeze with her sleeve/
Smiling and giggling, she acted naïve/
Today I'm back like the legendary Liu/
Revisiting her former neighborhood/
There remain only her old companions/
With her singing and dancing together/
They now ask the same price like her./
The poems of love we have written/
None of their lines I have forgotten/
Now who will be my company/
As I drink in the garden's open air/
And saunter outside the East City?/
The past is gone never to return/
I meant to relive its moment of jubilee/
Instead I find it filled with melancholy/
Raindrops pattering on the pool/

Golden willow branches hanging low/
I return on horseback in the evening cool/
In the yard reminiscent of sadness/
I find only a curtain of willow catkins.[24]

This poem contains a covert love story. Its narrative is complex, simple and yet elegant, rich in fine sentiments and thought-provoking.

Zhou Bangyan was an expert at manipulating rhymes and rhythms. His creations always fitted neatly together. He was the first poet to apply the four tones to *ci* poetry, making a clear demarcation between level and oblique tones, producing a melodious and refined effect, with "not a speck of commonness" (Shen Yifu of the Song Dynasty: *Guide Through the Maze of the Music Bureau*).

Zhou Banyan, as one of the most successful of the *ci* poets, and he exerted a great influence on the poets of the Southern Song Dynasty (1127–1279), such as Jiang Kui and Wu Wenying. It can be said that he was an important link between the *ci* poetry of the Northern and Southern Song dynasties.

The fresh look of the *ci* poetry of the Southern Song Dynasty

The *ci* poetry of the Southern Song Dynasty had a new and different appearance from that of the Northern Song Dynasty.

The female *ci* poet Li Qingzhao, who was active in the period which saw the Southern Song Dynasty emerge as the Northern Song Dynasty passed away, mainly wrote about the vicissitudes of the individual, but she also conjured up the spirit of her era, compelling her readers to mourn the ruin of the country and the breakup of families. Her representative work is "Slow, Slow Tune":

I've searched, looked, and groped,
But I still feel cold and solitary/
Which causes me to be all the more wretched/
The changeable weather of early spring/
Makes it hard for one to stay healthy/
Even two or three cups of rice wine/
Are not enough/
To fend off the cold of a windy night/
The sight of a skein of wild geese passing by/
Saddens me/
Because they are my old acquaintances.
The ground is covered with yellow flowers/
Now that they're badly withered/
Who would want to pick them?/
By the window all by myself/
I ponder how I can persist till the night/
Raindrops patter on the phoenix tree leaves/
Till the dusk/

Falling drip by drip/
How can the single word "worry"/
Define this state of affairs?[25]

The most influential *ci* poet of that time was Xin Qiji. His bold style earned him a rank alongside Su Shi, so that the two are often known as "Su and Xin." However, he was not as completely bold as Su Shi: the latter wrote *shi* poetry in *ci* form, while the former introduced prose features into *ci*. Xin Qiji introduced a plethora of subjects into his *ci* poems, ranging from discussions and reasonings to the classics and question-and-answer dialogues. In his *ci* poems we can find the eloquence of Mencius and the bizarre anecdotes of Zhuangzi; the outcries against injustice of Han Yu and the elaborate diction of Liu Zongyuan. His prose-tinged style of poetic writing, unsurpassed in its time, can really be considered a breakthrough in *ci* creativity. Every word is packed with vigor, and not a syllable is wasted. Let us look at his "Breaking a Military Formation * A Ci Poem of Heroism as a Message to Chen Tongfu":

Still drunk, we lit the lamps to seek our swords/
Awakened from dreams, we hear the camp horns/
For 800 *li* grilled meat under the banners/
Martial airs played upon 50 instruments/
Autumn maneuvers in the field/
On galloping steeds we plied our twanging bows/
Recovering lost land for the emperor/
Striving for everlasting fame/
But alas, our hair is turning grey.[26]

In his early years Xin Qiji was a righteous patriot, who joined Geng Jing's resistance army against the Jin invaders. Following his assassination of Geng Jing in 1162, his aide Zhang Anguo surrendered with his forces to the Jin. At that time, Xin Qiji was away on a mission to the Southern Song court to try to arrange joint resistance to the Jin. When, on his way back, he heard the news of Zhang Anguo's treachery, he stormed the Jin camp at the head of only some 50 men, captured Zhang Anguo and led the 10,000 or so remnants of Geng Jing's forces to Southern Song. Unfortunately he was let down by Southern Song in his ambition to expel the Jin and save his country and so his only recourse was to express his lofty aspirations and heartbreak in *ci* poems. A typical one is "Pure Serene Music * Staying up All Night Alone in the Wang Family Temple on Mount Bo":

Mice run helter-skelter around the bed/
Bats glide up and down around the lamp/
Wind rustling, rain pattering and pines whistling/
As if the tattered windows were whispering.

All my life I've been fighting north and south/
Now I've retired, haggard and gray-haired/
A cold wind piercing my quilt jolted me awake/
The land in my dream lingers even at daybreak.[27]

Some of Xin Qiji's *ci* poems deal with country life, as new material for *ci* creativity. For instance, "Pure Serene Music":

A low hut sits by a stream margined with grass/
Who are the gray-haired old man and woman/
Inebriated, talking in the pleasing dialect of Wu?
The eldest son is weeding the bean field in the east/
The second is making a coop for the chickens/
Upstream, the youngest is harvesting lotus seeds.[28]

Xin Qiji liked to include classical allusions in his ci poems, and freely quoted from China's dozens of ancient thinkers. It was this which, together with his spirit of patriotism, heroic demeanor and unique artistic style, made him outstanding in the *ci* arena of the Song Dynasty.

Patriotic *ci* poets contemporary with Xin Qiji were Zhang Xiaoxiang, Lu You and Chen Liang. The great vigor with which a *ci* poet expressed his noble nature is well exemplified in Zhang Xiaoxiang's "Remembering a Beauty * Crossing Dongting Lake":

Lake Dongting, Lake Green Grass/
Near the Midautumn night/
Unruffled, for no winds pass/
Like thirty thousand acres of jade bright/
A dot is this leaflike boat of mine/
The sky with pure moonbeams overflow/
The water surface paved with moonlight/
Brightness above, brightness below/
My heart with the moon becomes one/
Felicity to share with none.
Thinking of the southwest, where I passed a year/
To lonely pure moonlight akin/
I feel my heart and soul snow- and ice-clear/
Although my hair is short, my gown too thin/
In the immense expanse I keep floating up/
Drinking wine from the River West/
And using the Dipper as my wine cup/
I invite Nature to be my guest/
Beating time abroad and crooning alone/
I sink deep into time and place unknown.[29]

Lu You often describes his anguish in a noble way, as in his "Related My Innermost Feelings":

Alone, I went a thousand miles, long ago/
To serve in the army at the frontier/
Now to that fortress town in dreams I cannot go/
Outworn my sable coat of a cavalier.
The foe not beaten back/
My hair no longer black/
My tears have flowed in vain/
Who would have thought I would remain/
With a mountain-high aim/
But an old mortal frame?[30]

Chen Liang expresses his lofty and free spirit in his representative *ci* poem "Prelude to Water Melody * Farewell to Zhang Demao":

Not seeing southern troops for long/
Don't say their northern steeds can't run/
Single-handed, at once the thing is done/
After all, we are heroes millions strong/
His Majesty's envoy – what fun – /
Should eastward go like brimming river/
That eastward flows for ever/
We bend to the Jurchen tents now/
Another day to us they'll bow.
In the capital of our emperors/
And the land of the great and long/
Empire built by our ancestors/
Is there none who thinks it wrong/
To submit to the foe/
Whose stink of mutton wafts for miles/
Where's the spirit of heroes who died long ago/
When will our army beat the Jurchen ranks and files/
Why ask about the enemy's fate/
The sun of the Song Empire will soon radiate.[31]

Another *ci* poet of the Southern Song, Jiang Kui, started another trend in this genre, and his followers – Shi Dazu, Wu Wenying, Jiang Jie, Zhou Mi, Wang Yisun and Zhang Yan – formed the mainstream of the *ci* style in the latter part of the Southern Song period. Jiang Kui was noted for his "vapid" manner, which is also brought out in Zhang Yan's *The Wellspring of Ci Poetry*:

> The writing of *ci* poetry must be flexible and unpredictable, and possess romantic charm. It cannot be straightforward and definite; otherwise its

> meaning will be obscure. Jiang Kui's *ci* poems are like wild clouds that fly solitarily, and leave or stay without a trace. . . . The tunes of Jiang Kui's *ci* poetry, like "Faint Shadow" and "Hidden Fragrance" are not only flexible and romantically charming but also full of wit, thereby fascinating their readers.[32]

In Zhang Yan's eyes, vapidity was only one aspect of Jiang Kui's *ci* composition, and by vapidity he meant that Jiang Kui could describe the concrete as if it were abstract and conjure up broad images of the universe with a stroke of his writing brush. But there was another side to Jiang Kui, and that was his elegance. This meant a concentration of the author's feelings and mood, while avoiding flattery. Zhang Yan, in the work quoted above, says, "Mood is the predominant theme of *ci* poetry." And, citing Jiang Kui's poems "Hidden Fragrance" and "Faint Shadow," he says, "In vapidity there is mood." In my opinion, the words of Liu Xizai are an apt summing up of Jiang Kui's style: "Cool fragrance in hidden rhythms." The key words here are "cool" and "hidden." They blaze a unique trail, free from flattery, grandiosity and cleverness, and mark Jiang Kui as a poet of great influence on the Southern Song *ci* stage.

Jiang Kui was also a fine composer of music. His musical creations can be found in the six volumes of *Tunes by White Rock Taoist*. This work contains 17 songs in the *ci* mode, most of them composed by Jiang Kui. One of them is his "Hidden Fragrance":

> How many times did the bright moon/
> Shine upon me fluting by the plum bloom?/
> The beauty, aroused, came despite the cold/
> To join me in picking the plum blossoms/
> Forgetting the brisk literary rhetoric/
> Like He Xun, I'm growing old today/
> Beyond the bamboos a few blooms quaint/
> Scent our banquet with their perfume faint.
> Silent is the land south of the Yangtze River/
> It's too far to send the blossoms to her/
> Not to mention the snow falling at night/
> Holding a wine cup of blue jade in my hand/
> The plums bring her back to my mind/
> Forgetting not when we were hand in hand/
> Enjoying the plum trees laden with blossoms/,
> And the cool West Lake green and bright/
> Now, seeing all the plum blossoms fallen/
> I don't know when I will see her again.[33]

The *ci* poets of the latter part of the Southern Song, represented by Jiang Kui and Wu Wenying all had one thing in common, and that was a compactness of composition, which involved great attention to honing their words and verses until they were perfect and thus forming a group of literary figures with an extra-refined style.

Ci poetry in the Yuan, Ming and Qing Dynasties: successive bumper harvests

Of the Yuan Dynasty *ci* poets, Liu Yin was quite influential, with a reputation close to that of Su Shi. Zhang Zhu was also held in high esteem. The Mongolian poet Sadula wrote "Baiziling * Ascending to the Stone City" to commemorate his ascent of the city wall of Jinling, an erstwhile Six Dynasties (229–589) capital. This *ci* poem is steeped in the writer's feelings about the vicissitudes of history:

> I stare at the skyline of Jinling City/
> There's nothing I can see/
> But the relics of the kingdoms of Wu and Chu/
> There at one time six dynasties thrived/
> Now only the mountains have survived/
> Banners of battle used to blot out the sky/
> Sails of warships merged with the clouds/
> Fallen soldiers' bones amassed snowy white/
> The Yangtze River flows to the east/
> Taking with it many a strong man and hero.
> Quiet is the palace away from the capital/
> The passage traversed by the chariot royal/
> Is now covered with weeds year after year/
> At dusk, the paths in the forests are lonely/
> Only will-o'-wisps flicker in the blackness/
> The days were full of drinking and revelry/
> In the mirror the dancers looked young and pretty/
> Their hair, once black, is now as white as snow/
> This night enshrouded in the moonlight bright/
> Millennia of regrets witnesses the river Qinhuai.[34]

The achievements of the Ming Dynasty (1368–1644) *ci* poets have always been considered somewhat mediocre, and even such outstanding names as Liu Ji, Gao Qi and Yang Shen have been accused of lacking creative power. In the period which saw the end of the Ming and the beginning of the Qing Dynasty (1644–1911), Chen Zilong and his disciple Xia Wanchun attracted new attention to the *ci* genre. A representative piece by Chen Zilong is "Green Willow Tips * Spring Longing":

> The Xiuling Palace overlooks a plain/
> Above this mausoleum of the Han Chinese/
> Hangs a wisp of misty clouds/
> The roads are still thick with cloying dust/

Bordellos are bedecked with red candles/
Doing what they do are the courtesans.
A decade of awakening from fond dreams/
What was in the past that I'm recollecting/
Is replete with endless grief of parting/
Like slim willow branches and new cattails/
Like crows and wild geese in the evening/
Like a meadow to the horizon reaching.[35]

The language is fresh and lucid, the *ci* style is plaintive, and the whole poem is worthy of the hand of a master.

At the age of only nine, Xia Wanchun was an accomplished writer of *fu* poems in the ancient style. At the age of 15, he followed his father Xia Yunyi into the army to resist the Manchu invaders. Xia Wanchun was captured by the enemy, and died a martyr's death at the early age of 17. His *ci* poems are filled with enthusiasm and pathos. A representative one is "Plucking Mulberries":

Willow catkins are swept up by wind and rain/
Down on the ground, they roll like blobs of cotton/
Down on the ground, they roll like blobs of cotton,
Revealing the spring breeze's weakness at the pavilion.
Privately I relate my painful memory of a lost country/
To the Yangtze River that flows to the east/
To the Yangtze River that flows to the east/
Its whole length being filled with my grief.[36]

There was a revival of *ci* creativity during the Qing Dynasty; both poets and schools sprang up in abundance, and the theoretical part of *ci* composition made great strides. The Manchu *ci* poet Nalan Xingde was good at writing short lyrics, in crisp and fresh language. For instance, his "Everlasting Longing";

Across the rivers and over the ridges/
Heading for the Yu Passare the soldiers/
Late at night the barracks are still lit up/
A night of wind, a morning of snow/
Their rustling breaks many a dream/
A noise I never heard far off at home.[37]

Zhu Yizun started the Western Zhejiang School of *ci* poetry, a school which upheld pure elegance. His "Sound of Selling Flowers * Flower Terrace in the Rain" is a famous poem which expresses regret for the past and mourning for the present:

Sapped willows linger on by the White Gate/
Tides lapping the coastal city come and abate/

The Big and Small Changgan alleys are desolate/
Song clappers and wine banners have disappeared/
But fishing rods are still here with their bait.
A site of six dynasties lies grassy in cold autumns/
Platform after platform void of fallen blossoms/
Not to speak of a soul standing by the palace rails/
Carefree swallows fly at sunset to and fro/
What's happened to the land they care not to know.[38]

Chen Weisong was the doyen of the Yangxian School of *ci*. His *ci* style was very close to that of Xin Qiji. An example is "Southern Village * Composed on the Way to Xingtai":

An autumn wind chills our Bingzhou swords/
Its blinding gusts are raging like warlords/
Riding abreast, young men of Central China/
Looking wild and brave like heroes of old/
Shooting eagles while drunk in a forest of oaks.
Over our cups we remembered the Yan assassin/
His and others' tragic epics are never forgotten/
The hero's rumbling carriage is still sounding/,
Let's see if we can achieve the same.[39]

The Changzhou school of *ci* poetry, with Zhang Huiyan and Zhou Ji as the representative figures, emerged following the Jiaqing reign period (1795–1821) of Qing Emperor Renzong. It stressed "internal meaning and external words" to express its themes. A representative *ci* poem by Zhang Huiyan in this vein is "The Slow Tune of Mangnolia * Poplar Buds":

Though cleanly breaking from their branches/
Who recognizes the willow catkins as flowers?/
In double-layered curtains, the wind is hiding/
In the depth of draped tents, the rain is circling/
The swaying canopy the clouds are guarding/
They look for company throughout the spring/
Only to meet other fallen blooms in the evening/
They take off before touching the ground/
Unwilling to stand landing without a sound.
Bold but inhibited, they're doomed to isolation/
Lingering until spring comes to its conclusion/
Then they will fall and kiss the moonlit ground/
Accompanying the snow-like petals thereupon/
Together they're remembered as cold and clear/
Ignoring the injustice that they suffer in the spring/
They've become a cloud of grief to veil the hills/

Some have turned themselves into duckweed/
Staining the water of the pond like tears shed.[40]

This poem clearly pictures willow catkins, expressive of a kind of hidden but exalted loneliness. Zhou Ji's representative work in this vein is "Butterfly Enamored of Flowers":

Willow catkins bloom late every spring/
Along the lakeside road ten miles long/
Putting an end to a time of blossoming/
Finding nowhere to land as they fly around/
With the wind they leave, above the ground.
Broken walls and withered trees in full view/
Even though some flowers might survive/
The wind deva's jealousy would them destroy/
The river never stops its flow/
Despite the heaps of misty sand.[41]

There can be no doubt that there was a bumper crop of *ci* poetry of the Yuan, Ming and Qing dynasties. But creative spirit was not as strong as we could desire, and all we can say is that the output was continuous.

Notes

1 *Random Notes of the Jade Chicken*, Vol.1, Tang Guizhang, ed., *Edited Collection of Ci Talks*, Part 1, Zhonghua Book Company,1986, P. 74.
2 *The Wellspring of Ci Poetry*, Second Part, Tang Guizhang, ed., *Edited Collection of Ci Talks*, Part 1, Zhonghua Book Company, 1986, P. 255.
3 See Erbei's, Ren: *Preliminary Probe of Dunhuang Tunes*, Shanghai literature and Art Publishing House, 1954.
4 See Erbei's, Ren: *Dunhuang Tunes Collected and Edited * Ordinary Miscellaneous Tunes*, Shanghai literature and Art Publishing House, 1955.
5 *Complete Tang Poems*, Vol.28, Zhonghua Book Company, 1960, P. 408.
6 *Complete Tang Poems*, Vol.890, Zhonghua Book Company, 1960, P. 10056.
7 Yimang, Li: *Collected Teachings Among the Flowers*, Vol.1, People's Literature Publishing House, 1958, P. 1.
8 Yimang, Li: *Collected Teachings Among the Flowers*, Vol.2, People's Literature Publishing House, 1958, P. 31.
9 Antai, Zhan ed: *The Ci Poems of Li Jing and Li Yu*, People's Literature Publishing House, 1958, P. 73.
10 Guowei, Wang: *Comments on Ci Poetry*, People's Literature Publishing House, 1960, P. 197.
11 See Xingpei's, Yuan: *Research into the Chinese Art of Poetry and Ballads*, Revised and Enlarged Edition, Peking University Press, 1996, PP. 277–295.
12 [Yuan Dynasty] Toqto'a et al: *History of the Song Dynasty*, Vol.124, Zhonghua Book Company, 1977, P. 3345.

13 Zeng, Wu: *Casual Literary Notes from Nenggai Studio*, Vol.16 "At first, Liu Yong, a successful candidate in the highest imperial examinations, was keen on licentious songs and melodies, and spread them far and wide. Once he wrote a *ci* poem to the tune 'Crane Shooting into the Sky', which read, 'Though finding it hard, I still trade on my undeserved reputation for light drinking and crooning.' When announcing the successful candidates in the final civil examination in the palace hall, the Renzong Emperor did not include Liu Yong's name on the list. The emperor said, 'Go ahead and drink and croon. What do you need an underserved reputation for?'" Shanghai Ancient Books Publishing House, 1979, P. 480.
14 Guizhang, Tang ed: *Complete Song Ci Poems*, Zhonghua Book Company, 1956, P. 29.
15 Guizhang, Tang ed: *Complete Song Ci Poems*, Zhonghua Book Company, 1956, P. 21.
16 *On the Origin of Learning*, Collection 14, Vol.4, 1805, Yushan the Zhang's Zhaokuangge woodblock print.
17 *On the Origin of Learning*, Collection 14, Vol.2, 1805, Yushan the Zhang's Zhaokuangge woodblock print.
18 Guizhang, Tang ed: *Complete Song Ci Poems*, Zhonghua Book Company, 1956, P. 282.
19 Guizhang, Tang ed: *Complete Song Ci Poems*, Zhonghua Book Company, 1956, P. 280.
20 Guizhang, Tang ed: *Complete Song Ci Poems*, Zhonghua Book Company, 1956, P. 277.
21 [Song Dynasty] Zeng Zao says in his *Notes on Classical Poetry from Gao Studio*: "Shao You had the opportunity to pay his respects to Su Dongpo in the capital. The latter said, 'I didn't expect you to have styled your *ci* poetry after Liu Yong's.' Qin Guan replied, 'I may not be learned, but this is not true.' Su Shi asked further: 'Didn't you use words favored by Liu Yong, like the term ecstasy?'" See Guo Shaoyu's *Edited Talks on Song Poetry*, Zhonghua Book Company, 1980, P. 497.
22 Guizhang, Tang ed: *Complete Song Ci Poems*, Zhonghua Book Company, 1956, P. 459.
23 [Qing Dynasty] Tingzhuo, Chen: *Talks on the Ci Poems of White Rain Studio*, People's Literature Publishing House, 1959, P. 47.
24 Guizhang, Tang ed: *Complete Song Ci Poems*, Zhonghua Book Company, 1956, p. 595.
25 Zhongwen, Wang: *The Collected Works of Li Qingzhao Annotated*, People's Literature Publishing House, 1979, P. 64.
26 Guangming, Deng: *An Annotation to a Chronological Compilation of Xin Qiji's Ci Poems*, Vol.2, Shanghai Ancient Books Publishing House, 1981, P. 204.
27 Guangming, Deng: *An Annotation to a Chronological Compilation of Xin Qiji's Ci Poems*, Vol.2, Shanghai Ancient Books Publishing House, 1981, P. 172.
28 Guangming, Deng: *An Annotation to a Chronological Compilation of Xin Qiji's Ci Poems*, Vol.2, Shanghai Ancient Books Publishing House, 1981, P. 193.
29 [Song Dynasty] Xiaoxiang, Zhang: *The Collected Works of the Lakeside Lay Buddhist*, Vol.31, *Collected Writings of the Four Basic Branches of Literature*.
30 [Song Dynasty] You, Lu: *The Collected Works of Weinan*, Vol.50, *Collected Writings of the Four Basic Branches of Literature*.
31 Shuge, Jiang: *The Ci Poems of Chen Liang With Notes and Commentary*, People's Literature Publishing House, 1980, P. 26.
32 Guizhang, Tang ed: *Edited Collection of Ci Talks*, Zhonghua Book Company, 1987, P. 259.
33 Guizhang, Tang ed: *Complete Song Ci Poems*, Zhonghua Book Company, 1965, P. 2181. In the Preface, it says, "In the winter of Xinhai, I went to the place named Stone Lake in the snow. In a period of about a month, I asked people to write while I collected poetry and new verses normally deemed unorthodox. I composed these two *ci* poems,

and liked them very much. When I had them sung by my domestic singers, I found the lines sounding harmonic and mild. I therefore named them 'Hidden Fragrance' and 'Faint Shadow.'"

34 [Qing Dynasty] Yizun, Zhu ed: *The Loom of Ci Poetry*, Vol.29, Shanghai Ancient Books Publishing House, 1978, P. 667.

35 *Poems Throughout the Dynasties*, Vol.20, *The Complete Four Repositories* from the Pavilion of the Imperial Library.

36 *Additions to Xia Wanchun's Ci Poems*, Zhao Zunyue ed. *A Collection of Ming Dynasty Ci Poems*, Part 1, Shanghai Ancient Books Publishing House, 1992 photocopy, P. 432.

37 Xiuting, Zhao and Tongyi, Feng: *Drinking Water Ci Poems with Comments and Notes*, Vol.2, Zhonghua Book Company, 2005, P. 188.

38 [Qing Dynasty] Yizun, Zhu: *Collected Works of Pushu Pavilion*, Vol.24, *The Complete Four Repositories*, Pavilion of the Imperial Library.

39 Chengdao, Xia, and Zhang, Zhang eds: *Selected Ci poems of the Jin, Yuan, Ming and Qing Dynasties*, People's Literature Publishing House, 1987, P. 409.

40 Chengdao, Xia. and Zhang, Zhang eds: *Selected Ci poems of the Jin, Yuan, Ming and Qing Dynasties*, People's Literature Publishing House, 1987, P. 523.

41 Chengdao, Xia. and Zhang, Zhang eds: *Selected Ci poems of the Jin, Yuan, Ming and Qing Dynasties*, People's Literature Publishing House, 1987, P. 547.

8 *Qu* verses of the Yuan Dynasty

Yuan Dynasty *Sanqu*: a new form of singing

By the later stage of the Southern Song Dynasty *ci* poetry had developed to the stage at which it had become a one-sided pursuit of elegant diction and beautiful rhythms, and consequently something which only a minority of people appreciated. In the meantime, folk songs and tunes continued to evolve. During the Song and Jin (1115–1234) dynasties, the folk songs of the Jurchen and Mongolian nationalities gradually developed into a new kind of musical genre, which came to be called *sanqu*. This genre was able to describe human feelings and natural scenery just as well as the traditional *shi* and *ci* poems; and as *quci* it also became an important part of the Yuan Dynasty's poetic drama known as *zaju*. According to Sui Shusen's calculations in his *The Complete Sanqu of the Yuan Dynasty*," there were 3,853 short lyrics and 457 song sequences composed during the Yuan Dynasty, apart from miscellaneous compositions.

The course of development of Yuan *sanqu* can be broadly classified into two stages – the early and late parts of that dynasty. The leading dramatists of the first period included Guan Hanqing and Ma Zhiyuan, whose style was comparatively straightforward and natural.

There are 57 short poems ascribed to Guan Hanqing extant, and 14 sets of lyrics known as *taoshu* (including fragments). The authorship of some of these is disputed. Most of them have romantic love as their themes, and the speaker of many is a young woman. They are often accurate depictions of the motions of the female heart. Typical of the ones which describe the longing for a departed lover is "Sundered Love" [Four Pieces of Jade]:

> When you are gone/
> For you I long/
> When will my yearning end?/
> Leaning on the balcony rail/
> In snow-like willo down/
> The stream you went along/
> At the hillside makes a bend/

It is screened from view/
Oh, to be together with you![1]

Ma Zhiyuan's *Music Bureau of the Eastern Fence*, in one volume, contains 104 short poems and 17 *taoshu*. This is the largest number preserved of any of the *sanqu* writers of the early part of the Yuan Dynasty. In these works, Ma Zhiyuan mainly writes about the life of the recluse and his sedate pursuits; sighs for the present age and laments for the past; or natural scenery and the life of the vagabond. Ma's *sanqu* express his mourning over his unrecognized talents, his feelings of loathing for his times and his otherworldly attitude. His most famous short poem is "Autumn Thoughts" [Yue Mode * Clear Sky over the Sand]:

O'er old trees wreathed in rotten vines fly evening crows/
'Neath a tiny bridge beside a cot a clear stream flows/
Westward declines the sun/
Far, far from home is the heartbroken one.[2]

This work uses a series of objective scenes to bring out the sadness of the lonely traveler. The first three verses each use three linked images, which, in the original, pile up nine images without the use of connecting words, the connections between them being dependent on the reader's imagination. The beauty relies on the meaning, not on the words. Wang Guowei, in his *Comments on Ci Poetry*, comments, "It matches the beauty of the quatrains of the Tang poets."[3]

By the latter half of the Yuan Dynasty *sanqu* had developed to the point at which graceful expressions were principally sought after. Representatives of this style were Zhang Kejiu, Qiao Ji and Sui Jingchen.

Of Zhang Kejiu's short poems, over 700 are extant, the most of any Yuan *sanqu* composer. Zhang stressed form and pattern. He delighted in subtly carving his words and verses, pursued the elegance of *shi* and *ci* poetry, and avoided vulgarisms. His works were in stark contrast to those of his predecessors in the early part of the Yuan Dynasty. For instance, "A Spring Day by the Lake" [Huangzhong Mode * Reunion Under the Full Moon]:

The view from the pavilion is blocked by a mountain/
The site of the former Chu State cannot be seen/
In a dream last night I saw that beauty by my side/
On awakening, I was uncertain as to where she was fluting/
During the time when we were not together/
No one kept me company except/
The insensitive moon and the rhythmic tide/
Missing someone makes me age fast/
My soul is drifting like flying petals/
My eyebrows frowning like shriveled leaves.[4]

The theme is that of a girl longing for her lover in the far distant land of Chu. The "small tower" is where the lover lives. It is hidden in the verdant mountains, and can't be seen; only in dreams is the lover seen. The writer imagines that she is also waiting to see him. But such a meeting is no more than an "autumn moon" or a "spring tide." The autumn moon has no feelings; it cannot understand human thoughts, but it can arouse emotions in the human breast. The spring tide is reliable; it comes at certain times. It is not like the lover, who goes perhaps never to return. All this makes the girl careworn.

Qiao Ji's *Short Poems of Qiao Mengfu*, in one volume, contains ten groups of *taoqu*, second only to the works of Zhang Kejiu in number. Qiao Ji's style is also close to that of Zhang Kejiu in its elegance and lucidity. It also displays a tendency to stress craftsmanship of words and verses, as well as pleasant sounds. It was because of this that Zhang and Qiao used to be mentioned in the same breath Li Kaixian of the Ming Dynasty compared "Zhang and Qiao" to the Tang Dynasty's "Li and Du."[5] Qiao Ji's *sanqu* contain surprising turns of phrase, such as "As soon as the wind dies down/I slowly reel in my line/Pulling toward me a lakeful of stars" and "After returning home/ I hang up my fishing tackle/But I don't hang up my grief for the past and the present" ("The Fisherman's Song" [Zhonglv Mode * A Courtyard Filled with Flowers]). Again, "A skinny nag bears my poems to the end of the Earth/Weary birds pipe grief into all the rustic cottages" ("On the Way to Jinling" [Yue Mode * Leaning on the Railing]). And, "The limpid river is like water in the cup of the sky/The white geese form a cloud-grey line on high" ("Reflections on Parting" [Double Mode * The Passing Geese]). Qiao Ji's most representative work is "Looking for Plums" [Double Mode * Fairy of the Water]):

> I visited several villages during the cold winter/
> And, shoes covered with frost, both sides of the river/
> Searching the plum trees all over the solitary hill/
> I was unable to find the trace of a single flower/
> Then where on earth did the perfume come from?
> Looking back, I saw a beauty in her neat attire/
> The cold woke me up from my dreamy stupor/
> Of spring's end the melancholy flute is a reminder/
> Yellowish opaque moonlight filling the misty air.[6]

The writer tells us that he has wandered through the countryside, from village to village, in winter. North and south of valley streams he has pursued his course, gathering cold frost on his shoes. Finally he comes to an isolated wooded mountain. The cold wind from somewhere wafts a mysterious fragrance, and there suddenly appears a beautiful woman clad in white silk. Entranced, he falls into a swoon beneath a plum tree. The winter cold wakes him from a dream, and the sound of a flute awakens sadness in his heart. The moon has faded, and the twilight has passed into night. The tune played on the flute is "The Falling Plum Blossoms," giving rise to the verse, "The flute sings of chilly autumn, breaking my heart."

A particularly famous *taoqu* work by Sui Jingchen is "Emperor Gaozu Returns to His Home Village" [Banshe Mode * Shaobian]. In the *History of the Han Dynasty * Emperor Gao Section* it is recorded that Liu Bang, Emperor Gaozu of Han (reign: 206 BC–194 BC), returned to his home village and drank wine with his old acquaintances and relatives. In this account Liu Bang is shown to be both awe-inspiring and dignified, and at the same time friendly and approachable. But in his poem, Sui Jingchen does not follow the historical record; instead, he employs his own feelings to portray the emperor. When Liu Bang visits his home village, according to Sui Jingchen, his old neighbors look at him askance as they remember past times, and his show of dignity is portrayed as something ludicrous. At the same time, the poem makes the fawning approach used by the likes of Wang Xianglao and Zhao Manglang to the scene of the emperor being "escorted in his palanquin to the sound of trumpets" laughably obsequious. This *taoqu* is imbued with disdain for the feudal order and feudal rulers.

The *sanqu* and *zaju* of the Yuan Dynasty are collectively known as "Yuan drama" in the history of Chinese literature. Yuan drama shares an exalted place in that history along with Tang *shi* poetry and Song *ci* poetry.

Yuan *zaju* drama bursts onto the scene

The origin of Chinese drama can be traced back to the primitive songs and dances which accompanied the sacrificial rites of ancient times. But they only formed one aspect of drama, and cannot be regarded as dramas in the proper sense. In succeeding ages a number of factors contributed to the gestation of drama in the course of its development. For instance, the period that saw the transition from the Spring and Autumn Period (770–476 BC) to the Warring States Period (475–221 BC) also saw the appearance of clowns and other entertainers; athletic performers emerged in the Han Dynasty (206 BC–220 AD); and in the Tang Dynasty the "army recruitment play" was popular. These were all essential preparations for the full-blown drama.

It was in the Song Dynasty that drama proper emerged in China, with the advent of the *zaju* performance; this, together with the *yuanben*, or "storyteller's prompt books," was the fledgling form of the Chinese drama.

The Yuan *zaju* sprang up in the north of China as a new art form. Between the closing years of the Jin Dynasty and the early years of the Ming Dynasty a large number of *zaju* writers (nearly 200) and their works (over 162) appeared. This genre can be divided into Early and Late period forms. The former covers the latter part of the Jin Dynasty to the Dade reign period (1297–1307) of Yuan Emperor Chengzong, and the latter from that time to the end of the Yuan Dynasty, a span of about 60 years.

The former period is regarded as the golden age of Yuan *zaju*. The center of this drama form was the capital of the dynasty, Dadu (modern Beijing), and its most famous exponents were Guan Hanqing, Wang Shifu, Bai Pu, Ma Zhiyuan, Yang Xianzhi, Gao Wenxiu, Kang Jinzhi, Shi Junbao and Ji Junxiang.

Guan Hanqing wrote over 60 *zaju* dramas, of which only a dozen or so survive. The most important of these, which can definitely be ascribed to him and are representative of his achievements, are "The Injustice Done to Dou E," "Saving the Dusty Wind," "The Pavilion for Admiring the Moon," "Pavilion Overlooking the River" and "Guan Yu Meets His Formidable Foe with His Long Sword Alone."

"The Injustice Done to Dou E" is Guan Hanqing's representative work. The story goes that Dou Tianzhang, having borrowed money from Widow Cai which he is unable to repay, to pay off the debt delivered his daughter to the Cai household to be brought up as a future bride for the son of the house, who was in the capital taking the imperial examinations. The girl's name was changed to Dou E, meaning "Dou the Beauty." However, as soon as she reached marriageable age her husband-to-be died. Widow Cai was then inveigled by a rascal called Zhang the Mule into a scheme whereby she would marry Zhang while Dou E would be married off to Zhang's son. Widow Cai did indeed marry Zhang the Mule, but Du E refused to marry the son, whereupon the son threatened to poison Widow Cai, hoping that this would change Dou E's mind. When Zhang the Mule took the poison by mistake, and died, his son charged Dou E with the crime. The muddle-headed magistrate Tao Wu had Dou E tortured, but despite her suffering Dou E refused to confess to a crime she had not committed. It was only when the magistrate threatened to subject Widow Cai to torture that Dou E made a false confession, and was condemned to death. Just before her execution, Dou E made three predictions which would prove her innocence: that her blood would spurt out pure white; that snow would fall in that summer month; and that this would be followed by a three-year-long drought. Sure enough, these three predictions came true, and three years later, in his new capacity as an anti-corruption inspector, Dou E's father investigated the case and proved that his daughter had been innocent all along. The drama's poetic words set to music have a particularly moving artistic effect. Let us take a look at the song to the tune of "A Rolling Embroidered Ball," which Dou E sings in the torture scene:

> The sun and moon are looking down/
> The god of life and death is looking up/
> Heaven and Earth should know what's right and wrong/
> How can you let free the hooligan Yan Yuan?/
> You doom the good to poverty and a short life/
> And make the wicked long-lived and thriving/
> So even Heaven and Earth are but arrogant and cold/
> And push the boat in the direction of the current/
> Earth, how can you confuse truth and falsehood?/
> Heaven, you're unworthy of your name if you wrong the innocent/
> Alas, I can say nothing, but just shed tears.[7]

Guan Hanqing reveals the social contradictions and conflicts prominent in his time. In the course of depicting members of all levels of society, including the upper classes, such as generals, prime ministers, officials and influential families, and the common people, such as singing girls, he molds authentic images of human characters. But he does not confine himself to strictly real-life representations; his works contain a certain idealistic element, and he often gives non-realistic solutions to realistic problems. Sometimes he even goes so far as to ignore the logic of real life, giving happy endings to tragic stories. For instance, in "Saving the Dusty Wind" Zhao Pan'er uses coquetry to fool the local tyrant Zhou She into issuing a divorce certificate and freeing Song Yinzhang, who had fallen into Zhou She's cruel hands. Comparing the relative power of the two, Zhao Paner was in a much weaker position, but Guan Hanqing contrives to allow the underdog to come out on top. The arrangement of the plot of this drama has a very romantic coloring.

Guan Hanqing's use of language has been much praised. In his obituary of the playwright, Jia Zhongming lauds him as follows: "Exquisite words tumble out as naturally as pearls. He is a veritable wellspring of phrases of gold and jade. He has a Heaven-given talent to move one to the heart."[8] Wang Guowei says in his *Discussion of Song and Yuan Drama*: "Nobody like Guan Hanqing had been seen before. He forged his own phrases, and his songs plumbed the depths of human feelings. Every word had its unique connotation. He was the first and foremost of the Yuan dramatists."[9] Guan Hanqing laid the foundation stone of Chinese drama. He takes pride of place among the quartet of leading Yuan dramatists (The others being Ma Zhiyuan, Zheng Guangzu and Bai Pu.)

An Account of Ghosts collects 14 *zaju* written by Wang Shifu. Three have been passed down to us complete, and only fragments of two others. His representative work is "The Western Chamber."

"The Western Chamber," as it is popularly known, is the most accomplished romantic drama of traditional China, and one of the most influential. It is the story of a love affair between Zhang Sheng and Cui Yingying. It is also a warm celebration of the defiance of feudal mores by a young couple as they strive for the freedom to marry. The playwright, Wang Shifu, boldly lifts the lid off the irrationality of feudal teachings, and holds up for admiration those who defy and challenge the forces of feudalism. He so arranges the story that a triumphal outcome awaits the latter. In this drama, the author not only delineates images of people with different characters, as a breakthrough from the confused tangle that was the world of drama of his time, he successfully brings to the fore an ideological theme. In addition, the language of this drama shows a high degree of individuality, and the different dramatis personae all have distinct characteristics. The speech of Zhang Sheng is elegant and refined. He regularly expresses his real feelings, making a clean breast of his thoughts, sometimes to the extent of exaggeration but also tinged with humor. Yingying's speech is guarded but full of hidden meaning. In addition, it has a sentimental and fresh tone. The maid Hongniang's speech is bold and impertinent. She is astute and sharp, and everything she says hits the nail on the head. The diction used in this drama overall has a lyrical flavor. Its tunes are elegant and refined, encompassing the moods of the Song Dynasty *ci* poetry and the style of the Yuan Dynasty short poems. For abundance of poetic excellence "The Western Chamber" is rarely matched in Yuan *zaju*. Particularly in the act titled "Parting at the Long pavilion," emotion and scenery are well coordinated and the speech is sonorous. As an example:

> [Zheng Mode * Duanzhenghao]
> The sky is blue but cloudy/
> The fields are yellow with flowers/
> The westerly wind's blowing like a demon/
> The wild geese are migrating south/
> Who reddened the frost-covered forest in the morning?/
> I've been shedding tears for my love who's leaving.
> [A Rolling Embroidered Ball]
> I regret we didn't meet sooner/
> I hate parting in such haste/
> The withies are so long that I can't tie his horse trotting.
> If I could I'd beg the thin forest to catch the sun falling/
> I wish his horse were slow/
> And my carriage could follow/
> When I caught up, I was told to return/
> Because he had to rush to the civil exam/
> His "Goodbye" loosened the bracelets from my arms/
> My stare from the long corridor takes off my weight.
> Who could understand my grief at parting?
> [Daodaoling]
> Seeing them busy hitching the horse to the cart/
> I can't but feel anxious, as it broke my heart/
> Forget the blush and the silk blossom/
> I've lost the mood to doll myself up/
> The quilts and the pillows I'm grabbing/
> I'm ready to fall into a prolonged sleep/
> So my blouse will only my tears wipe away/
> How can I not feel depressed?
> How can I not feel depressed?
> Thus to me you must letters often write.
> [Conclusion]
> Surrounded by the mountains/
> A whip cracks loud in the dusk/
> Grief at parting filling the world/
> To carry them, can the carts perform the task?[10]

Bai Pu's representative work, "Rain on the Parasol Tree," deals with the story of Tang Emperor Xuanzong (reign: 713–756) and his concubine Yang Yuhuan. The playwright has an ambivalent attitude to the emperor: He criticizes him yet at the same time sympathizes with him. On the one hand, he finds the emperor's infatuation – to the extent that he nearly brings about the end of the Tang Dynasty – reprehensible; on the other, he admires the way the emperor's love for Yang Yuhuan never wavers. All in all, Bai Pu shows sympathy for his predicament. "Rain on the Parasol Tree" serves as a historical lesson, as it shows how Emperor Xuanzong's muddle-headed infatuation lays the groundwork for the An-Shi rebellion. At the same time it is a genuine paean of praise to love. The central character in the drama is Emperor Xuanzong, played as a middle-aged man. Thus it is a typical stage performance, but it is also, from the artistic point of view, a long lyric poem expressing the emperor's love for and attachment to Yang Yuhuan. The author is skilled at describing his characters' psychological world as well as in using physical surroundings to highlight his lyrical passages. In masterly fashion, he blends the characters' feelings with the atmosphere of their settings. For this he has received much favorable comment. Especially in the fourth act of this drama, in the part where rain falls on the parasol tree, the atmosphere is very well depicted.

Ma Zhiyuan's representative work is "Autumn in the Han Palace." The core of the plot is the journey of Wang Zhaojun, a consort of Han Emperor Yuan (reign: 48 BC–32 BC), beyond the Great Wall to become the wife of Khan Huhanxie, the leader of the Huns. The emperor had sent the rascally minister Mao Yanshou to tour his empire choosing beautiful girls for his harem, and painting their portraits for the emperor's approval. In Zigui County he came across the peerless beauty Wang Qiang, whose given name was Wang Zhaojun. He offered her one hundred ounces of gold to agree to become the head of the imperial harem. When the girl refused, Mao added some blemishes to her portrait to ensure that when she entered the palace she would be assigned to the drudges' quarters and never even see the emperor. One day, as she was whiling away the time playing on a zither, Emperor Yuan happened to overhear. Then he discovered how beautiful she actually was, and promoted her to a high position among his concubines. Mao Yanshou, his scheme foiled, fled to the Huns, taking with him an authentic portrait of the beautiful Wag Zhaojun. He inveigled the Hun khan into invading the territory of the Han Empire, and demanding Wang Zhaojun as the price for desisting. In the face of this demand, all the officials of the court, both civil and military, were helpless. Wang Zhaojun expressed her willingness to surrender herself to the Hun chieftain in order to bring about peace. The emperor bade her a tearful farewell after a formal banquet at a bridge over the River Ba. As she crossed the border, Wang Zhaojun turned to face the south, and poured a libation into the border river before jumping in herself and drowning. Emperor Yuan, hearing the mournful cry of a solitary goose one autumn evening, was overcome with longing for Wang Zhaojun, which was only increased by a glimpse of her in a dream that night. In the end, the Huns sent Mao Yanshou back as a prisoner, and expressed a desire for peace. Emperor Yuan had Mao Yanshou's head chopped off and offered as a sacrifice to the soul of his favorite concubine.

"Autumn in the Han Palace" is a hymn of praise to the patriotic integrity of Wang Zhaojun, and holds up for admiration her loyalty to the Han court. At the same time, it uses the image of Mao Yanshou to hold up for condemnation his type of avaricious, obsequious and corrupt officials, who would sell out their country for gain at the drop of a hat. The central character in this drama is Han Emperor

Yuan. Even though he is the ruler of the empire, he is unable to protect his favorite concubine, and in then end has to send her to the Hun chieftain in order to get the Huns to retire. This is his tragedy. The beautiful words and music of "Autumn in the Han Palace" are well suited to highlighting the feelings of the protagonists through descriptions of scenery. In the third scene, as Emperor Yuan is gazing at the departing Zhaojun and imagining how desolate and lonely he will feel as he wends his way back to the palace bereft of his love, he sings:

> [Plum Blossom Wine]
> Alas! I am sad looking at this vast open country/
> Where the grass is turning yellow and brown/
> Rabbits are greeted with frost in the morn/
> The hounds' have shed their fine hair/
> The people are holding their spears/
> The horses are carrying their gear/
> The carts are loaded with provisions/
> People gather on the hunting ground/
> Leaving the King of Han to his grief/
> I am seeing him off, holding his hand/
> He and his men will venture into the barren land/
> In my imperial carriage I return to Xianyang,
> Passing by the palace walls, the walls/
> Rounding the winding corridor, the corridor/
> Approaching the palace halls, the halls/
> The moon turns more and more yellowish/
> The night temperature is dropping and dropping/
> The crickets are moaning and moaning/
> The curtains are turning greener than green/
> I'd better stop thinking of the parting scene![11]

The verses of this "Plum Blossom Wine" lyrical song are very short, and in the second half the device of using the last word or phrase in the previous verse to start the next one is employed, as well as the techniques of overlap and zigzag. This is a perfectly apt way to express the tangled emotions of Emperor Yuan.

Kang Jinzhi's "Li Kui Shoulders Thorns" is a light-hearted drama. The story goes that an old man named Wang Lin runs a tavern in Apricot Blossom Village near Mount Liang. His only daughter, 18 years old, is called "The Local Beauty." On the third day of the third month two rascals called Song Gang and Lu Zhi'en arrive at the tavern pretending to be two stalwarts, Song Jiang and Lu Zhishen, of the nearby bandit fraternity of Mount Liang. They abduct "The Local Beauty." Now it just happens that on that same day another of the Mount Liang fraternity, Black Whirlwind Li Kui, drops by the tavern to drink. He is outraged to learn that Wang Lin's daughter has been kidnapped by his colleagues Song Jiang and Lu Zhishen, and hastens back up the mountain to take them to task. He causes a great uproar in the Hall of Loyalty and Righteousness, where the bandits gather.

In the end, Li Kui and Song Jiang bet their lives against each other, and proceed down the mountain to put their cases to the local magistrate. Li Kui, although he is getting deeper and deeper into error and seems about to lose his head, is fully confident of victory. The more he looks at Song Jiang and Lu Zhishen on the way the more they look to Li Kui like people who would do bad things, and he never ceases to jibe at them. Song Jiang and Lu Zhishen, meanwhile, are perfectly calm, confident that as soon as they meet Wang Lin their innocence will be established, and therefore do not bother to reply to Li Kui's taunts – a circumstance that only serves to increase the latter's suspicions. When Song Jiang goes in front, Li Kui reckons that he is walking fast because he is happy thinking he is "going to his father-in-law's house," and when he walks slowly, Li Kui thinks that Song Jiang is afraid of the magistrate. This dramatic irony causes the audience a great deal of amusement. But in the midst of the laughter there is an increasing sense of sympathy with Li Kui. Finally, Li Kui realizes his error when he comes face to face with Wang Lin. After the trio from Mount Liang leave, the original two blackguards return to the tavern, where Wang Lin plies them with wine. That same night, Wang Lin goes up the mountain to report that the two rascals are in a state of inebriation in his tavern. In the meantime, Li Kui has chopped a bunch of thorns, which he carries on his back up the mountain in repentance, and asks for punishment from Song Jiang and Lu Zhishen. First, he asks for a beating, and then to be accepted as a sworn brother by Song Jiang, hoping for forgiveness. Just at that moment Wang Lin arrives. Arms instructor Wu dispatches Lu Zhishen to help Wang Lin bring the villains up the mountain, where they are beheaded by Li Kui and Lu Zhishen. The drama ends in a round of congratulations.

"Li Kui Shoulders Thorns" was a breakthrough in Chinese dramatic art not only because the plot was based on a misconception but also because it relied on human nature for its authenticity. Through his description of the way the misconception developed, the author highlights how the heroes of Liangshan Marsh defend the people's interests, have a lofty sense of righteousness and dignity, and maintain close ties with ordinary folk. The drama especially successfully molds the character of Li Kui himself, as a man ever ready to spring to the defense of the mistreated. He is an honest and open-hearted person, always prepared to correct his faults. Although his manners are rough he has a special sensitivity for the beauties of Nature. In the first scene, in which he descends the mountain, Li Kui sings the praises of the scenery. His blunt but charming song is very attractive:

> [Zuizhongtian] Here fog envelopes the beautiful mountains,/And mists hang over the verdant Yangzhou. (Monologue) There's an oriole on that peach tree, picking and picking at the flowers, causing their petals to fall into the streamlet down below, creating a charming scene. Who told me so? Let me think. Yes, I've got it. It was him, my Brother Scholar. (Singing) This is the so-called, "Coquettish peach flowers run with water." (Monologue) Let me scoop up the peach petals and look closely. They're so pink! (Monologue with laughter) Look, how black my fingers are! (Singing) They are as beautifully pink as girls' blusher. (Monologue) You poor petals, let me set you free to catch

> up with your fellow petals. Let me follow you and follow you. Now I'm so occupied with the pursuit. (Singing) Before I know it, I've arrived at the ferry by the willow-shadowed Straw-bridge Tavern. (Monologue) No, I must stop. Otherwise, I will violate my brother's command. I must turn back. (Singing) Now I'm tantalized by this wine banner,/It – it is fluttering in the easterly wind on its curved pole.[12]

Ji Junxiang's representative work is "Zhao the Orphan." The story originates in the *Records of the Historian * The Zhao Family*, which recounts the enmity and struggles between the families of Tu'an Gu and of Zhao Dun and Zhao in the time of Duke Ling of the State of Jin and his overlord King Jing of Zhou (544–520) during the Spring and Autumn Period. Due to the demands of performance, certain artistic additions and changes have been made to the historical narrative within a rational scope. "Zhao the Orphan" consists of five acts and one interlude. The plot revolves round the hostility between the faithful courtier Zhao Dun and the rascally Tu'an Gu. The latter slanders his rival to Duke Ling, as a result of which over 300 of the Zhao family are executed. Zhao Dun's son Zhao Shuo had been married to the duke's daughter, who had given birth to a boy known as Zhao the Orphan. Tu'an Gu orders General Han Jue to shut the princess and her child up in the inner quarters and keep a close guard on them while he plots their deaths. The princess introduces into the palace the country physician Cheng Ying, and entrusts him with the task of smuggling the child out of the palace. She then hangs herself. As he is taking the boy out of the palace, Cheng Ying is discovered by Han Jue, who lets them both out before cutting his own throat.

When news of the escape reaches Tu'an Gu he orders that all babies under the age of six months be slaughtered. Cheng Ying confers with Gongsun Chujiu, an old retainer of Zhao Dun, on how to save the lives of Zhao the Orphan and the other infants. He gives his own son to Gongsun Chujiu, getting the latter to pretend that he is Zhao the Orphan. Cheng Ying then reports to Tu'an Gu that Zhao the Orphan is being sheltered by Gongsun Chujiu. Tu'an Gu has the baby brought him, and personally chops its head off. Despite torture, Gongsun Chujiu refuses to reveal the truth, and in the end commits suicide. At this point, the author goes very thoroughly into descriptions of the respective psychologies of Tu'an Gu, Gongsun Chujiu and Cheng Ying. To reward Cheng Ying for his supposed service, Tu'an Gu entrusts him with the raising of his young son (who is in reality Zhao the Orphan). Twenty years later, Cheng Ying paints a picture showing the truth about Zhao the Orphan's past, and shows it to the young man. With the help of the loyal retainer Wei Jiang, Zhao the Orphan kills Tu'an Gu, and gets revenge for his family. There are two prominent themes in this drama: One revolves around Tu'an Gu and his machinations against the Zhao family; and the other revolves around Gongsun Chujiu and Cheng Ying, and their heroic efforts to protect Zhao the Orphan. The conflict between these two runs through the whole of the drama and reveals itself in crisis after crisis.

"Zhao the Orphan" was the first Chinese drama to be introduced to Europe, where it received a comparatively warm welcome. It was translated into French in 1735, following which it was translated into English, German and Russian. The great French writer Voltaire adapted it as "The Chinese Orphan," which caused a great sensation when it was staged in Paris.

From approximately the end of the Dade reign period (1297–1307) of the Yuan Dynasty, the creative center of *zaju* gradually shifted from the capital Dadu in the north to the city of Hangzhou in the south. From this time to the end of the Yuan Dynasty was the last period of development of the Yuan *zaju*.

Both writers and dramas shrank in number in this last period, as did the quality of the works themselves. It was a period of decline for *zaju*, and the number of creators of this type of drama that we know of was only 20 or so, and the works of only about a dozen have come down to us. Apart from a few works by a handful of writers such as Zheng Guangzu, Gong Tianting and Qin Jianfu, most of the dramas of this period lack the realism of their predecessors. Their plots are taken mostly from historical stories, and advocate the feudal code of ethics and morals or the desire to lose oneself as a hermit in the wilds and seek the spirit world. Artistically, they are mediocre.

The most accomplished of the drama writers of this period was Zheng Guangzu. His representative work is "A Beauty Takes Leave of Her Soul." The plot derives from a short story called "A Story of the Leaving of a Soul", by Chen Xuanyou of the Tang Dynasty. In her seventeenth year, the beauty's (Zhang Qiannv) hand is sought by a young man named Wang Wenju. The girl sees that the young man is smitten with her, and she reciprocates his love. But the Qiannv's mother insists that Wang Wenju pass the civil service examination and make a career in some official capacity before he can marry. Qiannv sees Wang off to the capital at Broken Willow Pavilion, and then takes to her bed in a paroxysm of grief. Finally, her soul leaves her body and goes in search of young Wang. The soul alights on the boat he is traveling in. At the time, he happens to be playing his zither by the light of the moon. Qiannv's soul tells him that she has run away from her mother, and wants to accompany him to the capital. At first, Wang thought that this might be somewhat improper, but finally, convinced of the girl's sincerity, he allows her to accompany him to the capital. There, the young man is completely successful, and achieves the status of Number One Scholar. He sends a messenger with a letter informing Qiannv's mother of the good news. In the meantime, Qiannv is still lying in bed at home, stricken with illness. Every time she closes her eyes, she thinks she is with her lover. When she reads his letter, in which he says "I have gained the title of Number One Scholar. As soon as I am appointed to an official post I will return together with the young lady," Qiannv assumes that the young man has married somebody else, and collapses in a swoon. Three years later, Wang Wenju, having been appointed the local county magistrate, calls on Qiannv's mother together with her soul. Body and soul are thus reunited, and Qiannv and her lover celebrate their wedding. This story is permeated with romance and a happy-ever-after marriage, but it describes the image of Qiannv realistically and there is an appropriately hazy quality about the description of the psychology of the disembodied soul and a delicacy which transcends the original *A Story of the Leaving of a Soul.*

The lyrics of "A Beauty Takes Leave of Her Soul" are suggestive and full of hidden meaning. In the second act, when Qiannv is in pursuit of Wang Wenju, her song includes all the wit and interest of previous writers of *shi*, *ci* and *qu* verses. As follows:

> [Tusi'er]
> Look at the lonely ducks in the dusk by the distant river/
> And the crows on the old tree covered with vines/
> Hearken to the flute-notes from nowhere/
> The boatman sings lustily/
> Amid the creaking of his oar.
> [Shengyaowang]
> Near the pool of water peppers/
> I pull over my raft with my fishing gear/
> Cattails tattered, willows shriveled and reeds enfeebled.
> By the pond of water lilies/
> I pick the young lotus roots/
> A few houses appear by the misty water and moonlit sand.[13]

"Lonely ducks in the dusk" comes from Wang Bo's "Preface to the Teng Wang Pavilion," "crows on the old tree covered with vines" comes from Ma Zhiyuan's "Clear Sky over the Sand" and "the misty water and moonlit sand" comes from Du Mu's "Moored by the Side of Qinhuai River." These quotations are all finely mingled in the song.

The Southern Opera of the Song and Yuan Dynasties and its regional coloring

The Song and Yuan Southern Opera was a type of opera which flourished in southern China from the end of the Northern Song Dynasty until around the end of the Yuan Dynasty and the beginning of the Ming Dynasty. The term Southern Opera is an abbreviation for "Southern Tunes and Opera Scripts," and was originally simply "Opera Scripts," but as it originated in the Wenzhou region of Zhejiang Province, in the southern part of China, it came to be called "Southern Opera" to distinguish it from the northern *zaju*. It was also called Wenzhou or Yongjia (another name for Wenzhou) *zaju*.

Southern Opera first appeared in Wenzhou in the period which saw the end of the Northern Song and the birth of the Southern Song dynasties. Wenzhou had all the conditions conducive to the growth and development of this genre – it was an outward-oriented trading port, had a comparatively well-developed commerce and was economically prosperous, and was overwhelmingly populated by urban residents. At first, the authorities tried to ban this new type of entertainment, but the enthusiasm of the local people ensured that it spread. It was in Lin'an (now called Hangzhou) that Southern Opera fully developed into a mature stage art.

Lin'an was the capital of the Southern Song Dynasty and had a large number of artistic venues. According to the "Tales of the Old Capital," there were 23 venues in and around the city with special facilities for holding drama performances. Besides, there was a number of strolling player companies, and with the flourishing of this entertainment sector came companies writing and editing new scripts in large numbers, which contributed to the further development and process of maturity of the Southern Opera.

Following the overthrow of the Southern Song Dynasty by the Mongol Yuan Dynasty, the northern *zaju* began to move south, and as it did so, Southern Opera fell into a decline. Xu Wei said in his *Record of Talks on the Southern Ci Poems*: "In the early years of the Yuan Dynasty the northern zaju began to spread southward, and soon became fashionable, sidelining the Southern *ci* poetry. At the same time, Southern Opera began its process of decline."[14] Thus he explains the situation. In the last years of the Yuan Dynasty, Southern Opera absorbed some of the strong points of the zaju, a situation of revival emerged, and this laid the foundation for its transmission through the Ming and Qing dynasties.

The Southern Opera scripts came mostly from the hands of lesser literati and artists. For the most part, they mirror the complicated social conditions of the Song and Yuan periods, and the likes and dislikes of the common people. About a third of these scripts deal with marital problems: Some praise the fight for freedom of marriage, like "On the Wall and on a Horse" (See *Record of Talks on the Southern Ci Poems*, Scraps of Tunes). Others tell of scholars who abandon their wives as soon as they achieve fame, and enter a rich man's mansion as a prospective son-in-law. This type of drama is known as an "estrangement" play; an example is "Wang Kui Rejects Guiying" (mentioned in *Record of Talks on the Southern Ci Poems*, but no longer extant).

The Southern Operas of the Song and Yuan dynasties were originally created by the people, and their scripts were transmitted from master to pupil. Add to that the fact of active discouragement by the authorities, and the result was that there were few opportunities to publish the scripts and so comparatively few have been preserved. It has been calculated that 238 scripts of this type were once extant, but no more than one tenth of these have survived[15] and only five in their original form. These five are "The Number One Scholar Zhang Xie," compiled by the Jiushan Book Association during the Song Dynasty, "A Son of an Official Family Takes the Wrong Path of His Life," newly edited by The Genius of Old Hangzhou during the Song Dynasty, "The Young Butcher," compiled by Xiao Dexiang of the Wulin Book Association during the Yuan Dynasty, "The Story of the White Rabbit," compiled by the Yongjia Book Association during the Song Dynasty, and "The Story of the Lute," compiled by Gao Ming of the Yuan Dynasty. Twelve scripts were revised during the Ming Dynasty, of which the most famous are "The Story of the Thorn Hairpin," "The Pavilion for Admiring the Moon" and "The Story of the Slaughter of a Dog." These three, together with "The Story of the White Rabbit" (The full title of which is "The Story of Liu Zhiyuan Meeting the White Rabbit") comprise the "Four Great Operas," and are referred to as the "Jing," "Liu," "Bai" and "Sha."

"The Story of the Lute" tells the tale of Zhao Wuniang and Cai Bojie. This story had become a staple of oral folk literature as early as in the Southern Song Dynasty. In one of his works, the Southern Song poet Lu You mentions a blind performer singing the story of Cai Zhonglang (Cai Yong) in his "Mooring my Boat by a Village and Returning on Foot": "In Zhao Family Village as the sun sank behind the ancient willows/An old blind man with a drum on his back /Took up his position in the square/When he passes away will there be anyone to take over his tale?/Meanwhile, the whole village listens to the story of Cai Zhonglang."[16] Tao Zongyi of the Yuan Dynasty records a Jin Dynasty drama script titled *Cai Bojie* in his *Notes on Resting from the Plow in Southern Village * A Catalog of Drama Scripts*. Xu Wei of the Ming Dynasty, in his *Record of Talks on the Southern Ci Poems * Old Editions from the Song and Yuan Dynasties*, gives pride of place to a script titled "Cai Erlang and the Virtuous Girl of the Zhao Family," and appends this comment: "The old tale that Cai Yong was killed by a thunderbolt due to his betrayal of his family and abandonment of his wife is a sheer vulgar fabrication. But the tale has become the most popular among all theatrical performances."[17] Cai Bojie is a negative character in literature, who, as soon as he scores top marks in the civil service examination, abandons his parents and wife, and eventually comes to a sticky end.

Gao Ming's "The Story of the Lute" is based on "Cai Erlang and the Virtuous Girl of the Zhao Family," and the most important alteration is that of Cai Bojie into a positive character of the utmost loyalty and filial piety. He does not want to leave home, but is quite content to remain in his native fields. However, he is by nature weak-willed, and the pressures of the outside world soon lead him into confusion and grief. He is meek and yielding to the point at which he lets anyone push him around. All this time, his sorrow accumulates in his heart. After he becomes adopted into Prime Minister Niu's household as a prospective son-in-law he seeks out a servant whom he asks to deliver a letter home for him. He is overheard by the daughter of the house, and is forced to confess what is on his mind to her, but at the same time swears her to secrecy. In the meantime, Cai Bojie's first wife, Zhao Wuniang, has been scrupulously guarding the womanly virtues of chastity and filial piety; since her husband left, she has been devoting herself heart and soul to the service of her mother-in-law, giving her the best food to eat and herself living on scraps. She even sells her own hair to buy a coffin for her mother-in-law. All these actions have an individual significance in that they show the tenacious and praiseworthy nature of her character. While extolling such feudal moral values, "The Story of the Lute" also reveals the dark side of feudal society, such as the despotism and unfairness of Prime Minister Niu, and the way the local officials were corrupt and bent the law for their own purposes. In addition, the drama gives a convincing picture of rural starvation in those days.

"The Story of the Lute" is Gao Ming's creative masterpiece. In the *Record of Talks on the Southern Ci Poems*, it says, "Tradition has it that the author took three years to complete this drama, working night and day in a small room, before he was satisfied that it was worthy of the stage." As this is a merely traditional account it is not necessarily credit-worthy; however, we can see from the script itself how painstaking was the process the author went through to complete it. The artistic accomplishment of "The Story of the Lute" is well worth the praise it has received. There are two threads of development throughout this play, which criss-cross and interlock, joining the fates of the two protagonists, Cai Bojie and Zhao Wuniang, and two locations, the capital and their hometown Chenliu. Cai Bojie gains fame and fortune, only to lose his freedom, and in consequence sinks deeper and deeper into repentance and gloom. Meanwhile, Zhao Wuniang, taking up the burden of household responsibility that Cai Bojie has cast aside, daily pines for his return. While one enjoys wedding festivities, whiling away the summer by a lotus pond and appreciating the full moon at the Mid-Autumn Festival, the other has to live on scraps of food and even to cut and sell her hair to buy her mother-in-law a coffin. The contrast between the two leads to a fine dramatic effect. The language, and the characters, their personalities and situations are all well matched in "The Story of the Lute." The language at times approaches the colloquial, and at times the sublime, but it is always in perfect harmony with the protagonists' psychology in any situation they find themselves in.

Notes

1 Shusen, Sui ed: *The Complete Sanqu of the Yuan Dynasty*, Zhonghua Book Company, 1964, P. 156.
2 Shusen, Sui ed: *The Complete Sanqu of the Yuan Dynasty*, Zhonghua Book Company, 1964, P. 242.
3 Guowei, Wang: *Comments on Ci Poetry*, People's Literature Publishing House, 1960, P. 221.
4 Shusen, Sui ed: *The Complete Sanqu of the Yuan Dynasty*, Zhonghua Book Company, 1964, P. 758.
5 [Ming Dynasty] Jide, Wang: *Patterns of Melodies*, Vol.4, *Random Discussions (No.39, Second Part)*: "Li Zhonglu wrote a preface for two *xiaoling* (a form of *ci* poetry) poems by the Yuan Dynasty poets Qiao Mengfu and Zhang Xiaoshan. In the preface, he stated that they could not match the Tang Dynasty poets Li Bai and Du Fu. According to him, it is more appropriate to compare Wang Shifu to Li Bai and Ma Zhiyuan to Du Fu. Qiao and Zhang could only be matched with Li He and Li Shangyin," *A Collection of Commentaries on Classical Chinese Drama*, Vol.4, China Theater Publishing House, 1959, P. 156.
6 Shusen, Sui ed: *The Complete Sanqu of the Yuan Dynasty*, Zhonghua Book Company, 1964, P. 622.
7 Jisi, Wang chief ed: *The Complete Operas of the Yuan Dynasty*, Vol.1, People's Literature Publishing House, 1990, P. 198.
8 [Yuan Dynasty] Sicheng, Zhong: *An Account of Ghosts * Guan Hanqing*, Shanghai Ancient Books Publishing House, 1978, P. 8.
9 Guowei, Wang: *Discussion of Song and Yuan Drama * Essays on the Yuan Stage, Posthumous Works of Wang Guowei*, Vol.15, The Commercial Press, 1940.
10 Jisi, Wang chief ed: *The Complete Operas of the Yuan Dynasty*, Vol.2, People's Literature Publishing House, 1990, P. 293.
11 Jisi, Wang chief ed: *The Complete Operas of the Yuan Dynasty*, Vol.2, People's Literature Publishing House, 1990, P. 122.

12 Jisi, Wang chief ed: *The Complete Operas of the Yuan Dynasty*, Vol.3, People's Literature Publishing House, 1990, P. 190.
13 Jisi, Wang chief ed: *The Complete Operas of the Yuan Dynasty*, Vol.4, People's Literature Publishing House, 1990, P. 590.
14 Chinese Opera Research Institute ed: *A Collection of Commentaries on Classical Chinese Drama*, Vol.3, China Theater Publishing House, 1959, P. 239.
15 For reference: Nanyang's, Qian: *An Overview of Drama Texts*, Shanghai Ancient Books Publishing House, 1981.
16 [Song Dynasty] You, Lu: *Collected Works of Lu You*, Zhonghua Book Company, 1976, P. 870.
17 Chinese Opera Research Institute ed: *A Collection of Commentaries on Classical Chinese Drama*, Vol.3, China Theater Publishing House, 1959, P. 250.

9 *Chuanqi* Opera in the Ming and Qing Dynasties

The rise of *Chuanqi* Opera and their Ming Dynasty heyday

The early period of the Ming Dynasty saw a low ebb in opera creativity, and the *zaju* of that period was no more than a faint reverberation of the Yuan Dynasty *zaju*, with no works of value appearing.

But in the mid-Ming period (the 16th century) a new genre of *zaju* arose and flourished – *Chuanqi* Opera. "*Chuanqi*" was a name applied to different genres of works appearing in different eras. It was applied to genres as different as Tang Dynasty vernacular short novels and the ballads and *zaju* of the Song Dynasty. In the Ming Dynasty it was applied to full-length operas, to distinguish them from the Song and Yuan *zaju*. The *Catalog of Songs* by Huang Wenyang of the Qianlong reign period (1736–1795) of the Qing Dynasty, divides the drama scripts from the Song and Yuan dynasties onward into the two categories of *zaju* and *Chuanqi* Opera. Wang Guowei in his *Discussion of Song and Yuan Drama* follows him, as do subsequent historians of Chinese literature.

Famous *Chuanqi* Opera which emerged from the mid-Ming period on include Li Kaixian's "Story of the Precious Sword," the hero of which is Lin Chong; Liang Chenyu's "The Story of the Laundry Beauty," the protagonists of which are Fan Li and Xi Shi; and "The Story of the Cry of the Phoenix" (author unknown but thought to have been Wang Shizhen or one of his pupils). This is a story of the conflict between eight upright ministers, headed by Xia Yan, and Yan Song and his son. It draws its inspiration from actual events, and is well worth our attention.

In those days there were two schools of drama, one represented by Shen Jing and known as the Wujiang school, and the other represented by Tang Xianzu and known as the Linchuan school. The former included the writers Shen Zijin, Lv Tiancheng and Wang Jide, who stressed musicality, and the latter included Meng Chengshun, who stressed acting talent. In his *Patterns of Melodies*, Wang Jide says,

> Tang Xianzu and Shen Jing had always been at odds. Observant of conventional standards, Shen Jing fussed over the rules and never ventured a single step beyond the limit nor deviated in a crude manner. Tang Xianzu, however, preferred doing what he liked, and tended to depart from the classics and

> rebel against orthodoxy. His writing skills proved to be as dexterous as those of the Goddess of the Loom. Nevertheless, his language was so awkward that it might twist the tongues of his readers. Shen Jing once said, "I would rather sacrifice skillfulness for adherence to the rules. It is my way of writing that lines may not read smoothly unless they are chanted." He used to make changes to the rough sentences found in Tang Xianzu's "Return from the Dead". Lv Yusheng showed the revised copy to Tang. The latter was unhappy, and wrote back to Lv, retorting, "You'd rather suffer yourself in order to covet favor from others. I stick to my principles. I don't care if my writings break the tongues of all my readers." That was how the two dramatists conflicted in terms of their aspirations and interests.[1]

Shen Jing came from Wujiang in Jiangsu Province. He strictly adhered to the pattern of the Kunshan melodies. His *Thirteen Tunes of the Nine Palaces of the South*, include 7 *Chuanqi* Opera under the name of his study: *Seventeen Chuanqi Opera from Shuyu Study*. Of particular importance is one about the legendary hero Wu Song titled, "Story of the Righteous Knight."

Tang Xianzu was from Linchuan in Jiangxi Province. He authored five *Chuanqi* Opera – "The Story of the Purple Flute," "The Story of the Purple Hairpin," "The Story of the Return of a Soul" (also called "The Peony Pavilion"), "The Story of the Southern Bough" and "The Story of Handan." The four latter ones center on dreams, so they are classified together as the "Four Dreams of Linchuan" or "Four Dreams of the Yuming Hall." The first two source their material from a Tang Dynasty novel titled, "The Story of Huo Xiaoyu," with the second being a reworking of the first. "The Story of the Southern Bough" and "The Story of Handan" source their material from two Tang Dynasty novels titled "The Tale of the Lord of the Southern Bough" and "The Story of the Pillow."

Tang Xianzu's most important work is "The Peony Pavilion," in 55 acts. The story goes that in the early years of the Southern Song Dynasty Du Liniang, the daughter of Magistrate Du Bao, at the instigation of her maid Spring Fragrance, goes on an outing to enjoy the spring. Feelings of romance are stirred within her, and in a dream she meets a gallant young scholar named Liu Mengmei, who is holding a bunch of willow twigs. Unable to conquer her longing for him upon awakening, she sickens and dies. Her soul meets the young scholar again, and with the help of the willow tree she comes alive again, and the two formally marry. In his "Dedication," Shang writes;

> People like Li'niang are true lovers, who are unaware of the source of their affection and faithful to their beloved all their lives. For them, they can live and die, and after death they can come back to life again. Those who live but cannot die or when they are dead cannot come back to life are not true lovers. . . . Therefore they are not reasonable people and cannot be reasoned with. How can those who claim that reason never exists know that feelings do exist?[2]

The main theme of this drama is the way it emphasizes the strength of love and opposes the fetters that feudal morality imposes on love. It sets emotion against reason, and lauds individual freedom and liberation. This had a positive resonance in the Ming Dynasty, when the drama was written and when the weight of feudal ethics was particularly burdensome. The characterization in "The Peony Pavilion" is fresh, and its plot intricate. The language is refined. An example of its excellence can be found in the tenth act "Awaken From a Dream," when Du Liniang sings:

> [Zaoluopao] There used to be colorful blossoms everywhere,/But in their place now are these dry wells and broken walls./When were those good old days?/Where is that family that gladdened the heart? (Monologue) But my grandpa and grandma never mentioned such a beautiful picture. (Chorus) Flying in the morning and falling at dusk,/The clouds shroud beautiful pavilions,/The rain is sliced by gusts of wind,/The decorated barge floats on the misty waves./All these beautiful scenes are transitory.[3]

Following the emergence of the two schools, another excellent Tale of Fantasy was "The Story of the Jade Hairpin." This is a story of love between the young scholar Pan Bizheng and the Taoist nun Chen Miaochang. Yet another is "The Story of Red Plum," by Zhou Chaojun. This tells the story of the love between Pei Yu and Li Huiniang in the closing years of the Southern Song Dynasty. It also starkly reveals the evil nature of the rascally official Jia Sidao.

Kun Opera, which appeared in the area of Suzhou in the second half of the 16th century, reached maturity and achieved popularity in the late Ming and early Qing dynasties, even becoming the most fashionable form of drama in China as a whole. A famous example of this was "A Record of Unimpeachable Loyalty," by Li Yu. It tells the story of the antagonism between Zhou Shunchang of the Donglin court faction and Wei Zhongxian during the Tianqi reign period (1621–1628) of the Ming Dynasty. Ordinary townspeople led by Yan Peiwei band together to support Zhou and engage in a factional fight in one scene. The same author's "A Handful of Snow" tells how Yan Shifan, the son of Yan Song, coveting a jade cup, brings a false charge against Mo Huaigu. Li Yu wrote "The Mistake Involving a Flute," which tells of the vicissitudes that the lovers Han Shixun and Zhan Shujuan have to weather before they can get married. His "Journal of Leisure Time" is worth attention for its systematic dramatization.

Highlights of Qing Dynasty *Chuanqi* Opera

The two most famous *Chuanqi* Operas to appear during the Qing Dynasty were "Longevity Hall" by Hong Sheng and "The Peach Blossom Fan" by Kong Shangren. The plot of the former is based on the dalliance between Tang Emperor Xuanzong and his concubine Yang Yuhuan, which runs like a thread through the story, involving issues of politics and history. At the same time, it conveys the author's feelings about the rise and fall of governments, and we get a glimpse of how he sums up the lessons of history. The plot is wide-ranging and the drama's structure is grand and varied. Moreover, the arias well represent the characters and their individuality. In Act 38, "Playing a Tune," Li Guinian, during his wanderings in the land south of the Yangtze River, sings to the accompaniment of his lute of the episode of the Yuyang mutiny:

> [Liuzhuan]
> To the Rainbow-feather Garment tune they were dancing/
> When suddenly battle drums came from Yuyang rambling/
> Battle reports flooded in from the frontier/
> Throwing the court into a panicky atmosphere/
> Noisily, hurriedly and in distress, they fled in swarms westward/
> Tagging behind the imperial carriage was the pretty concubine/
> Suddenly the soldiers gathered, cursing and threatening mutiny/
> Forcing the loving and caring imperial couple to separate/
> Instantly creating a tragedy involving a marvel of beauty.[4]

"Longevity Hall" was an instant success. In his "Preface to Longevity Hall," Xu Lin says, "For a time, this music became a hit at feasts of rich families and in restaurants and brothels. Beautiful girl singers added even more appeal."

Through the story of the love between the scholar Hou Fangyu of the Society of Classical Learning Restoration and the renowned singing girl Li Xiangjun of Qinhuai, "The Peach Blossom Fan" traces the rise and fall of the late Ming Dynasty. In this process, it reveals the evil deeds of the rascally eunuchs Ruan Dayue and Ma Shiying, who collude to bring false charges against worthy officials, and cause calamity for the state and the people. The author skillfully uses the gift of a fan inscribed with a poem from Hou Fangyu to Li Xiangjun as a motif which runs through the whole drama. The conflict with Ruan Dayue only serves to bring the lovers closer together. And it is then that Hou Fangyu gives Li Xiangjun the fan as a token of his love. The two are separated, and while Hou undergoes a series of political encounters Li is brought face to face with the corruption of the Southern Ming court. Ma Shiying tries to get the girl to marry Tian Yang, a member of his court faction, but she steadfastly refuses, leaving spots of her own blood on the fan. Yang Wencong recognizes the bloodstains as forming an image of a blossoming branch of a peach tree. Later, the girl denounces the wicked officials to their faces at a formal banquet. The image of Li Xiangjun is of an honest and upright person. In his "Tentative Comments on The Peach Blossom Fan," Kong Shangren says, "The peach blossoms are the bloodstains of a beautiful woman and the bloodstains are a symbol of the preservation of chastity; Li Xiangjun would die rather submit to being shamed by the villainous officials. The latter, in turn, are the dregs of eunuch society, who are devoted to dissipation and the acquisition of power and riches for themselves, and have formed faction wherewith to gain their ends. In the process, they undermine 300 years of efforts by the Ming emperors."[5] This passage is a good summing up of what "The Peach Blossom Fan" is all about.

Both "Longevity Hall" and "The Peach Blossom Fan" are *Chuanqi* Opera based on historical material, but they also have a practical significance. How to handle historical material is a problem even today which requires the full attention of the creative dramatist. And so the experience of these two *Chuanqi* Opera deserves our close attention.

Notes

1 [Ming Dynasty] Jide, Wang: *Patterns of Melodies*, Vol.4, *Random Discussions (No.39, Second Part), A Collection of Commentaries on Classical Chinese Drama*, Vol.4, China Theater Publishing House, 1959, P. 165.
2 [Ming Dynasty] Xianzu, Yang: *The Peony Pavilion*, People's Literature Publishing House, 1982, P. 1.
3 [Ming Dynasty] Xianzu, Yang: *The Peony Pavilion*, People's Literature Publishing House, 1982, P. 43.
4 [Qing Dynasty] Sheng, Hong: *Longevity Hall*, People's Literature Publishing House, 1958, P. 171.
5 [Qing Dynasty] Shangren, Kong: *The Peach Blossom Fan*, People's Literature Publishing House, 1982, P. 3.

10 The structure and style of *ci* and *qu*

The formats of *ci* and *qu*

Ci is lyrics set to music, and the musical measures were known as Yan music, inherited from the Sui and Tang dynasties. The musical measures applied dictated a series of form and stylistic characteristics for this genre.

First, there were certain tonal patterns and rhyme schemes. This was a musical score called a *cipai*. Some *cipai* were originally connected with the content of the *ci* poem or song, for instance, Bai Juyi's "Fair South Recalled." This poem focuses on the poet's remembrance of the scenery and life in the land south of the Yangtze River. Later generations, however, concentrated on the *cipai* as a tune, without any necessary connection with the original content of the poem. And so, the *cipai* gradually became nothing more than tunes; some *ci* poets even went so far as to adopt traditional *cipai* simply to indicate the titles of their *ci* poems, for instance, "Remembering a Beauty," which precedes the title of Su Shi's "Memories of the Past at Red Cliff." What these *cipai* represented in cadence and score was originally sometimes vehemently delivered and sometimes in a lingering and meandering way. These scores, unfortunately, have not been handed down,[1] and we can only guess at what they sounded like with reference to the mood and rhyme schemes of the large numbers of works which remain. We can say that *ci* poems like "Remembering a Beauty" and "The River Is All Red" were accompanied by vigorous tunes, and that *ci* poems like "Slow Tune of Magnolia" and "A Courtyard Filled with Flowers" were accompanied by cheerful tunes. However, when later *ci* poets chose the tunes for their works they generally seem to have paid no attention to the original cadences of those tunes, simply depending on the rhyme schemes and the patterns of level and oblique tones.

The same *ci* poem can have different tonal patterns and different rhyme formats. In 1715 Wang Yiqing presented to the Kangxi Emperor (reign: 1662–1723) a catalog of *ci* poems containing a total of 8263,206 variations of such patterns and rhymes, and since the discovery of the records in the Dunhuang Grottoes early in the 20th century, and the compilation of the *Complete Song Ci Poems* and other such books, which contain about 1,000 such variations, we conclude that the total of such *ci* formats must be large indeed.

In addition, taking into account the elaborateness and simplicity of *ci* tunes, and the long and short natures of the poems themselves, we can divide *ci* into three rough categories: short, medium and long. In his *Random Discussions on the Music Bureau*, Song Xiangfeng says:

> The poetry called *ling*, or short *ci* poetry, is what musicians call *xiaoling* (small *ling*). The poetry known as *yin* and *jin* is what the musicians refer to as "middle notes." The poetry known as *man*, or slow tempo, is known to musicians as "long notes." The poetry not referred to as *ling*, *yin*, *jin* or *man* but *xiaoling*, "middle notes," and "long notes" follows folk convention, and is therefore easy to understand. It is also inclusive of popular themes.[2]

It is generally reckoned that a *ci* poem of fewer than 58 characters is a short one, one of 59–90 characters is a medium-length one, and one of over 91 characters is a long one. But, of course, in practical terms the division is not so clear-cut. The short poems originated as banquet entertainment in the Tang Dynasty; medium-length *ci* poems include the *yin* and *jin* types. The former were the introductory melodies that accompanied Chinese opera, and the latter were part of the main opera arias. The long poems were called slow melodies or simply "slow," in contrast to the brisker shorter ones.

Ci also have different formats as regards their sections – single, double, three-tier and four-tier. A single-melody tune only has one section. A two-melody tune usually dominates two sections, known as upper and lower stanzas or parts. This is the most common *ci*. Three- and four-tier sections are called long tunes.

There is a definite connection between the format and style of a *ci* poem. Short lyrics are in fact "short," something like a quatrain in *shi* poetry. These often include in a hidden way profound skill. The long melodies, which are winding and meandering, also display profound skill in their variety of expression. The qualities of the medium-length melodies are somewhere in between these two.

A prominent characteristic of *ci* poems is that the verses are uneven – They can be from one character to ten. However, the five- and seven-line format is not necessarily shaped as two-plus-three or four-plus-three, but can have a wide variety of changes. The Song Dynasty poets mostly based themselves on the common speech sounds of their time when composing rhymes, and their rhyme schemes were looser than those used for *shi* poems. In his *Correct Rhymes for Ci Poems*, Ge Zai of the Qing Dynasty divides 106 rhymes into 19 sections, which he terms orthodox. His classification of the rhyme schemes of *ci* poems into level-oblique series is all-encompassing, with almost every character having either a level or oblique tone. And in the name of the tune to which a *ci* is to be recited the oblique tones are listed as either high, low or entering. However, some characters can be either level or oblique. The rhythm too of a *ci* depends on the different demands of its attached tune, and does not necessarily depend on a balance of level and oblique tones. Here we will cite a few commonly seen *ci* tune patterns:

"Like a Dream" by Li Qingzhao, 33 characters, single melody

O, O, O, L, L, O	Last night the wind was strong and the rain fine/
O, O, O, L, L, O	Sound sleep did not dispel the taste of wine/
O, O, O, L, L	I ask the maid who's rolling up the screen/
O, O, O, L, L, O	The same crab-apple tree, she said, is seen/
L, O	But don't you know?/
L, O	But don't you know?/
O, O, O, L, L, O	The red must languish and the green must grow.

"Pusaman" by Li Bai, 44 characters, double melody

L, L, O, O, L, L, O	O'er the woods the smoke weaves a screen/
L, L, O, O, L, L, O	Cold mountains form a belt of green/
O, O, O, L, L	Dusk envelops the tower high/
O, L, L, O, L	Where someone utters a longing sigh.
L, L, L, O, O	On marble steps she waits in vain/
O, O, L, L, O	Only to see the birds fly back again/
O, O, O, L, L	Where should she gaze to see her dear?/
O, L, L, O, L	Nothing but pavilions far and near.

"Hexinlang (Congratulations to the Bridegroom)" by Xin Qiji, 116 characters, double melody

O, O, L, L, O	That I should have aged so!/
O, L, L; L, L, L, O	And my fellows, how many remain?/
O, L, L, O	Life spent with naught to show/
O, O, L, L, L, O, O	But hair turned white in vain/
O, O, L, L, O, O	Yet with a smile I part/
O, O, O; L, L, L, O	From all that is mundane/
Whereof nothing gladdens the heart./	
O, O, L, L, L, O, O	From all that is mundane/
Whereof nothing gladdens the heart./	
O, L, L; O, O, L, L, L, O, O	Charming are mountains green/
I expect the feeling to be/	
L, O, O	Mutual, for we/
O, L, O	Are alike in mood and mien.
L, L, O, O, L, L, O	I sit at the east window, goblet in hand/
O, L, L; L, L, O, O	My thoughts in Peach Blossom Land/
O, L, L, O	The poet bemoaned scattered friends/
O, O, L, L, L, O, O	He was a philosopher and drinker true/
O, O, L, L, O, O	Unlike those who/
Of fickle fame felt proud/	
O, O, O; L, L, L, O	I turn back crying/
An angry blast, and dark clouds flying/	
O, O, L, L, L, O, O	I cannot see the men of old/
O, L, L; O, O, L, L, O	Rather a pity they cannot see me/
L, O, O	But even my fellows, all told/
How many really know me?/	
O, L, O	But two or three.

Even the composition of *qu* poetry was based on the demands of the accompanying melody. The accompanying melodies of *qu* verse and *ci* poetry had some differences, but here we cannot go into the details.

The stylistic characteristics of *ci* and *sanqu*

Discussed above is the basic patterns of both the *ci* and *qu* forms of poetry, and we can now make a comparison between *ci* and *qu* on the one hand and *shi* poetry on the other, through a comparative explanation of the stylistic characteristics of *ci* and *qu*.

Song Dynasty scholars discussed the stylistic characteristics of *ci*. The *Series of Poetic Notes by Fisherman Recluse of the Tiao River* quotes Wang Zhifang's *Discussion of Shi Poetry*:

> Su Dongpo often showed Wujiu and Wenqian his short *ci* poems, and asked if they could match Shaoyou's. The two answered, "Shaoyou's works are like short *ci* poems; but yours are like rhymed poems."[3]

From this material we can see that in the eyes of Chao Buzhi and Zhang Lei, *shi* and *ci* are stylistically different. In his "Quatrains for Poem Review," Yuan Haowen has this to say about Qin Guan's *shi*-like ditties:

> "As a lover's tears are like the raindrops on peony petals/So the feeble branches of a rose resemble the limbs of a reclining beauty." Compared with Han Yu's lines in his *Mountain Crags* poem, these lines seemed to be written by a female.[4]

From the above two verses from Qin Guan's "Spring Sun," and comparing it for instance with Han Yu's "Mountain Rocks," an ancient-style poem with seven characters to a verse, we can see that its protagonist is a young woman. The woman's beauty perhaps spills over into the stylistic characteristics of the diction. If this is so, then Su Shi's grandiose *ci* poems can naturally be considered to be *shi* poems. And an examination of Yan Zhu's couplet *ci* poems may solve a problem. In his "Silk-Washing Stream" there are the following two verses: "The blossoms fall, come what may/Like a monk recognizing the swallows' return." These two verses were used in the seven-character poem "For the Eyes of Magistrate Zhang and Wang the Proofreader" Wang Shizhen, in his "Extracts from the *Collected Ci Poems Among the Flowers* and *Selected Ci Poems from a Humble Cottage*" quotes these two verses when he makes a distinction between *shi* and *ci* poetry. He says that they do not resemble the *shi* style, probably because they have too much "feminism" in them.[5]

Concerning the differences of style between *shi* and *ci* poetry, there is some controversy. In his "Preface to Selected Ci Poems," Zhang Huiyan says that the form of *ci* poetry is "full of twists and turns and subtleties." Mr. Wang Guowei says in his *Deleted Pieces of the Comments on Ci Poetry*: "The form is *ci* is subtle and lends itself to embellishment. *Ci* can express things which *shi* cannot, but at the same time it cannot plumb the depths of *shi* expression. *Shi* is characterized by expansion, *ci* by pithy diction." Mr. Miao Yue, in his "Discussion of *Ci*," points to four characteristics of the genre: "brevity," "lightness of essence," "narrowness of focus" and "vague domain."

The opinions expressed above all have something to do with the music that accompanies *ci* poetry. *Ci* poetry was devised as a banquet entertainment, and would be sung by professional entertainers to the accompaniment of music. The singers would be comely teenage girls hired to assist at the feasting. Political doctrines and other weighty matters were expressed in poetry using the *shi* format; the *ci* format was utilized to convey contents and feelings that were felt to be unsuited to or awkward for orthodox *shi* poetry. And so, right from the very beginning, *ci* poetry became something which developed confined to places of entertainment. It was, so to speak, doomed to be regarded as a "feminized," frivolous or "entertainment" literature.

However, the above summary only applies to *ci* poetry written in the Five Dynasties and early Northern Song Dynasty periods. Starting with Su Shi, the *ci* format underwent revolutionary changes, until it could hold its own alongside *shi* poetry as a literary genre. It was no longer necessarily either "feminine," "gentle," "subtle" or "meticulous." Its poets started to utilize various writing methods and subject matter very close to those used for *shi* poems. In this way, *ci* poetry got a new lease of life.

But because the patterns of *ci* and *shi* poetry were different, as were their respective musical arrangements and their functions (For instance, *shi*, unlike *ci*, could be used as a civil service examination subject), their styles could not avoid being different. And the differences manifested themselves in their respective weightiness, factors of entertainment and seriousness, and whether their accompanying music was light or symphonic. In *ci*, the poet left himself free space to roam in, where he did not need to disguise his feelings, but could unburden himself of them comparatively freely and thereby more easily perceive the true nature of his feelings. *Shi* poems had originated as songs to be sung, but after a long period of evolution they had adopted a serious coloring, in much the same way that a person tends to adopt a grave demeanor after donning a uniform. But a person cannot always be clad in a uniform, and *ci* can be compared to ordinary clothes which a person can slip into when he wants to be freer and more informal.

Sanqu includes single ditties and groups of songs. The single ditties were the basic form of *sanqu*, whereas the groups of songs were suites formed of two or more ditties in the same register and with rhymes, generally at the end.

The pattern and style of the *sanqu* were also different from those of *ci*.

1. Both *qu* and *ci* have long and short verses, but those of *qu* are uneven; a short verse has only one or two characters, while a long one can have 20–30. For instance, Ma Zhiyuan's [Nanlv Mode * Golden Sutra]: "In the westerly wind at night/Eagles and hawks fly high/Hemmed in by common folk from Central China/How sad/Old friends, do you know my predicament?/I would like to climb up to the pavilion/But cannot find a ladder."[6] And Guan Hanqing's "Not Yielding to Old Age" [Nanlv Mode* A Branch of Blossoms]: "I am a clattering copper bean that cannot be cooked by steaming and boiling, and nor can it be hammered flat or popped by frying. All the time, however, my juniors try to get it into their elastic multiple-layered brocade pullover that cannot be hoed, axed, untied or shaken open."[7]
2. In *ci*, there are no extra characters inserted for balance or euphony, while in *qu* this is permissible. In the latter, the combination of the main and inserted characters not only maintains the pitch of the tune, it also adds to the liveliness

and colloquial flavor of the language. An example is Zhong Sicheng's "No Title" [Drunk in Peace and Tranquility]:

The talented (but poor) are the best/
The base (but affluent) are no friends/
(With) plaster I mended (the) old cave dwelling/
(To open) a school for young beggars/
(Wearing) a half-new official gauze cap/
(Donning) a half-length jute robe/
(Tying) a frayed black girdle/
I now (become) a charming teacher.[8]

3. *Sanqu* uses rhymes more densely than *ci* does; in fact in some *sanqu* every verse contains a rhyme. The alternation of level and oblique tonal rhymes is permitted in *qu* but not in *ci*. An example is Xu Zaisi's "Spring" [Reading the Golden Sutra]:

Swallows tend to return to their old abode/,
Mandarin ducks perch on warm sand/
Willows everywhere to which horses can be hitched/
He asked if there's a wine shop in the village ahead/
"Red apricot flowers by the pink wall beneath the swing.[9]

To sum up, the syllables and use of rhyme in *sanqu* are freer than in *ci* poetry, and *sanqu* is thus closer to and more suitable for the expression of natural speech than *ci* poetry. The appearance of *sanqu* marked a stage in the liberation of *shi* poetry.

The style of *sanqu* can be divided into two parts – the colloquial and the unrestrained. This is far from the courtly diction used in all types of *shi* poetry, and marks *sanqu* as much freer than *shi* poetry. *Sanqu* can adopt the solemn manner of *shi* and the soft one of *shi*. But at the same time it has to contain elements of humor, slickness and unconventionality, so that it bears the attitude of an intelligent person who is also an unfettered outsider looking at the world with a far-off mocking and yet compassionate eye. When written well, *sanqu* is colloquial and free-and-easy; when written clumsily, slick and glib.

The structure of *zaju* and *Chuanqi* Opera

Simply put, the scripts of Yuan Dynasty *zaju* divided each section into four acts, with each act closed by a curtain fall. Each act would be both a unit of the plot and of the musical structure. Moreover, each act would have its own set of tunes, which could be many or few, but all would belong to the same register (or mode). The first tune would make clear the title of the register, and the last one usually was played in the finale of the same register. The first act of "The Injustice Done to Dou E" uses the Xianlv Mode, which pursues the following sequence: Applying

Crimson Lipstick, The Dragon of the Turbulent River, The Oil Gourd, Happiness on Earth, Half, The Flowers of the Rear Hall, Song of Youth, Feelings Attached to Grass, and Finale. The four acts used different registers, but the general practice was: Xianlv for the first act; Zheng or Nanlv for the second; Zhonglv for the third; and Double Mode for the fourth. Each libretto corresponded to one complete register.

The word *xiezi*, or prologue, was originally applied to a wedge inserted to stabilize wooden joints. The Yuan *zaju* borrowed this term to indicate a short, independent section distinct from the four acts. One *xiezi* was often inserted before the first act, as a sort of synopsis of the play to follow; others divided the acts as light entertainment. It was common for a *zaju* to have one prologue; some scripts have two, and there are even scripts which have no prologue at all. The prologue was short and pithy, with single-melody accompaniment.

We can say that the structure of the *zaju* scripts was made up of four acts and a prologue. But of what elements were the scripts composed? These were threefold:

1 Music and singing. Music and singing were mainly used to express emotions, but also to embellish the scenes. In Yuan four-act dramas it was usually one leading protagonist who did the singing. As the core part of Yuan *zaju*, music and singing were bound by a strict format, and each act had its own rhyme scheme.
2 *Binbai*, or spoken parts. The spoken parts of Yuan *zaju* were subordinate to the sung parts. Some of the spoken parts would be in blank verse, and some would be rhymed. The latter could be in the form of *shi* poems, or could be just ordinary speech. An example of the former occurs in "Li Kui Shoulders Thorns," when Song Jiang appears on the stage: "The gorge stream gurgles before the stronghold gate/Wild flowers adorn my glossy-green turban/The apricot-yellow flag bears these seven words/For Heaven justice, for the people salvation." In "The Injustice Done to Dou E" has another. When "Doctor Better than Bian Que" appears on the stage, he recites the following: "Practicing as a physician, one gets plenty of hospitality/Medicines can be got free from the grass/A doctor can't bring the dead back to life/But he can bring death to the living." In the third act of "Pavilion Overlooking the River," as Bai Shizhong exits the stage, he recites the following: "I see the flag hoisted aloft/I hear once more good news." *Binbai* can be divided into dialogue, monologue, aside (the scripts call this *beiyun*, or "remarks from the back"), inserted speech (the scripts call this *daiyun*, or "incidental remarks," in which speech is inserted into a sung part), and others. *Binbai* has an important function in the Yuan *zaju* by helping to indicate shifts in the plot; the lyrics of the songs and the messages of the *binbai* form a harmonious whole. In addition, *binbai* generally have a humorous and satirical element, which helps to regulate the atmosphere of the drama. Thus, *binbai* is an essential, organic part of the Yuan *zaju*. In the Yuan Dynasty *binbai* was written based on the northern pronunciation. The best dramatists used lively *binbai* in brief sentences to bring out their protagonists' characters.

3 Directions. This includes a performer's main movements, expressions, dance movements, etc. For instance, directions for "performing tragedy," "conducting warfare," "dancing," "cry of the goose," etc.

We should also note in passing the formal title of the drama, which is composed of an antithetical couplet of two or four verses, which summarizes the plot and at the same time announces the title of the script. An example is the formal title of "Li Kui Shoulders Thorns": "Title: Wang Lin of Apricot Blossom Manor Brings a Lawsuit. Formal Title: Li Kui of Liangshan Marsh Bears Brambles."

There are, roughly speaking, four character roles in Yuan *zaju*: *Mo*, *Dan*, *Jing* and *Za*. *Mo* is a male role, somewhat equivalent to *Sheng* in Peking Opera. The main male role is called *Zheng Mo*, and subordinate male roles are called *Fu Mo* or *Xiao Mo*. *Dan* is a female role. The main female character is called *Zheng Dan*, and the subordinate female roles are called *Fu Dan* or *Wai Dan*. *Jing* is a sturdy, evil or clownish character, and can be either male or female. There are also *Gu* (official), *Bolao* (old man), *Pu'er* (old woman), *Lai'er* (child) and *Xisuan* (scholar or poor literatus) roles. In each of the four acts of Yuan *zaju* one performer assumes the singing task all the way through. The *Zheng Mo* and the *Zheng Dan* are the ones who perform the chief singing roles, the former's part being described as the *Mo Ben* in the script, and the latter, the *Dan Ben*.

The differences between the Southern Opera and *zaju* can be summed up as follows:

1 *Zaju* are divided into acts, Southern Operas into scenes. The basic format of *zaju* is four acts and a prologue. It is compact, and the plot is succinct. Southern Opera has no fixed number of scenes, and its length is quite flexible. For instance, "Zhang Xie the Number One Scholar" has 53 scenes, "The Young Butcher," 21 and "The Story of the Lute," 42.
2 In *zaju*, only one person (*Zheng Dan* or *Zheng Mo*) usually sings; in Southern Opera, either one person or several can sing, and can sing in the form of dialogue or chorus.
3 In *zaju*, each act ends in one rhyme in one register; in Southern Opera, the scenes don't necessarily end in one register, and the rhymes can alternate.
4 *Zaju* official titles come at the end of the script; in Southern Opera, at the beginning. *Zaju* don't have an introductory speech, whereas Southern Operas are opened by a subordinate male role performer giving a synopsis of the plot. This began to be called *Kaichang* in the Ming Dynasty. The drama proper began with the second scene. The *Kaichang* consisted of two stanzas, one describing the author's intention, and the other giving the gist of the story.
5 The music of *zaju* was mostly based on the registers, which was a narrative ballad form, while that of Southern Opera was based mainly on the folk songs of the southeast coast region (such as the "rural tunes" and "village ditties" of the *Record of Talks on the Southern Ci Poems*), and later absorbed some of the *ci* tunes common during the Song Dynasty. In addition, the southern and northern opera tunes differed in style, structure and method of expression.

The characteristics of the *Chuanqi* Opera genre were close to those of the Southern Opera. They too eschewed the four-acts-and-a-prologue format, and one script could be divided into a dozen to 40–50 scenes, making the work quite long. It was this lengthening that made necessary the introduction to the whole drama and to the author's purpose in the first scene. The musical accompaniment to the *Chuanqi* Opera was intricate, with changes in the register. All the roles were allowed to sing, either individually, in answer to each other or in chorus. The differences between the roles in this regard were minimal. Both the *Chuanqi* Opera and the Southern Opera were large-scale, multi-scene song-and-dance productions. The main differences between them were in the eras they appeared in and their respective musical arrangements.

Interim summary

Both *ci* and *sanqu* were lyrics to be sung. They flourished and were popular partly because they received a constant stream of nourishment from the common people and partly because literary figures, especially great writers paid a great deal of enthusiastic attention to these genres. Absent the former, these genres would have quickly withered; absent the latter, they would have found it difficult to reach the heights that they did. Here I would like to discuss the importance of the participation of great writers. Those who made particularly important contributions to the development of *ci* and *sanqu* were Bai Juyi, Wen Tingyun, Wei Zhuang, Feng Yansi, Li Yu, Ouyang Xiu, Liu Yong, Wang Anshi, Yan Jidao, Su Shi, Huang Tingjian, Zhou Bangyan, Li Qingzhao, Lu You, Fan Chengda, Xin Qiji, Jiang Kui, Yuan Haowen, Guan Hanqing, Ma Zhiyuan, Liu Ji, Chen Zilong, Wang Fuzhi, Chen Weisong, Zhu Yizun, Nalan Xingde, Zhang Huiyan and Wang Guowei. Among these men were great writers of *shi* poetry and of prose essays. There were also scholars of great courage and vision who created a poetic genre called *shiyu*, developed from *ci*, and thereby constantly raised the later to new levels. But, taking another look at the creative efforts exerted in the field of *ci* for singing at this time, although there was no shortage of fine and popular pieces, we cannot help feeling that in general they did not reach the standard they should have. If there had been more high-caliber poets and advanced scholars engaged in this work, as in olden times, *ci* for singing would have made even greater strides.

Zaju, Southern Opera and *Chuanqi* Opera were stage dramas, and Chinese stage dramas had very distinct national characteristics, two of the major ones being the following:

1 Appeal to the imagination. There is an absence or shortage of stage props. The background to the actions of the protagonists is expressed by their actions, singing and dialogue. From this comes the abstract and stylized nature of Chinese operas.
2 Chinese stage plays from beginning to end are operas, and music is at their core. As singing is the central element in the makeup of the drama, Chinese people often talk about "listening" to a stage play, and in the old days theaters

were arranged in such a way that the audience did not necessarily face the stage. Once one understands the central place occupied by music in Chinese drama, one won't find this unusual.

Classical Chinese Opera is a most precious intangible cultural legacy. We must pay positive attention to how Chinese Opera suits the tastes of today's audiences, but we must be careful not to reject this tradition completely. No matter how Chinese Opera is reformed, the basic elements that make up Chinese Opera must be preserved; its elementary characteristics cannot be changed.

Notes

1 *Ci* poems and tunes from the Dunhuang Grottoes preserved in a number of collections. Jiang Kui's: *Collected Tunes by White Rock Taoist*, 17 self-created tunes contained.
2 Guizhang, Tang ed: *Edited Collection of Ci Talks*, Zhonghua Book Company, 1986, P. 2500.
3 [Song Dynasty] Zi, Hu: *Series of Poetic Notes by Fisherman Recluse of the Tiao River*, First Part, Vol.42, People's Literature Publishing House, 1962, P. 284.
4 [Song Dynasty] Haowen, Yuan: *Collected Works of Mr. Yishan*, Vol.11, *Collected Writings of the Four Basic Branches of Literature*.
5 Guizhang, Tang ed: *Edited Collection of Ci Talks*, Zhonghua Book Company, 1986, P. 686.
6 Shusen, Sui ed: *The Complete Sanqu of the Yuan Dynasty*, Zhonghua Book Company, 1964, P. 239.
7 Shusen, Sui ed: *The Complete Sanqu of the Yuan Dynasty*, Zhonghua Book Company, 1964, P. 173.
8 Shusen, Sui ed: *The Complete Sanqu of the Yuan Dynasty*, Zhonghua Book Company, 1964, P. 1351.
9 [Yuan Dynasty] Zaisi, Xu: *Sanqu Collection by the Sweet Studio*, Shanghai Ancient Books Publishing House, 1991, P. 96.

Part 3

The novel

The Chinese novel is divided into two types: those written in the classical language (*wenyan*) and those written in colloquial language (*baihua*). They are not only distinguished by the language used, but also by their origin, authorship and readership, and so they had a widely divergent course of development. The *wenyan* novel appeared earlier than the *baihua* novel did. The authors and readers of the former tended to be aristocrats and scholars, while those of the latter included some of the commoner urban dwellers as well. The two did, of course, influence each other, but this influence came mainly from the *wenyan* works, especially in the aspect of source material.

The traditional catalogs of novels are quite a jumble, containing works which would not nowadays be considered novels; for instance, some early ballad materials have been classed as novels. In this book I will provide the necessary historical background, but I will not stick slavishly to the traditional viewpoint, and will confine myself within the accepted concept of the novel as it has evolved in modern times.

11 The concept of the novel and its debut

The early concept of the novel

There is a vast difference between the understanding of what constituted a novel in ancient and modern times. Many works which were termed "novels" in ancient times would not be so termed today. There is no doubt that the study of the history of the Chinese novel would have to focus on those works which would fit the modern concept of the novel, but would also have to include those works which the ancients considered to be novels; only in this way can an understanding of the overall course of the development of the Chinese novel be achieved.

The term "novel" first appears in the "External Things" section of the miscellaneous chapters of the *Zhuangzi*: "Those who dress up their small tales to obtain favor with the magistrates are far from being men of great understanding."[1] "Small tales" are contrasted with "great understanding." This means trifling matters unconnected with government or ideology. Later, "small tales" came to have a different connotation from that in the *Zhuangzi*, but nevertheless works considered "small tales" or "novels" never managed to attain the status of elegant literature. In this regard, two aspects are closely related.

In the early years of the Han Dynasty (206 BC–220 AD) there was a great vogue for collecting writings, paving the way for the submission of books to the imperial court. Emperor Wu (reign: 140–86 BC) pursued a policy of building libraries, and established special offices for writing and collecting books, among which were the works of novelists. In the reigns of emperors Cheng and Ai (32 BC–1) the father-and-son pair of Liu Xiang and Liu Xin edited the works in the imperial book depository, and presented a digest *Seven Outlines* to the imperial court. The historian Ban Gu relied on this digest to write *Records of Art and Literature * A Short Discussion on Shi and Fu Poetry*. Novelists are included in this chapter – at the very end – marking the first time for novels to be recorded in a work of history. In fact, novel was the most numerous category at 1,380 volumes out of 4,324. Ban Gu, according to *Seven Outlines*, said that "Novelists spring from the ranks of petty officials whose job is to listen to street gossip. Confucius said, 'Even in the meanest alleys, there is always something worth noting. A gentleman is not made from someone who holds himself aloof and shuns the mud.' That is how such talk is preserved; the trifling knowledge of the back streets is written down and not forgotten. But all this is nothing but the thoughts of the lowliest type of people."[2] This, of course, is the authoritative and partial judgment of a historian and archivist. He considered that novels were composed from "alley gossip" and "the chatter of the lanes," but what the novelists gathered and wrote down became a genre to be taken into serious consideration. Of course, this "back-alley chatter" consisted of scraps of hearsay, anecdotes and shallow garbled opinions. It may have been trivial, but it always presented something to grasp hold of, and so it did not perish. As such, wasn't it similar to the sort of stuff that the modern tabloids feed on? Ban Gu very clearly pointed out that the novel originated in the traditions of the common people, and this is very significant for our identification of the origin and development of the novel.

Huan Tan of the Eastern Han Dynasty gives a further explanation of the novel in his *New Discussion.* He says, "It is clear that the writers of novels used colloquial language to form metaphors and lessons, and their short works are meant as guides to personal conduct and wholesome family life."[3] Three levels of meaning are contained in these words: First, novels are brief pieces of writing, the language of which is often couched in the form of aphorisms. For instance, we find in the *Spring and Autumn Annals Annotated by Gu Liangchu * Second Year of Duke Xi* : "As the saying goes, 'When the lips are gone, the teeth are cold.'"[4] This type of saying is longer than the usual metaphor, but suitable for fitting into a piece of writing of short length. The latter has been defined by Wang Chong in his *On Balance * Telling Shortcomings*, as "Two feet and four inches is all a sage needs to express himself."[5] From this we can see that the standard short book in the Han Dynasty was measured in feet and inches, and short books, those which did not record the classics, were called "short books arranged by length."[6] Second, the characteristic of the novel was metaphor or analogy, which in turn was regarded as a rhetorical device. And so we can see that the novel was already considered to have a literary flavor. Third, although the novel was short and not held in esteem by Confucians, nevertheless, its social function was determined by its being reckoned beneficial to self-cultivation and the healthy running of a family. Huan Tan's comment represents the new understanding of the novel that emerged in the Han Dynasty.

The Wei, Jin and Southern and Northern Dynasties: the original format of the novel

Following the period of the Wei and Jin dynasties (220–420), there was a new development of the concept of the novel. At the same time, the novel emerged in its basic format.

Most of the 15 so-called novels described in the "Monographs" chapter of the *Annals of the Han Dynasty* are the words of soothsayers and suchlike persons. The historian Ban Gu, in his commentary on the *Yu Chu's Tales of the Zhou*, says, "In the time of Emperor Wu there was a group of soothsayers and minor officials who were from south of the Yellow River and were known as the Attendants of the Yellow Carriage."[7] Zhang Heng, in his *fu* poem "Western Capital," included in the *Selected Works of Literature*, says, "The 900 novels all basically come from Yu Chu."[8] Li Shan quotes Xue Zong (a man from Wu State of the Three Kingdoms) as saying, "Novels are an art of pronouncements by physicians and wizards."[9] Xue Zong's words are obviously quoted from the *Annals of the Han Dynasty*, but his identification of novels with "pronouncements by physicians and wizards" and his claim that petty officials were the first novelists was a brand-new point of view. At the same time, there appeared in the area of the country ruled by the Wei Dynasty a genre called "comic novels." In the section on Wei in the *Annals of the Three Kingdoms * Biography of Wang Can*, we find, "Handan Chun's given name was Zhu and his literary name was Zishu, was a man of great scholastic attainments and was adept at all styles of penmanship. He was fond of a certain Cao Zhi, whom he once invited to his home. At first, Cao Zhi just sat there and did not say a word. As the day was hot, he asked for water to bathe himself. He then applied face powder. Kowtowing and slapping his bare chest, he performed an exotic sword dance while reciting several thousand words from a comic novel. Finally, he said to his host: 'Who else in Handan can do that?'"[10] The so-called "comic novels" seemed to have involved some kind of humorous performance involving exotic dances and acrobatics, something like the solo modern comedian's patter, accompanied by gestures. Chun of Handan was the author of the *Forest of Laughter*, and he seems to have been an accomplished humorist. Cao Zhi, on the other hand, was of an aristocratic lineage. When he first met Chun he performed something similar to what was to be found in the *Forest of Laughter*, determined not to be outdone by Chun. From this, we can infer that what were contained in that book were jokes and other kinds of humorous stories.

It is interesting to note that Xue Zong's theory of novels being an art of physicians and soothsayers, and the record in the *Outline History of the Wei Dynasty* of humorous novels are in perfect agreement with the two genres of stories of weird happenings and outstanding people which emerged in the period of the Wei, Jin and Southern and Northern Dynasties (386–589).

These latter novels, or "mystery novels," are mostly tales of supernatural beings and their magic arts, ghosts and hauntings, strange happenings and monsters, and are closely connected with Taoism, Buddhism and shamanism.

Magic and magicians are attested from the most ancient times in China, in the form of shamanism. In those days, people believed that the Lord of Heaven was the source of man's blessings and disasters; all major enterprises had to get the approval of the Lord of Heaven before they could be embarked upon. This attitude led to a habit of making sacrifices and divinations, interpreting dreams and praying for rain, and similar activities. However, it was not just anyone who could address the Lord of Heaven – only those specially qualified could do so. These were the shamans. During the Shang Dynasty (16th century–11th century BC) the shamans were the cultural representatives of the slave-owning class, and kept all culture and knowledge in their own hands, having a most exalted position in society. They were the sages who preceded Confucius. Despite the fact that the social status of the shamans declined in later years, superstitious beliefs kept a tight hold of the people's minds. Stories of magic powers continued to circulate widely, and formed the material for the "mystery novels."

The wizards were an offshoot of the shamans, emerging in the latter half of the Warring States Period (475–221 BC). They claimed to be able to speak with the spirits and to hold the secret of longevity. They engaged in the search for the elixir of immortality, and officiated at the sacrifices to the Lord of Heaven, who was supposed to dwell on the summit of Mount Tai, and at which the emperor himself was present, and at lesser mountains. According to the *Records of the Historian*, they were fond of boasting and giving exaggerated accounts of how they had seen members of the spirit world, who lived for several hundred years, and how they had seen dates as big as melons and plums as big as gourds, etc. Their stories were enshrouded in mystery, with no evidence of their authenticity whatsoever. For example:

> A man of the State of Qi, Li Shaoweng, lived for 200 years, and his countenance was still that of a young boy. The emperor had great faith in him, appointing him commander of Wencheng. When his wife died, Li Shaoweng said that he could contact her spirit. One night, sitting alone in his campaign tent, by the light of a candle he dimly saw his deceased wife. He couldn't help but stare at the apparition.[11]

It was because The First Emperor of Qin (reign: 246–209 BC) and China's first unifier, and Emperor Wu of the Han Dynasty put their trust in wizards and yearned to become immortal that such charlatans appeared in great numbers and wizardry flourished. At the same time, stories of the supernatural emerged in an endless stream, providing the material for the mystery novels.

Taoism struck root among the people in the latter part of the Eastern Han Dynasty, first of all in the forms of "Five Pecks of Rice" Taoism and "Great Peace" Taoism. Following its connection with a peasant uprising at the close of the Han Dynasty, Taoism started to exert widespread influence in society. After the Jin Dynasty (265–420), Ge Hong, Tao Hongjing, Kou Qian and others founded various Taoist sects, with names such as "Yao Tao" and "Gui Tao," which dabbled in contact with spirits, ghostly transformations and efforts to prolong life. The propagation of such religions and superstitions were also important sources of contents for the mystery novels.

In the first year (2 BC) of the Yuanshou reign period of Emperor Ai of the Western Han Dynasty Buddhism was introduced into China. At first, this foreign religion blended well with China's native superstitious thought, and became a vehicle for its transmission to the upper echelons of society. After the Jin Dynasty, Buddhism became melded with the school of metaphysics known as the Dark Learning. With support from the ruling class, Buddhism flourished exceedingly during the Southern and Northern Dynasties period. In fact, Emperor Wu of Liang (502–557, one of the Southern Dynasties) became a monk on three occasions, and his ministers spent a lot of money getting him released from his monastery. With the spread of Buddhism came popular tales of weird happenings connected with this religion; these also became fodder for the mystery novels.

To sum up, the mystery novels are a catalog of stories based on religious beliefs and superstitions stemming from shamanism, wizardry, Taoism and Buddhism. The authors of the mystery novels for the most part were not literary men but followers of wizardry, Taoism and Buddhism themselves – people like the Taoist Wang Fu, who wrote *Records of the Miraculous*, and the Buddhist Wang Yan, who wrote *Tales of the Ominous and Auspicious*. The *Record of Ten Provinces* was written by a necromancer by the name of Dongfang Shuo, who was incidentally very much a necromancer himself. The motive for writing such stories was to spread religious propaganda and get people to "find religion through the spirits." Nevertheless, there were some mystery novels produced by the hands of literary men, such as Zhang Hua's *Natural History* and Gan Bao's *In Search of Spirits*. These novels were not out-and-out religious propaganda, but they still had a heavy tinge of superstition.

A large number of novels focused on outstanding personages appeared during the Wei, Jin and Southern and Northern Dynasties period, catering to the fashionable taste of the time, and as a result of a vogue to discuss in lofty terms the affairs of noble families and scholars. Even as early as in the Eastern Han Dynasty, Ban Gu's *History of the Han Dynasty* contained a section titled, "Model Personages Ancient and Modern," in which such people were arranged as nine types, and by the end of that dynasty there had grown up a fashion of using scholars as yardsticks for judging people. Guo Tai, for example, gained a reputation for judging people in this way, so much so that scholars were graded only after an appraisal by Guo. In the *History of the Later Han Dynasty * Biography of Xu Shao* we find: "Both Shao and Jing had great reputations. They liked to discuss their fellows, and every month they would issue a formal appraisal in writing, which became known in the south as the 'First of the Month Critique.'"[12] Cao Cao's character is gauged by his habit of using humble words and giving lavish gifts. Xu Shao says that Cao Cao was "an able government minister and a stalwart in a time of confusion."[13] Disparagement or praise by one of these pundits often determined the success or failure of a person. Once a person had received a high appraisal he would be sought after by the emperor for an official post, and so such criticisms received much attention. Wen Qiao was once appraised as follows: "Number two among those across the Yangtze River, and he was often mentioned in the conversations of his contemporary celebrities. His halo often dimmed when compared with even the ones that trailed the number-one assemblage."[14] In a few elegant words, the situation is summed up neatly.

Following the Wei and Jin dynasties, among the scholar-gentry there flourished, apart from the judging of character, also lofty discourse and the formation of the Dark Learning. Previously, during the latter years of the Han Dynasty, scholars had often openly criticized political affairs and the court, a phenomenon termed "sincere discourse." After the Disasters of the Partisan Prohibitions, numerous scholars of reputation keen on political criticism were slaughtered, so others did not dare to discuss state affairs, instead, they began to confine themselves to debating the Dark Learning. "Speech dealt with abstruse matters, and no longer appraised individuals."[15] The Dark Learning they got involved with mainly comprised the Taoist philosophy of Laozi and Zhuangzi, together with the Confucian ethical code and Buddhist doctrines. They led easy-going and eccentric lives. Anyone who shunned discussion of the Dark Learning was considered unqualified to be a true scholar. But those who could debate the Dark Learning and hold their own at drinking parties, and led dissipated lives found favor in the eyes of such worthies as Ruan Ji, Ji Kang, Wang Dao and Xie An, and became famous names. As an example of their unorthodox ways, we can quote Yin Zhongkan: "If I go for three days without reading the [Taoist classic] *Moral Classics (Dao De Jing)*, the root of my tongue becomes stiff."[16] As to the debate between Sun An'guo and Yin Hao, "When the two attendants ate, they were so slow that the food had to be heated four times. The host and guest threw the deer-tail whisk to each other irritatedly during their debate, so much so that the hair of the tail fell all over the dishes, and both forgot to eat until dusk."[17] Liu Ling stripped naked in somebody else's house, and when somebody mocked him, he said, "The universe is my house, and this dwelling is my trousers. What are you gentlemen doing in my trousers?"[18] He often rode in a carriage pulled by deer, holding a jug of wine, and with an attendant following behind carrying a spade on his shoulder. He said, "If I die, he can bury me on the spot."[19] Another example is that of Zhong Hui, who wrote an essay which he was eager to show to Ji Kang but was afraid to. He ended up throwing it over Ji Kang's wall and running away. It was the custom in ancient times to air one's clothes in the sun on the seventh day of the seventh [lunar] month. Ruan Ji's nephew Ruan Xian was poor, and he and his family lived in a southern slum. Ruan Ji's household, by contrast, was wealthy, and lived in the northern part of the city. On the seventh day of the seventh month Ruan Ji's family put out their fine silks to air, while Ruan Xian, having no sumptuous clothing, raised in his courtyard a pair of "calf-nose" shorts. When someone asked him why, he answered, "I had to conform to the custom, yet I am still a vulgar man. So that's my response to you."[20] There was another of these eccentrics named Hao Long, who, while everyone else was airing clothes on the seventh day of the seventh month, lay supine in a sunny spot. When asked what he was doing, he replied, "I'm airing my writings."[21]

Nowadays we find such antics hilarious, but in the social atmosphere of the time eccentric behavior could enable one to make a name for oneself, and even open the way to high office for those so inclined, and so scholars paid great attention to this behavior. It was this social atmosphere too that led to the production of novels dealing with the words and deportment of famous literary figures. The modern writer Lu Xun hit the nail on the head when he called the *New Words for the World* a "textbook for leading scholars." As soon as Pei Qi's *Forest of Words* came out there was a rush all over the country to transcribe it, and every fashionable young man had to have a copy. This type of novel not only created a great stir among the ordinary people, it even attracted the attention of the emperor himself. One example of this was when Emperor Wu of the Liang Dynasty ordered Yin Yun to write a *Novel* for him.

There are more than a dozen types of mystery novels extant, with 28 we know of having been lost. That makes over 40 types altogether. Judging them by their contents, they can be divided into three categories:

1 Geographical oddities such as the *Classic of Strange Ghostly Happenings*, written by the man with the pen name of New Moon in the East, and Jin Dynasty Zhang Hua's *Natural History*. A later novel, *The Floating Crops of the Eighth Month*, is particularly imaginative:

 An old story has it that the Milky Way is connected to the oceans on Earth. In recent times there was a man who lived on an islet in the sea. Every year in the eighth month without fail a floating field of crops would appear. The man thought that this was curious, and so he built a pavilion on it from which he could harvest the crops. After ten days he thought he could see the sun, moon and stars, while all below him was hazy. He also discovered that he could no longer distinguish between day and night. After another ten days he suddenly arrived at a grand city with magnificent buildings. He could see among the distant palaces a number of girls weaving. He then saw a man leading an ox to water. The man asked the traveller in astonishment: "How did you get here?" The latter explained what had happened, and asked where he was. The answer was, "Go back, sir, and ask Yan Junping of Shu Prefecture. Then you will know." So the traveller, staying where he was, returned to his own time. Then he went to Shu Prefecture, where he recounted his adventure to Yan Junping, who explained that in a certain year, on a certain day of a certain month a strange star had intruded into the Herd Boy Constellation (Altair). It turned out that this coincided exactly with the time the islet-dweller had arrived at the Milky Way.[22]

 This story shows the author's imagination extending to space travel. It is a complete account in itself, and as such provides food for thought.

2 Ghost stories and bizarre events, like *A Series of Strange Tales* by Cao Pi of the Wei Dynasty (220–265), *In Search of Spirits* by Gan Bao of the Eastern Jin Dynasty (265–420), *Sequel to In Search of Spirits* by somebody using the famous name of the poet Tao Qian, *Record of Putting Things Right* by Wang Jia of the Jin Dynasty and *A Sequel to the Fantasies of Qi* by Wu Jun of the Liang Dynasty. In the *Sequel to In Search of Spirits* there is a story titled, "The Pure Girl of the White Water," which tells of how a poor but honest young farmer named Xie Duan takes a snail home with him and keeps it in his house. He then finds that upon his return from work each day there is a meal prepared for him. Eventually he finds out that the snail is really the Pure Girl of the White Water, who has been sent by the Milky Way to keep house and cook for him. When she departs, she leaves the snail's shell behind, which always ensures that the young man never goes short of food. After this episode, Xie Duan goes on to prosper.[23]

3 Buddhist lore and strange spiritual happenings, as exemplified in *Tales of the Ominous and Auspicious* by Wang Yan and *Stories of Unquiet Souls* by Yan Zhitui, both of the Northern Qi Dynasty (550–577). In the former book there is a story about a Buddhist believer named Liu Ling, whose father dies of a sudden illness. A shaman warns him that three members of his family are destined to die. A neighboring Taoist tells Liu Ling that this is because he has embraced the foreign faith of Buddhism, and if he doesn't change his religion his household is doomed to destruction. So Liu Ling converts to Taoism. As a testament to his change of faith, he sets fire to his Buddhist texts and images, but the fire consumes his whole house, leaving the scriptures and images gleaming in the night just as before. The Taoist insists that the Buddhist religion should be driven back to the foreign land it came from. That very night, Liu Ling was stricken by paralysis and the Taoist developed a severe ulcerous condition. Within a month, both were dead.[24]

Gan Bao's *In Search of Spirits* is a representative work of this genre, preserving as it does a number of folk myths and legends. These anecdotes, although they inevitable contain some elements of superstition, reflect in a roundabout way the social contradictions of their times, expressing contemporary loves and hatreds, as well as aspirations, wrapped up in pleasing fantasy. An example is *Han Ping's Wife*:

> In the Song Dynasty (960–1279) there was a man named Han Ping, who was a functionary in the household of Kang Wang. He married a woman by the name of He. She was very beautiful, and Kang Wang conceived a passion for her. Ping hated the king, and for that the latter imprisoned him and condemned him to the hard labor of building city walls. Han Ping's wife smuggled a note to her husband, which said, "The rain pours down without end. The river is big and the water deep. At sunrise, be on your guard." Kang Wang got hold of the note, and showed it to his attendants, none of whom could make head or tail of it, until one of them, named Su He, said, "The first line expresses her sorrow. The second line means that she cannot come to him, the third line means that she intends to die." Soon thereafter, Han Ping killed himself. His wife then secretly made rents in her clothes, and, mounting a terrace with Kang Wang, suddenly threw herself from the top of the terrace. Kang Wang's attendants tried to prevent her fall by grabbing her gown, but it came away in their hands, and so the woman died. In her girdle was found another message, which said, "It is better for you, My Lord Kang Wang, to live, and better for me to die. My only request is that you inter my remains together with those of my late husband." Kang Wang flew into a rage when this was read to him, and refused to accede to the dead woman's plea; instead, he ordered that her corpse be buried in a place within sight of her late husband's tomb, saying, "I will make sure that you two are as separated in death as you were in life!" In the course of time, a large tree grew out of each of the tombs, and before long started to lean toward each other, until both their branches and roots intertwined. Then a pair of mandarin ducks, one

male and one female, came and nested in the branches. They stayed there all day, with their necks entwined and uttering mournful cries, which so moved the people of Song that they gave the trees – now one growth – the name of "Longing for Each Other Tree." This was the origin of the name "Longing for Each Other." The people of the south call these birds the souls of Han Ping and his wife. In Suiyang, Henan Province, there is a Hanping City, and a song about him can still be heard there today.[25]

As for novels about outstanding personages, there are extant two types of such collections: *Miscellaneous Records of the Western Capital* and *New Words for the World*. Lu Xun's *Dredging up Old Novels* enumerates six types, in three categories:

1 Humorous stories, such as the *Forest of Laughter* by Handan Chun. This book contains jokes which are still told today. For example, A poor man of the State of Chu read in the book *Huainanfang* (*Prescriptions of Huainan*) that "a mantis hunting a cicada uses a leaf as camouflage." He could not determine which of a bunch of fallen leaves under a tree would make him invisible, so he scooped up several bagfuls of leaves, and took them home. He tried every one of the leaves by holding it in front of himself and asking his wife if he had become invisible. Eventually his wife was so exasperated that she said what he wanted to hear. He then went to a market with the leaf and tried to steal something right under the noses of others. A constable dragged him off to a magistrate, who, after learning about the folly, released the man without any punishment. Another story of foolishness tells of a man surnamed Taoqiu, who divorced his wife simply because he found her mother homely. Yet another tale relates the story of two men embroiled in a fight: A bites off B's nose but accuses B of inflicting the injury on himself. When people wondered how B could possibly bite off his own nose when it was right above his mouth, A retorted, "He did so by standing upon his bed."
2 Unofficial histories, such as the two volumes of the *Miscellaneous Records of the Western Capital*. This book was written by Ge Hong under the name of Liu Xin, and contains anecdotes of people of the Western Han Dynasty, along with the palace system of the time and customs and habits, and adornments. There is a flavor of the exotic about the stories.
3 Trifling tales, as exemplified by *Forest of Words* by Pei Qi and *Master Guo* by Guo Chengzhi, both of the Eastern Jin Dynasty (317–420), *New Words for the World* by Liu Yiqing of the Song Dynasty, and *Secular Words* by Shen Yue and *Novel* by Yin Yun, both of the Liang Dynasty.

Liu Yiqing's *New Words for the World* is a representative novel of outstanding personages.

Liu Yiqing was a nephew of Liu Yu, Emperor Wu (reign: 420–423) of the Song Dynasty (one of the Southern and Northern Dynasties). In the *History of the Song Dynasty*, his biography was attached to that of Liu Daogui, King of Linchuan. In fact, he was said to be Liu Daogui's adopted son and heir, and rose to be the royal secretary. The *History of the Song Dynasty* also says that he was fond of literature and ceremony, and gathered scholars around him from near and far.[26] *New Words for the World* was probably the work of many hands. It is in 36 chapters, with titles such as "Virtuous Conduct" and "Spoken Language." It records anecdotes and achievements of outstanding personages from the end of the Han Dynasty to the Eastern Jin Dynasty (together with a handful from the Western Han Dynasty). It mainly recounts the antics and subterfuges of worthies of the Wang, Xie, Gu and Chi clans, and quite a number are taken from the *Forest of Words* and *Master Guo*. Indeed, the language used is similar to that used in these books. Liu Xiaobiao of the Liang Dynasty wrote a commentary for it, using for reference over 400 ancient works to fill in many historical details. Most of these works are no longer extant, but scraps of them have been preserved which have proved of interest to later generations.

New Words for the World preserves for us many aspects of life in the period from the Han Dynasty to the Jin Dynasty, including society, politics, ideology, religion, literature, the lifestyles of the upper classes and the people's habits and customs. All these things are of great value for researchers into history the social sciences and literature.

New Words for the World also has great literary value among novels of extraordinary personages. It shows skill in delineating character, often by describing only a handful of words or actions, vividly painting a protagonist's personality and peculiarities, in fact revealing his or her psychological world. For example:

> When Gu He served as a subordinate of the Governor of Yangzhou Prefecture, he had to present himself before the king on a monthly basis. At first, he came but parked his chariot outside the office building of the governor. On his way to meet the Prime Minister, Lord Zhou Ji passed by Gu He but immediately turned back and came up to him, who was attentively and calmly catching lice from within his clothes. Going up to him and pointing at his bosom, Zhou Ji asked, "What do have in there?" While still busying himself, Gu He replied in a leisurely manner: "It's a place hard to fathom." Arriving at the Prime Minister's office, Zhou told him, "You have among your prefecture officials a person with extraordinary talent."[27]

New Words for the World is also good at narrative description; in a few well-chosen words it can aptly describe a complicated series of events. For example:

> The king of Wei, Cao Cao, was to receive an emissary from the Huns. However, he made Cui Jigui take his place for fear that his own uncomely countenance might not lend him enough overawing power to the representative of a faraway country. Cao Cao himself then stood by Cui Jigui, sword in hand. After the meeting, Cao Cao sent a special agent to ask the emissary: "What do you think of the king of Wei?" The emissary answered, "The king looked

> very elegant, but the stalwart holding a sword by his throne was a true hero." Hearing this, Cao Cao sent his men to hunt down the emissary and kill him.[28]

This whole episode is covered using only 69 Chinese characters, but these words are succinct and pregnant with meaning, resulting in a true-to-life panoramic image. Hu Yinglin once commented on this passage as follows: "On reading these words, the true face and spirit of the people of the Jin Dynasty are clearly before us, in words limitlessly profound."[29] This quality comes through again in the story of Wang Ziyou going to visit his friend Dai, a piece of writing that beautifully combines the techniques of prose and verse:

> Wang Ziyou lived on the north side of a mountain. One night, there was a heavy fall of snow. Unable to sleep, Wang opened his door, called for wine and gazed at the whiteness all around. Then, strolling back and forth and reciting a poem of appealing for reclusion by Zuo Si, he suddenly thought of his friend Dai Andao. As Dai lived in Shan County, Wang took a skiff there that same night. On reaching his friend's door, Wang Ziyou abruptly turned back and went home again. When someone asked him why he had done so, Wang replied, "I set out in high spirits, but when my excitement faded I thought, 'Why do I need to see Dai?'"

Again:

> When Zhong Hui completed his *Four Theories on Aptitude and Quality*, he was keen to show it to Ji Gong. He tucked the volume into the breast of his gown, and set off for Ji Gong's house. But when he got there, he was seized by a sudden fear that Ji Gong might criticize the work, and so he flung the book down outside Ji Gong's door, and scampered away.

The categories of division used by Tang Dynasty (618–907) historians and catalog experts as regards the concept of the novel tended to follow traditional theories. In his *History of the Sui Dynasty * Record of Classics and Documents*, Wei Zheng divides all writings into four groups – classics, histories, works of philosophy and collections. He puts novels into the "works of philosophy" category, and says, "Novels are made up of street talk and back-alley gossip."[32] This is a traditional point of view. The *Annals of the Sui* Dynasty gives a more complicated account of the novel, including in this category such works as *Arts Ancient and Modern*, *Illustrated Devices of Accuracy* and *Water Ornaments*, which concern the arts, crafts and amusements.

Notes

1 [Qing Dynasty] Qingfan, Guo: *Collected Works of Zhuangzi Interpreted * Miscellaneous Chapters * External Things*, *Collected Works of the Philosophers*, Vol.3, Shanghai Bookstore, 1991, P. 399.

2 [Han Dynasty] Gu, Ban: *History of the Han Dynasty*, Vol.30, *Records of Art and Literature * Sketches of the Philosophers, Zhonghua Book Company*, 1962, P. 1745.
3 *Selected Works of Literature*, Vol.31, Jiang Yan's: *A Poem Modeled After Commandant Li's*, Selected and Annotated by Li Shan, Zhonghua Book Company, 1977 photocopy of the Hu woodblock print.
4 *Spring and Autumn Annals Annotated by Gu Liangchu * Second Year of Duke Xi, Commentary on the Thirteen Classics*, World Bookstore photocopy of the Ruan woodblock print, P. 2392.
5 [Han Dynasty] Chong, Wang: *On Balance * Telling Shortcomings, Complete Collection of the Works of the Philosophers*, Shanghai Bookstore, 1991, P. 125.
6 [Han Dynasty] Chong, Wang: *On Balance * Telling Shortcomings, Collected Works of the Philosophers, Shanghai Bookstore, 1991*, P. 125.
7 [Han Dynasty] Gu, Ban: *History of the Han Dynasty * Records of Art and Literature*, included in the annotation *Yu Chu's Tales of the Zhou*, Zhonghua Book Company, 1962, P. 1745.
8 [Tang Dynasty] Shan, Li and Yanji, Lv: *Selection of the Major Writings of Six Officials*, Vol.2, *Collected Writings of the Four Basic Branches of Literature*.
9 [Tang Dynasty] Shan, Li and Yanji, Lv: *Selection of the Major Writings of Six Officials*, Vol.2, *Collected Writings of the Four Basic Branches of Literature*.
10 [Jin Dynasty] Shou, Chen: *Annals of the Three Kingdoms*, Vol.21, Zhonghua Book Company, 1963, P. 603.
11 *The Story of Emperor Wu of the Han Dynasty*, see *Dredging up Old Novels, The Collected Works of Lu Xun*, Vol.8, People's Literature Publishing House, 1973, P. 454.
12 [Song Dynasty of the Southern Dynasties] Ye, Fan: *History of the Later Han Dynasty*, Vol.68, *Biography of Xu Shao*, Zhonghua Book Company, 1965, P. 2235.
13 [Song Dynasty of the Southern Dynasties] Yiqing, Liu: *New Words for the World*, Middle Volume, "Mirror of Knowledge" selection and commentary by Liu Xiaobiao from Sun Sheng's *Miscellaneous Words, Collected Writings of the Four Basic Branches of Literature*.
14 [Song Dynasty of the Southern Dynasties] Yiqing, Liu: *New Words for the World*, Middle Volume, "Critical Appraisal," *Collected Writings of the Four Basic Branches of Literature*.
15 [Tang Dynasty] Xuanling, Fang: *History of the Jin Dynasty*, Vol.19, *Biography of Ruan Ji*, Zhonghua Book Company, 1974, P. 1361.
16 [Song Dynasty of the Southern Dynasties] Yiqing, Liu: *New Words for the World*, First Volume, "Literature," *Collected Writings of the Four Basic Branches of Literature*.
17 [Song Dynasty of the Southern Dynasties] Liu Yiqing: *New Words for the World*, First Volume, "Literature," *Collected Writings of the Four Basic Branches of Literature*.
18 [Song Dynasty of the Southern Dynasties] Yiqing, Liu: *New Words for the World*, Last Volume, "Capriciousness," *Collected Writings of the Four Basic Branches of Literature*.
19 "Accounts of Celebrities," *New Words for the World*, First Volume, "Literature," Selection and Commentary by Liu Xiaobiao, *Collected Writings of the Four Basic Branches of Literature*.
20 [Song Dynasty of the Southern Dynasties] Yiqing, Liu: *New Words for the World*, Last Volume, "Capriciousness," *Collected Writings of the Four Basic Branches of Literature*.
21 [Song Dynasty of the Southern Dynasties] Yiqing, Liu: *New Words for the World*, Last Volume, "Ridicule," *Collected Writings of the Four Basic Branches of Literature*.

22 Ning, Fan: *Natural History Corrected*, Vol.10, *Miscellaneous Discourses*, Last Volume, Zhonghua Book Company, 1980, P. 111.
23 Wang Shaoying editing and commentary: *Sequel to in Search of Spirits*, Zhonghua Book Company, 1981, P. 30.
24 [Northern Qi Dynasty] Yan, Wang: *Tales of the Ominous and Auspicious, see Dredging up Old Novels, The Collected Works of Lu Xun*, Vol.8, People's Literature Publishing House, 1973, P. 621.
25 Wang Shaoying editing and commentary: *In Search of Spirits*, Vol.11, Zhonghua Book Company, 1979, P. 141.
26 [Liang Dynasty] Yue, Shen: *History of the Song Dynasty*, Vol.51, *Biography of Liu Daogui*, Zhonghua Book Company, 1974, P. 1477.
27 [Song Dynasty of the Southern Dynasties] Yiqing, Liu: *New Words for the World*, Middle Volume, "Generosity," *Collected Writings of the Four Basic Branches of Literature*.
28 [Song Dynasty of the Southern Dynasties] Yiqing, Liu: *New Words for the World*, Last Volume, "Demeanor," *Collected Writings of the Four Basic Branches of Literature*.
29 [Ming Dynasty] Yinglin, Hu: *Scribblings From Shaoshi Mountain Cottage*, Vol.29, 1896 corrected version by Guangya Publishing Company.
30 [Song Dynasty of the Southern Dynasties] Yiqing, Liu: *New Words for the World*, Last Volume, "Capriciousness," *Collected Writings of the Four Basic Branches of Literature*.
31 [Song Dynasty of the Southern Dynasties] Yiqing, Liu: *New Words for the World*, First Volume, "Literature," *Collected Writings of the Four Basic Branches of Literature*.
32 [Tang Dynasty] Zheng, Wei et al: *History of the Sui Dynasty*, Vol.34, *Record of Classics and Documents*, Zhonghua Book Company, 1973, P. 1013.

12 The impetus behind the novel

From the Tang Mystery novels to the *Strange Tales from a Chinese Studio*

The Tang novels carried on the tradition of the Wei, Jin and Southern and Northern Dynasties, to produce works such as the *Miscellaneous Literary Sketches Collected at Youyang* and *Yunxi's Friendly Commentaries*. But the real representatives of the novels produced during the Tang Dynasty were the mystery novels, which were a new type of short pieces of writing in the vernacular which emerged during the heyday of the Tang. The general name for these novels probably derives from the title of a collection of novels by Pei Xing – *Mystery Tales*. In the *Talks on Poems by Chen Shidao*, written by Chen Shidao of the Song Dynasty, we find, "Fan Zhongyan created a fantasy world in his *Records of Yueyang Tower* by his use of parallel prose in descriptions. Yin Shilu, after reading it, exclaimed, 'A mystery genre of writing indeed!'"[1] From this we can see that the mystery novel was already a popular genre in the early Song Dynasty. Tao Zongyi of the Yuan Dynasty (1206–1368), in his *On Leaving off Plowing*, says, "In the Tang Dynasty emerged the mystery novel, in the Song the opera, the humorous anecdote and the novel, and in the Jin the script drama and the operatic drama." It is clear that the mystery novel ranked beside the opera and the drama as a literary genre in its own right. Hu Yinglin of the Ming Dynasty (1368–1644), in his *Scribblings from Shaoshi Mountain Cottage*, divides the novel into six types, of which the second is the mystery novel, testifying to its qualification as a genre of the novel. This is the origin of the title "mystery novel" that we use today.

The mystery novel was a new genre of the novel developed during the Tang Dynasty. It differed from the Six Dynasties (229–589) "tales of mystery" novel in several respects: First, the latter dealt mainly with ghosts and supernatural happenings, whereas the Tang mystery novels, although they told of the weird and wonderful, nevertheless, sourced their material from real life. Lu Xun said, "The authors of the mystery novels concentrated on literary grace and thought for their appeal, very different from the ghost story tellers of old."[2] Second, the "tales of mystery" presented supernatural happenings as if they had really happened, and not as if their authors were consciously writing novels, whereas the authors of the Tang mystery novels did not try to hide the fact that they were engaged in the creation of novels. Hu Yinglin said, "All the stories of supernatural transformations which attained their heyday in the Six Dynasties period were pure fantasy, and not necessarily just constructs of the imagination; in the Tang Dynasty there was a conscious interest in the curious, and the form of the novel was used to express this in a literary manner."[3] Again, Lu Xun: "Just as with poetry, the novel underwent a change in the Tang Dynasty. Although it did not eschew the marvelous altogether, the writing was more subtle and elegant, and, unlike the coarse and slapdash style of description used in the Six Dynasties period, the plot evolves slowly and in a more gradual manner, and it is this that marks the beginning of the novel in the true sense of the word."[4] Thus it can be seen that the appearance of the mystery novel was a major step in the history of the novel in China, marking its achievement of maturity.

Some people consider the mystery novels of the Tang Dynasty to be urban literature, reflecting the lives, thoughts and interests of urban dwellers. But there is some reason to treat this judgment with caution. First of all, the writers of the Tang mystery novels were all feudal landed gentry, and their works circulated among that class of people; the ordinary people of the towns were not necessarily the readers, and if they were they did not necessarily identify with the life and characters written about. Worth noting is Zhao Yanwei's remark made in his *Loose Notes of the Cloud-Covered Foothill* about candidates for the imperial examinations presenting their works of the mystery novel genre to famous or influential figures before the examinations took place. Writers who used their mystery novels to demonstrate scholarship and win fame are worthy of recognition. Their action had nothing to do with whether they were townspeople or not. Secondly, the mystery novels of the Tang Dynasty mostly reflected the life, thinking and emotions of the scholar-bureaucrats of the time. Take the love stories in the "Three Words" for example, the townspeople protagonists of "An Oil Seller Wins the Queen of Flowers," "Miss Du in Anger Sinks the Jewel Box," and "Jin Yu'nu Beats the Heartless Man" – all craved for freedom from the humiliating life to which the feudal system had subjected them and defied the conventional social hierarchy. They represented the emerging middle-class townspeople. Moreover, there are differences between certain of the Tang mystery novels; for instance, between *The Story of Li Wa* and *The Story of Cui Yingying* on the one hand and *The Story of Huo Xiaoyu* on the other. The first two were created on the basis of the tastes and standards of the feudal landed gentry. In the first novel, Li Wa helps the dissolute young scholar Ying Yang turn his life around, from being a beggar to passing the imperial civil service examination and becoming an official, thus traversing the standard career path of a young member of the feudal ruling class. The girl not only earns the gratitude of the young man but even a commendation from the emperor himself. The author finally gasps out praise for Li Wa, saying, "Indeed, the integrity of this singing girl could not be surpassed even by the heroines of old!"[5] Apart from her social standing, where among the townsfolk could a girl like Li Wa, who is compared to the heroines of old, be found? Yingying is the daughter of noble house. At first she is bashful and graceful, later self-sacrificing, and finally bears no grudge despite the wrong done to her. This is entirely to the taste of Zhang, who is typical of the dissipated young scholars of the feudal ruling class of the time. Meeting Yingying, he has no problem toying with her while he himself has yet to achieve success, but he just as easily casts her aside once he achieves fame. Then, he not only divests himself of any trouble in caring for Yingying's welfare or in taking responsibility for his conduct, he even curses her as a slut, and washes his hands of his own reprehensible behavior. Zhang's swaggering conduct quite naturally drew the admiration of the feudal literati of those times. In clear contrast to these two novels is *The Story of Huo Xiaoyu*, which has a somewhat deeper social resonance inasmuch as it is a powerful indictment of the Tang Dynasty system of dominant families. Nevertheless, the author of this novel did not write it from the standpoint of the townsfolk, nor is Huo Xiaoyu a model for the new bourgeoisie.

But *The Story of Li Wa* and *The Story of Huo Xiaoyu* have something in common, and that is sympathy and praise for the female sex. In the love relationship between Li Wa and Ying Yang, the former takes the initiative; she has ideas and power, and dares to take action; by comparison, the young man is weak. In the case of the love affair between Huo Xiaoyu and Li Yi, the girl is wronged but gets her revenge. This attitude toward women is indicative of a new tendency, well worth noticing.

The Story of Li Wa could be called the best of the Tang Dynasty mystery novels. As part of the category of novels which traces the redemption of a young rake, it breaks no new ground, but its genius lies in the fact that the heroine both brings Ying Yang low and then rescues him. She plays two different roles, and in the course of changing from one to the other she changes from an ordinary singing girl to a brave and resourceful mature woman of action. The episodes in which she takes the young man under her wing, treats his illness, helps him purchase the books he needs, supervises him as he studies and gets him an opportunity to take the civil service examination, in which he comes out top – this type of maternal love is described with great artistic appeal. In the course of this, Li Wa's internal world is minutely and exquisitely described. In addition, the description of the dirge-singing contest between the east and west markets in Chang'an at the mourning hall is both moving and absolutely lifelike, and as such is of value as a piece of social history.

It is rather a complicated problem to identify the wellspring of the Tang Dynasty mystery novel, and space does not permit many examples to be cited here. But I believe the following few should not be glossed over:

> A great peasant uprising at the end of the Sui Dynasty (AD 581–618) dealt a serious blow to China's powerful families, and land reform during the following Tang Dynasty increased the strength of the small landowners of the middle and lower classes. In addition, the civil service examinations became more open to such people, affording them opportunities to rise into the official ranks and become a dynamic force in society. Many of the writers of the Tang Dynasty came from this stratum. They were well acquainted with social life and the lives of the lower classes, which infused a rich spirit of

creativity into their work. The way that the Tang mystery novels reflect in a wide-ranging way the social life and progressive thought of that time is intimately connected with the efforts of these people.

The Tang Dynasty was a time of rapid economic advance; agriculture, handicrafts, trade and international commerce all reached a stage of unprecedented prosperity. This was especially true of the economic development of the cities, and Chang'an, Luoyang, Yangzhou, Chengdu in particular saw huge increases in population. It was here that representatives of every class and walk of life were to be found – officials, landlords, literati, swashbucklers, merchants, handicraftsmen, Buddhist monks and Taoist priests, singing girls, etc. This kaleidoscope of social relations, with the resulting anecdotes and tales provided a rich mine of materials for the novelists. It turned out that the short and rough type of novel which had emerged in the Six Dynasties period was not adequate for the demands of the new materials, and so appeared the mystery novel, which was longer, had a more complicated plot and paid more attention to delineating character.

The Tang Dynasty was an era when the arts and literature all flourished in China, and the achievements of the other literary genres such as poetry and ballads, and the essay influenced the mystery novel. From the mid-Tang onward, poems and ballads became more and more attuned to the daily life of society, creating an atmosphere conducive to the development of the Tang mystery novel. It was in fact in this era that the mystery novel broke free from the restraints of the stories of the supernatural. As a result, a large number of novels were produced reflecting daily life and of a high artistic standard. In the late Tang period, however, as realism gradually weakened in poetry and ballads, so it did in the mystery novels, public taste showed a return to the old fashion for the bizarre and the supernatural.

The mystery novel was not the only genre embraced by popular literature in the Tang Dynasty; popular among the common folk were the "marketplace" novel and a type of novel in alternate prose and verse which were new forms of literature suited to the requirements and interests of the townspeople. According to the *Miscellaneous Literary Sketches Collected at Youyang*, "One day at the end of the Taihe reign period of the Tang Dynasty, I went to enjoy some miscellaneous performances to celebrate my younger brother's birthday. Among the performances, there was storytelling, where Bian Que (扁鹊) was referred to as Biǎn Que (褊鹊), i.e., the vowel in his surname was pronounced with the falling-rising tone."[6] A line in Li Shangyin's poem "To My Beloved Son" reads, "Either to tease the guest for his dark countenance,/Or to laugh at Deng Ai for stuttering."[7] Based on this evidence, Lu Xun comes to the conclusion that there were professional story-tellers already in the Tang Dynasty, among whom were those who told stories from the Three Kingdoms Period (220–280). According to the *New Book of the South* by Qian Yi of the Song Dynasty, the Tang Dynasty saw "most of the open-air theaters in Chang'an concentrated around the Ci'en Temple, while the smaller ones clustered around the Qinglong Temple, and the even smaller ones around the Jianfu and Yongshou temples."[8] In the Tang Dynasty too the courtyards of Buddhist temples were where acrobatic performances were held, and these later evolved into temple fairs. This was the atmosphere in which "marketplace" novels, the discourses of monks and their associates, and alternate-prose-and-verse novels flourished. In his *Tales of Repayment and Retribution*, Zhao Lin says:

> A monk named Wenxu often spoke to public gatherings. On the pretext of preaching Buddhist teachings, he talked nothing but obscenities. Lawless people related his bawdy tales with great gusto to other another, while ordinary men and women were only too pleased to listen. Listeners filled the temple and worshiped him as a saint, calling the venue the Performing Institute of Monks. While mimicking the monk's tones, they turned his stories into songs.[9]

The so-called "ordinary men and women" are mostly about urban commoners. In his *Record of a Pilgrimage to Tang China in Search of the Buddha's Law*, the Japanese monk Ennin says, "In every couple of streets there is a temple where colloquial stories are told." And he cites Master Wenxu as an outstanding storyteller. From this we can see how flourishing this folk art of reciting and singing was at that time. It was the "marketplace" novel, the storytelling and the recital-and-singing art of the Tang Dynasty that gave birth to the novel in the colloquial language in China; right from the start, the colloquial novel had an indissoluble connection with the common people of the towns.

The development of the mystery novel, which reached its heyday in the Tang Dynasty, began to flounder in the Song Dynasty. The mystery novels of the latter dynasty were far inferior to those of the Tang, and the two following dynasties – those of the Yuan and the Ming – failed to produce literary works of a high standard. It was not until the early years of the Qing Dynasty (1644–1911) that the novel in the classical language reached a new peak, with the emergence of Pu Songling's *Strange Tales from a Chinese Studio*.

Pu Songling (1640–1715), styled Liuxian (Last of the Immortals), was a resident of Zichuan, the present Zibo in Shandong Province. In his youth he was eager to make a name for himself. He passed the lowest civil service examination, but failed several times to advance further, and in consequence spent the rest of his years in poverty and disappointment. His *Strange Tales from a Chinese Studio* contains 491 short novel-like stories. These fantastic stories of fox fairies and the like are also bold exposures of various kinds of dark social phenomena. His mordant criticism and trenchant satire earned for his work a reputation of being a "personal litany of anger." *Strange Tales from a Chinese Studio* is rich in criticism, but the spearhead of this criticism is aimed at officials, both powerful and petty. Pu Songling mercilessly castigates their avarice, their obsequiousness, their fatuousness and their shamelessness. This is particularly evident in such stories as "The Cricket," "Xi Fangping" and "The Wolf Dream." The latter goes as follows: A certain Mr. Bai had an elder son named Bai Jia, who was an official in a distant town. In a dream, Mr. Bai seemed to approach his son's dwelling, only to find it guarded by a huge wolf. Nearby was a pile of bleached bones. When he awoke,

Mr. Bai sent his younger son with letter to warn Bai Jia. But Bai Jia brazenly said to his brother: "The power to promote and demote resides in one's superiors, not in the common people. When one's superior is pleased, one gets raised to a fine official position. How can one's care for the common people please one's superior?" The following year, by means of bribery, Bai Jia obtained a promotion. On the way to his new post he was set upon by robbers and had his head chopped off. An immortal appeared, and restored his head to his shoulders, but deliberately put it on backwards, saying, "An evil man should not be restored to a normal shape." Bai Jia, although he had regained his life, then became a symbol of a wicked man. In this story, Pu Songling is aiming his critical barb at the dark side of the civil service examination system, involving both the examiners and the candidates. In "Suqiu" examiners are called "dim-eyed," and in "Yu Qu'e" they are called "vagabond bad-news ghosts." In "An Official in the Editorial Service in the Palace Library" a blind monk is said to be able to tell the quality of an essay simply by using his nose. Three candidates take the examination at the same time, and to their surprise the worst essay comes top of the list. The blind monk sighed apologetically, and said, "I am blind in my eyes, not in my nose, but I'm afraid that the examiner is blind in the nose." He then sniffed samples of writing of all the examiners until he came to one, at which he paused and vomited against the wall. In a voice like thunder, he said, "This was the examiner who judged those essays!" This is pungent criticism indeed.

But at the same time Pu Songling praises the lighter side of the society of his time. He expresses hope, and molds ideal types of people. Some of them are indeed fox spirits, but they delight in helping others, they have a sturdy sense of resistance to injustice and are faithful in love. Examples are Hongyu, Yingning, Qingfeng, Xiaocui and The Green-clad Girl. The author, while giving these heroines authentic human appearances and natures, at the same time allows their original characteristics to be brought into play. In this, he displays consummate and subtle artistic skill. Hongyu is a fox spirit who helps the poor scholar Feng Xiangru marry a lady from the Wei family. The local bully Censor Song is attracted by the girl's beauty, and seizes her after sending his henchmen to beat Feng Xiangru's father to death and injure the young man himself. Then a stalwart with a bushy beard kills Censor Song to avenge Feng Xiangru. Feng Xiangru, however, is thrown into jail, and his infant son is taken from him and abandoned on a mountainside. When the distraught Feng Xiangru leaves the prison Hongyu appears once more, holding the boy. Father and son are reunited, and Hongyu remains to help Feng Xiangru reestablish his household. Yingning's mother is a fox, who brings up her daughter alone after her husband dies. Yingning grows up to be an innocent and straightforward young woman, with impeccable manners. She would never on any solemn occasion laugh uproariously; only at her wedding does she laugh out loud, and then the ceremony cannot go ahead as normal. Pu Songling has a lot of affection for this girl, calling her "my Yingning."

The stories in the *Strange Tales from a Chinese Studio* have plots displaying many twists and turns, but they are all closely knit. The characters of the protagonists have differences in their similarities and similarities in their differences. The language used combines ancient expressions from the pre-Qin period, and those of the two Han Dynasties, the Tang and the Song, with colloquial parlance, forming a fresh and lively style, both elegant and pithy. For these reasons, *Strange Tales from a Chinese Studio* is an incomparable artistic achievement among China's short mystery novels written in the classical language.

The storytelling in pleasure quarters

The period of the Song and Yuan dynasties saw at the same time the decline of the novel in the classical language and the rise of that in the vernacular. The Song mystery stories all contained a moral lesson as well. "The Song Dynasty was a time when Neo-Confucianism reached its zenith, and this philosophy had its effect on the contemporary novel; a novel which did not have a moral lesson was considered as being not up to the mark."[10] The format of the Song and Yuan mystery novels was still confined within that of the Six Dynasties period, but the Song and Yuan dynasties saw a great historical change in the Chinese novel, when the *huaben (script for story-telling)* emerged. These, commonly referred to as "storytellers' prompt books," were different from the classical-language novels in subject matter, ideological theme and artistic style. This was a new type of literature which sprang from the class of the common people of the cities.

As handicrafts and commerce developed during the period of the Song and Yuan dynasties, the commodity economy saw a certain growth in prosperity, accompanied by an expansion of the bourgeois class. In the larger cities there sprang up a concentration of pleasure quarters, called *washe* or *wazi*, literally meaning "tile-roofed cottages." Meng Yuanlao, in his *Brilliant Record of the Dream of the Eastern Capital*, says of Kaifeng, the capital of the Northern Song Dynasty (960–1127): "was home to such entertainment compounds as the large-sized Sang Family *Wazi*, the Mid-Sized *Wazi* near the north side, and the Small-Sized Inner *Wazi*. Together they housed more than 50 entertainment venues, of which the Mid-Sized Inner *Wazi*, Lotus Booth, Peony Booth, Inner *Wazi*, Goblin Booth and Elephant Booth were the largest. Together they could accommodate several thousand spectators."[11] Zhou Mi's *Tales of the Old Capital* records 23 such places of entertainment in Hangzhou during the Southern Song Dynasty (1127–1279). He also says that storytelling (*shuohua*) was particularly popular as part of the entertainment of pleasure quarters. The *huaben* were scripts of the storytellers. The audiences of the storytellers mostly came from the lower classes of the town-dwellers, and they particularly liked artistic depictions of people of their own class; so the stories were replete with handicraftsmen, traders both medium and petty, singing girls and gallants.

The Accomplished Gaffer, in his *A Record of the Capital's Landscape*, says that there were four types of storytelling in Hangzhou during the Song Dynasty. He does not say what they were, and scholars of this genre are divided on the matter. However, we can be fairly sure of three types – the novel, the exposition of the scriptures and the historical tale. The Song and Yuan *huaben* extant today are mostly of the first and last types.

Novels which served as short *huaben* were also called "silver," because they were accompanied in performance on silver pipes and flutes. These short stories, which were different from what had previously been called "novels," were partly recited and partly sung. They gathered their material from a wide range of sources – some from the stories of heroes and mystery tales of previous dynasties (like "Zhang Lao" of *Sequel to Records of the Supernatural*, which was combined with a performance of *Zhang Gulao Meets and Marries a Literary Girl while Planting Gourds*, which originated in *Novels Ancient and Modern*), and some from real life and social gossip. *Records of the Chats of a Drunken Old Man*, edited by Luo Ye, in its "Origin of the Novel" chapter lists eight types of novel the titles of which are self-explanatory: Ghosts, Boudoir, Romance, Courtroom, Sword and Club (both recounting the deeds of swashbuckling heroes), Witches and Immortals. To these, we can add *A Record of the Capital's Landscape* and *Dreaming of the Old Capital*, as well as "gaining fame and making a fortune" (stories of people becoming rich and famous) and "*the iron horseman*" (stories of warfare).

Representative Song and Yuan *huaben* novels are "Polishing the Jade Bodhisatva" and "The Wrongfully Executed Cui Ning." The heroine of the first of these, Xiuxiu, is the daughter of a craftsman who specializes in mounting paintings and calligraphy. She is skilled at needlework, and is accepted as a servant in the house of Magistrate Wang of Xian'an Prefecture. In the Wang mansion is a young jade worker named Cui Ning, who falls in love with Xiuxiu. Magistrate Wang is pleased with this state of affairs, and expresses his willingness for the pair to become engaged. Later on, the mansion catches fire. The young couple takes advantage of this to flee to far-distant Tanzhou, where they marry and set up a jade-processing shop. Magistrate Wang, however, finding out where they are, pursues them, kills Xiuxiu and drives her parents to suicide. Cui Ning is flogged and banished. Xiuxiu's spirit follows him to his place of exile, Jiankang Prefecture, where they set up a household once more. Magistrate Wang again finds out where they are. He pursues them, but is thwarted when Xiuxiu gets Cui Ning to join her in death. This novel exposes the tyranny of the feudal ruling class while extolling the spirit of resistance of people of the lower urban class.

Compared to the novel form of the *huaben*, the historical *huaben* are much longer, and it took several sessions to complete one reading; in addition, they deal exclusively with stories from history. They were often called "popular" stories, meaning that they were couched in popular language. They were recited exclusively, with no sung parts. In the Ming and Qing dynasties, the word "popular" was often written using a similar character meaning "criticism," indicating that they had some commentary content.

Representatives of the Song and Yuan period historical novels are contained in *The Five Kinds of Illustrated Vernacular Fictions*, which appeared in the Zhizhi reign period (1321–1323) of the Yuan Dynasty. There are three volumes for each type of story, and they all follow the same format – illustrations followed by text. The five types are *King Wu Marches against the Tyrant Zhouh*, *Yue Yi's Attempt at the State of Qi in the After Set of the Spring and Autumn Annals of Seven States*,

Popular Stories of the State of Qin Conquering the Other Six States, *Popular Stories from the History of the Former Han Dynasty* and *Annals of the Three Kingdoms in Plain Language*. The last-mentioned, dealing with the history of the Three Kingdoms of Wei, Shu Han and Wu (220–280), already contains the main plot of the later novel titled, *Romance of the Three Kingdoms*. A particularly important historical *huaben* is the *Stories from the Great Song Dynasty During the Xuanhe Reign Period*, which contains mainly historical tales of the last years of the Northern Song Dynasty. It is in this book that Song Jiang and 36 other characters who are prominent in the later novel *Outlaws of the Marsh* first appear.

The emergence of the Song and Yuan *huaben* marked a "major turning point in the history of the novel in China."[12] In subject matter, language and structure they were different from the novels written in the literary language. They were a new literary form firmly rooted in the colloquial language of the townspeople, and as such laid a firm foundation for the flourishing of the classical novel. The earliest-known collection of *huaben* novels is the *Huaben of the Qingping Mountain Hall*, edited and published by Hong Pian in the Jiajing reign period (1522–1567) of the Ming Dynasty. Originally comprising 60 stories, only 29 are extant.

The influence of the Song and Yuan *huaben* was wide-ranging, becoming a model for writers from the middle of the Ming Dynasty. During the Tianqi reign period (1621–1628) Feng Menglong edited three compilations of Song and Yuan *huaben*, titled respectively *Bright Words of Explanation to the World*, *Ordinary Words to Alarm the World* and *Immortal Words for Awaking the World*. Collectively, they are known as the "Three Words." In the Chongzhen reign period (1628–1644) Ling Mengchu edited two books titled respectively *Pounding the Table in Surprise* Part 1 and *Pounding the Table in Surprise* Part 2. These are called the "Two Poundings." The "Three Words" have altogether 120 chapters, of which about two-thirds are Ming Dynasty *huaben*. A large proportion of the content consists of the themes of love and marriage. Representative works are "Yu Tangchun in Distress Finds a Husband," "Miss Du in Anger Sinks the Jewel Box" and "An Oil Seller Wins the Queen of Flowers." In the first one, a court minister returns to his ancestral home, leaving his son Wang Jinglong in the capital to continue his studies. The young man falls in love with a courtesan, Yu Tangchun, fritters away all his money and property, and is expelled from the bordello by the scheming bawd. He is reduced to begging. With the help of Yu Tangchun, he returns home and applies himself once more to his studies. Passing the provincial examination, Wang Jinglong goes up to the capital to take the metropolitan examination. He searches for Yu Tangchun, but in vain, for she has been sold to Shen Hong, a merchant from Shanxi Province. Shen Hong's wife poisons her husband and lays the blame on Yu Tangchun. Bribed, the local magistrate forces Yu Tangchun to confess under torture, and then casts her into prison. By this time, Wang Jinglong had passed the highest examination, and was appointed imperial inspector for Shanxi Province. Investigating Yu Tangchun's case, he finds her innocent. They end up married. What readers sympathize with in this story is the vicissitudes suffered by the innocent singing girl Yu Tangchun, and what they admire is the fact that Wang Jinglong does not forget his old love when he attains career success. The theme of "Miss Du in Anger Sinks the Jewel Box" is different from the preceding novel inasmuch as it castigates people who turn their backs on righteousness in their greed for gain. The story goes that Li Jia, the son of a senior government official, is studying in the capital, when he falls in love with a courtesan named Miss Du Shi. She is keen to marry the young man, but the latter is reluctant for fear of his father. When Li Jia runs out of money, the madame of the bordello throws him out. The girl spends all her savings to buy herself out of the madame's clutches, and accompanies Li Jia back to his hometown. On the way, they meet a certain Sun Fu, who, taken with Miss Du Shi's beauty, offers to buy her from Li Jia for 1,000 pieces of gold. Just as the transaction is about to take place, Miss Du Shi takes out her jewel box, which she has taken along secretly, and throws its precious contents one by one into a river. Then, bitterly berating the two young men, she throws herself in the river and drowns. "An Oil Seller Wins the Queen of Flowers" is set in the period of the Jin invasion from the north in the early 12th century. Fleeing the invaders, Yao Qin, a girl of the Song Dynasty capital of Bianliang, becomes separated from her parents. She is reduced to the calling of courtesan to make a living, changing her name to Meiniang. Her price increases steadily as she becomes in great demand among the customers, who give her the name "Queen of the Flowers." A poor young man called Qin Zhong who makes a living by selling oil saves up his coppers until he can procure a meeting with Meiniang. The girl, however, comes back drunk, takes no notice of Qin Zhong, and goes straight to bed. In the night, she wakes up ill. Qin Zhong takes care of her, and wins Meiniang's affections. Later, the son of the magistrate of Fuzhou, on account of a slight by Meiniang, shamefully maltreats the girl, and abandons her in the wilderness. Fortunately she is rescued by Qin Zhong, and the two get married. And so, a lowly oil seller, by his sincere love, wins the heart of Meiniang, the "Queen of the Flowers" – a story of the triumph of love over power.

The "Two Poundings" comprise 40 volumes altogether. Ling Mengchu compiled them from a mishmash of stories old and new, with the result that the contents are somewhat mediocre. "A Trafficker Chances upon Special Tangerines: A Persian Merchant Finds Turtle Shells to Be Invaluable Treasures" tells of Wen Ruoxu, a crafty merchant, who makes a surprise fortune while doing business overseas, and becomes a rich merchant in Fujian Province. It is a novel highlighting the overseas trading activities undertaken during the Ming Dynasty and the daring spirit of the merchants.

Notes

1 [Qing Dynasty] Wenhuan, He ed: *Notes on Poems Through the Ages*, Zhonghua Book Company, 1981, P. 310.

2 *A Brief History of the Chinese Novel*, Vol.8, *Tang Mystery Literature*, First Part, *The Collected Works of Lu Xun*, Vol.9, People's Literature Publishing House, 1973, P. 212.

3 [Ming Dynasty] Yinglin, Hu: *Scribblings from Shaoshi Mountain Cottage*, Vol.36, 1896 copy corrected by Guangya Book Company.

4 *A Brief History of the Chinese Novel, The Collected Works of Lu Xun*, Vol.9, People's Literature Publishing House, 1973, P. 211.

5 *The Story of Li Wa*, Li Shiren ed, *Complete Novels of the Tang and Five Dynasties Periods*, Vol.1, Shaanxi People's Publishing House, 1998, P. 631.
6 [Tang Dynasty] Chengshi, Duan: The 4th Volume "Disparaging by Accident" of the sequel to Miscellaneous Literary Sketches Collected at Youyang, *Collected Writings of the Four Basic Branches of Literature*.
7 [Tang Dynasty] Shangyin, Li: "To My Beloved Son," *The Poems of Li Shangyin Annotated*, Vol.3, Shanghai Ancient Books Publishing House, 1979.
8 [Song Dynasty] Yi, Qian: *New Book of the South*, First Edition of the Collected Literary Works, P. 46.
9 [Tang Dynasty] Lin, Zhao: *Tales of Repayment and Retribution*, Vol.4, Shanghai Ancient Books Publishing House, 1979, P. 94.
10 Xun, Lu: *The Historical Changes in the Chinese Novel*, Lecture 4 "The Song Dynasty 'Talks' and Their Influence," *The Collected Works of Lu Xun*, Vol.8, People's Literature Publishing House, 1983, P. 331.
11 [Song Dynasty] Yuanlao, Meng: *Brilliant Record of the Dream of the Eastern Capital*, Vol.3, Classical Literature Publishing House, 1956, P. 12.
12 *A Brief History of the Chinese Novel, The Collected Works of Lu Xun*, Vol.9, People's Literature Publishing House, 1983, P. 332.

13 Full-length *zhanghuiti* novel of Ming and Qing Dynasties

The formation of the full-length *zhanghuiti* novel

As detailed above, in the Song and Yuan dynasties the novel was essentially a short *huaben*; lengthy historical anecdotes were not included in the novel genre. Separate were the historical stories and "critical" tales, the boundary between which was very clear. From the Ming Dynasty onward, the concept of the novel underwent a change – medium and long works began to include novels, "critical" tales and the so-called romances, the demarcation lines between which gradually became blurred; in this process, the *huaben* came to be called "short novels." For example, Xie Zhaozhe of the Ming Dynasty includes in his *Five Miscellaneous Literary Sketches* the full-length novels *Outlaws of the Marsh* and *Romance of the Three Kingdoms*. Qian Zeng of the early Qing Dynasty, in his catalog of popular novels titled, *Bibliography of So-It-Is Garden* the 12 volumes of the *Ancient and Modern Romance of the Three Kingdoms*. In the *Reading Notes of the 53rd Year*, we find, "The *Romance of the Three Kingdoms* is basically a novel." Similarly, in the *Two Kinds of Essays Jotted Down at the Autumn Rain Temple* we read, "The *Romance of the Sui and Tang Dynasties* is a novel." By this time, the term "novel" had taken on a very expanded meaning, so that the concept of the novel was approaching its modern meaning.

The *Romance of the Three Kingdoms* was China's first full-length *zhanghuiti* novel [The *zhanghuiti* novel is divided into chapters, the synopsis of each of which is introduced by a set of rhyming couplets]. Its appearance marked the reaching of a new stage for the Chinese novel. Its author, Luo Guanzhong, lived at the end of the Yuan Dynasty and into the early years of the Ming Dynasty. Basing himself on the *Annals of the Three Kingdoms* by Chen Shou and its annotations by Pei Song, the author drew widely on the stories of the Three Kingdoms as presented in dramas and historical *huaben*, and finally used his own artistic creativity to produce the masterpiece known as the *Romance of the Three Kingdoms*. The novel describes the tangled political, diplomatic and military conflicts of the Three Kingdoms of Wei, Shu and Wu (20–280), but it does not cling slavishly to the historical facts; many of the incidents are fabrications, so much so that it could be called a "heroic romance."[1] For a long time, *Romance of the Three Kingdoms* was used as a textbook of popular history. Its presentations of the craftiness of

Cao Cao, the magnanimity of Liu Bei, the lofty intellect of Zhuge Liang, the integrity of Guan Yu, the gallantry of Zhang Fei and the courage of Zhou Yu leave an indelible impression on all who meet them in the pages of *Romance of the Three Kingdoms*. Luo Guanzhong assesses the merits and demerits of the leaders of the Three Kingdoms depending on their loyalty or otherwise to the ruling house of the preceding Han Dynasty, and those of their officials both civil and military depending on their loyalty or otherwise to their masters, so that, for instance, the rascally Cao Cao has under him upright ministers. In fact, the officials are judged on whether they display loyalty to the leaders of their own camp, the particular camp they belong to being considered unimportant. The word "loyalty" runs throughout the *Romance of the Three Kingdoms* (The righteous behavior of Guan Yu and Zhang Fei toward Liu Bei is construed as "loyalty.")

The *Romance of the Three Kingdoms* deals mainly with warfare; in fact, more than 40 battles are described in the book. Scenes of warfare predominate, but almost none of them are identical. Some are all-out pitched battles, such as those at Guandu and Red Cliff. These are described in meticulous detail, but the author does not confine himself to the battlefield scenes. He goes to great lengths to delineate the complicated bilateral or multilateral military and diplomatic relations developing along with the clashes. The grand sweep of Luo Guanzhong's writing combines with his minute attention to detail to produce a lively literary rhythm. The *Romance of the Three Kingdoms* uses plain yet sonorous language, in which poetic effects are not lacking. Examples of the latter are episodes such as "Three Calls at the Thatched Cottage," "Versed in Both Polite Letters and Martial Arts" and "Using Reed-clad Boats to Borrow Arrows." Let's take a look at part of Chapter 48:

> But suddenly amid the merriment was heard the hoarse cry of a raven flying toward the south.
>
> "Why does the raven thus cry in the night?" said Cao Cao to those about him.
>
> "The moon is so bright that it thinks it is day," said they, "and so it leaves its tree." Cao Cao laughed. By this time he was quite intoxicated. He set up his spear in the prow of the ship and poured a libation into the river and then drank three brimming goblets.
>
> As he lowered the spear, he said, "This is the spear that broke up the Yellow Scarves, captured Lu Bu, destroyed Yuan Shao, and subdued Yuan Shu, whose armies are now mine. In the north it reached to Liaodong, and it stretched out over the whole south. It has never failed in its task. The present scene moves me to the depths, and I will sing a song in which you shall accompany me."

Zhuge Liang and Cao Cao are the two most important characters in the *Romance of the Three Kingdoms*. Many outstanding stories are woven around them. The successful depiction of the images of these two stems from their multifaceted natures. Zhuge Liang is the embodiment of intelligence, as illustrated in the episodes called "Eloquent Debates Against a Hall of Learned Lords with Witty Remarks" and "Using Reed-clad Boats to Borrow Arrows." He is also the model of a competent prime minister – he is throughout loyal to Liu Bei and Liu Chan and he is good at uniting the people around him. Finally, he dies as a result of wearing himself out in devotion to his duties. His master, Liu Bei, while not a man of rare gifts or outstanding military talent, and of no more than average brain power, has two advantages: One is that he shares in the glory of the Han Dynasty as a relative of the imperial uncle, and the other is that he is a good judge of character and knows how to use people, and so is perfectly confident in recruiting and using geniuses like Zhuge Liang. Let's take a look at the episode in which Liu Bei, on his deathbed at Baidicheng, entrusts his son and successor to the care of Zhuge Liang: "The former ruler, weeping, said, 'Your talent is tenfold that of Cao Pi [a rival warlord]. You are the man to knit together the allies and establish the state on a firm foundation, and accomplish the great task of empire. If my heir needs support in anything, I know you will give him the support he needs. But if he turns out to be wanting in talent, you must make yourself the lord of Chengdu.' Hearing this, Kong Ming [Zhuge Liang] broke out into a sweat all over, and was at a complete loss. He flung himself on the ground, and in tears wailed, 'How could I dare fail in my duty to remain loyal to the very end?'" Thus, Zhuge Liang is virtually forced to swear an oath that he will never try to usurp the throne. As a result, Zhuge Liang finds himself helping the feckless Liu Adou to consolidate his rule. At one point, Zhuge Liang is lashed to Adou's chariot and forced to take part in a completely pointless battle. This is one more example of how Zhuge Liang is successfully portrayed as a loyal prime minister. Cao Cao is presented as having a character that is crafty, scheming and treacherous, partly by revealing how he murders people and cuts heads off in his dreams. His one abiding principle can be summed up in his own words: "I'd rather betray the whole world than have the whole world betray me." He slaughters the whole family of Lv Boshe, because it arouses his morbid suspicion, even though they have treated him well. Cao Cao is clever and able to plan well, but the flaw in his character – his utter lack of morality – arouses aversion in the reader.

The significance of the *Romance of the Three Kingdoms* for modern times lies partly in its store of wisdom which serves as a source of enlightenment in many aspects for people of today. It can be said that this is a great collection of human wisdom, and a comprehensive manual of military strategy couched in a literary form. Here, the various kinds of knowledge are focused on one single end – how to overcome the enemy. This can be done by bringing one's mental powers to bear on how to handle the multifarious connections involved in a rivalry, how to give full play to advantages and sidestep limitations, and how to make use of contradictions. In this regard, the reader's attention is drawn to the two characters Zhuge Liang, as the epitome of wisdom, and Cao Cao, as the arch-plotter.

Outlaws of the Marsh is another famous full-length *zhanghuiti* novel which emerged in the period covering the end of the Yuan Dynasty and the beginning of the Ming Dynasty. Its main author [There are thought to have been collaborators] was Shi Nai'an. Its theme is an uprising in the closing years of the Song Dynasty, led by a man called Song Jiang. It recounts the progress of this rebellion from its start to its conclusion, when the rebels accept an imperial amnesty, join in the crushing of the Fang La uprising and put an end to their lawlessness. Song Jiang's motto is "Do Virtuous Deeds on Behalf of Heaven," and his goal in life is to eradicate corrupt officials. The novel gives descriptions of a whole host of heroic characters with totally fresh insights into their natures, including Song Jiang, Wu Yong, Wu Song, Li Kui, Lu Zhishen and Lin Chong. The backgrounds of these men reflect the realities of the various classes of people at that time, and symbolically explains the contemporary situation of "the people rebelling against official oppression." Most of the men who have sought refuge on Mount Liang [which is protected by a marsh, hence the name of the novel] have been driven there by a history of injustice and suffering. In this regard, the author's most meticulous and successful depiction is that of Lin Chong. But some men are inveigled into joining the band by a variety of tricks that Song Jiang uses in order to increase his power and influence. Lu Junyi is the most representative of such men. Originally, he had no connection with the Liangshan outlaws at all, but Song Jiang racks his brains to get Lu Junyi to join them, and when he does, Song Jiang makes him the top commander. The plot here is complicated, and a little forced; Lu Junyi makes little contribution to the Liangshan band, and the reader may think that he is something of a superfluous character in the novel.

The structure of *Outlaws of the Marsh* is somewhat special. Heroes from everywhere flow to Liangshan Marsh like rivers to the sea. Before they ascend the mountain to join the outlaws in their stronghold, each has a complicated history, and it is in their individual stories, which are juxtaposed one against the other, that their characters are revealed. Once they ascend the mountain they become as drops of water in the ocean, and are no longer centers of attraction in themselves. For that reason, the focus of the narrative then shifts to another person, and the writing rediscovers its dramatic element. *Outlaws of the Marsh* is written in lively colloquial language, which nevertheless is not lacking in poetic flavor; especially outstanding in this regard are episodes such as "Wu Song Kills a Tiger on Jinggang Ridge" and "Arms Instructor Lin Seeks Refuge in a Mountain Shrine During a Snowstorm." An extract from the latter reads as follows: "(Lin Chong) staggered on through the snow, weaving his way and only able to plod ahead because the north wind was at his back. The snow was falling thick and fast, and just as he thought he couldn't go another step he saw ahead of him an old shrine." This is a very vivid piece of writing.

Outlaws of the Marsh and *Romance of the Three Kingdoms* have something in common in that they both extol heroic deeds. This appealed widely to the reading public in the context of the tangled social contradictions prevailing in the Song and Yuan dynasties. The depiction of the protagonists is similar in both novels; Song Jiang in *Outlaws of the Marsh* comes across as very like Liu Bei in *Romance of the Three Kingdoms*, and Wu Yong in the former is depicted in a very similar way to the way Zhuge Liang is described in the latter. In addition, the character of Li Kui in Outlaws of the Marsh has similarities with that of Zhang Fei in *Romance of the Three Kingdoms*. How far the subject materials of the two novels influenced each other in the course of being transmitted orally is a subject worthy of research.

It was in the mid-to-late Ming Dynasty that the creative writing of full-length novels reached the period of its greatest prosperity. It was at this time that the classic works *Journey to the West* (written by Wu Cheng'en), *Enshrined as Spirits* (edited by Xu Zhonglin), *New Records of the States* (edited by Feng Menglong and re-titled *Records of the States of the Eastern Zhou Dynasty* after revision by Cai Yuanfang of the Qing Dynasty) and *Plum in a Golden Vase* (written by the Laughing Lad of Lanling) appeared. Of these, *Journey to the West*, *Plum in a Golden Vase*, *Enshrined as Spirits* and *Records of the States of the Eastern Zhou Dynasty* had the widest impact.

Journey to the West took shape in the middle period of the Ming Dynasty. Its core is a historical incident, the journey of the Tang Dynasty monk Xuanzang to India in search of the Buddhist scriptures, and it has been creatively embellished. It contains a mixture of both Buddhist and Taoist elements, but the author's aim is to exalt the former at the expense of the latter. The first seven chapters tell of the birth of Sun Wukong, the Monkey King, and how he creates an uproar in the Dragon Palace and then in the Heavenly Palace, until the Buddha buries him under five mountains. From Chapter 8, the story of Xuanzang's journey to the western regions in search of the scriptures begins. The monk takes three disciples with him; besides the Monkey King, there are also Pigsy and Friar Sand. After overcoming 81 difficulties, they finally return with the scriptures. These 81 difficulties are the bases of 81 episodes, which form the main body of the novel. Of these episodes, some of the most interesting are "Three Strikes at the White Bone Demon," "Three Waves of the Plantain Fan," "Passing Through Gaolaozhuang Village" and "Passing Through the Cave of the Silken Web." In these stories appear supernatural incidents of all kinds, and the abilities and personalities of the ghost and demons associated with them are most vividly depicted. But the most rounded descriptions in the whole book are those of the Monkey King and Pigsy.

The episode of the Monkey King's causing an uproar in the Heavenly Palace has been seen as an analogy for a peasant uprising. But there are many difficulties with this analysis. For instance, the Monkey King is depicted as a lovable rascal, naive, lively and full of clever tricks. Through the Monkey King, the reader can once again experience the joy and mischief of his long-lost childhood. We admire the Monkey King, and are drawn by him unconsciously back to our own early days. To readers of tender years he is a friend here and now, while for adult readers he is a good friend of bygone times. It is through a child's eyes and a child's mind that we should appreciate the Monkey King's pranks and the way he battles ferociously to defend his master the Tang monk. Through expressions such as "nimble and resourceful" and "good-humored joker,"[2] doesn't Shi Nai'an display his affection for the Monkey King? Pigsy, however, is a multifaceted character, not a straightforward one. He is upright, simple and hardworking, while sometimes he can be crafty, lazy, cowardly, opting for the easy way out and inconsistent. He is the most wavering of the four pilgrims and the one most likely to desert the group. In Pigsy we see the heights and depths of human character.

From pleasure quarters to study

The appearance of *Plum in a Golden Vase* was an important landmark in the history of the Chinese novel, signifying the transition from the complete formation of the *huaben* to the creativity of the writer's study.

This novel, by describing the three aspects of Ximen Qing – an official of Qinghe County, an evil bully and a rich merchant, and the degenerate lifestyles of his household, lays bare the darkness and corruption of the feudal society of the later years of the Ming Dynasty. At the same time, it describes the various social impacts of the burgeoning factors of capitalism. The background to the novel is the court of Emperor Huizong (reign: 1101–1126) of the Song Dynasty, the four powerful rascally clans of the Gao, Yang, Tong and Cai, the sale of official posts and titles, and the accompanying embezzlement and corruption, and the universal unrest that all this caused. The story starts with the poisoning of Wu Song's elder brother Wu Da by Ximen Qing and Wu Da's wife Pan Jinlian. Ximen Qing already has a wife, Wu Yueniang, and a concubine, Li Jiao'er. In addition, he has taken another concubine, Yu Lou, the widow of a rich merchant, and gained a huge amount of wealth thereby. At the same time, Ximen Qing is having an affair with Li Ping'er, the wife of his neighbor Hua Zixu, who happens to be involved in a lawsuit. Li Ping'er entrusts Ximen Qing with 60 silver ingots to use for bribes, and a large number of jewels for safekeeping. Ximen Qing manages to get Hua Zixu released through the influence of Cabinet Minister Cai, who sends an order to the governor of the Kaifeng prefecture. When Hua Zixu gets out of prison and learns that his property is almost all gone, he dies of apoplexy. Just as Ximen Qing is about to take Li Ping'er in marriage, he himself is involved in a lawsuit. Li Ping'er then marries Jiang Zhushan, and uses her deceased husband's wealth to enable Jiang to open a pharmacy. Meanwhile, Ximen Qing manages to bribe his way out of trouble, get rid of Jiang Zhushan and take Li Ping'er as another concubine. Li Ping'er gives birth to a son, who is given the name of Guan'ge Er. On the occasion of the birthday of Cai Jing, Ximen Qing journeys to the Eastern Capital to offer his congratulations, taking with him 20 shoulder poles full of presents. Cai Jing takes Ximen Qing as his adopted son. When Li Ping gives birth to a son, Ximen Qing dotes on him, but the jealous Pan Jinlian raises a fierce cat, which she hopes will bite the baby to death, and this the cat eventually does do. The baby's mother Li Ping also dies, of grief. In the meantime, due to Cai Jing's influence, Ximen Qing has been promoted to the position of magistrate over 1,000 households. In this post, he becomes even more avaricious and lecherous. Eventually his excesses result in his death. All this time, Pan Jinlian has been consorting illicitly with her son-in-law Chen Jingji. The maidservant Chun Mei is also a partner in these orgies. In order to break up this trio, Wu Yueniang sells Chunmei to Garrison Commander Zhou as a concubine, and gets Madame Wang to take Pan Jinlian away. At first, Chun Mei is a favorite with the garrison commander, but she too dies as a result of her carnal excesses. Pan Jinlian is killed by Wu Song, and Wu Yueniang spends the rest of her days mourning by Ximen Qing's spirit table.

Through its description of Ximen Qing and his activities, *Plum in a Golden Vase* lays bare the social phenomenon of collusion between officials and businessmen to perpetrate outrages. Ximen Qing's wealth was accumulated by trickery and fraud, and he used it for no other ends but bribery and the pursuit of pleasure. This was a common syndrome in China's feudal society. The importance of *Plum in a Golden Vase* lies in the fact that it was not recited for an audience but written to be read by individuals. It had left the earlier stage of the novel, which had been based on recital, and moved on to embody the characteristics of the modern novel. Although this novel has the basic approach of excoriating evil and recommending goodness, its detailed lascivious descriptions dilute somewhat this overall theme. In the context of the history of the Chinese novel, the special features of *Plum in a Golden Vase* are (1) The negative characters play leading roles in both number and importance; (2) There is a tendency toward naturalism; (3) the description brings out real-life situations; and (4) There is a great deal of salacious content. These four aspects reinforce each other, and in fact have contributed to the popular concept of *Plum in a Golden Vase* as being a chiefly pornographic novel. But since lascivious description was not uncommon in the drama scripts of the mid- and late-Ming Dynasty, accurately reflecting the social mores of time, perhaps this is not surprising.

Wu Jingzi's *The Scholars*, written in the early Qing Dynasty, takes as its theme the civil service examination system as the object of its satire, presenting the disparate images of a large number of literary figures. They are both comical and pitiful. Fettered by desire for fame and wealth, some grow old and die enslaved by the eight-legged essay, proficiency in which was necessary to answer the examination questions, and doomed to spend meaningless lives. Zhou Jin and Fan Jin are two classic examples. The former is 60 years old, and has failed the exam many times. He has to eke out a living teaching in a village school, and all the while having to put up with the sneers and slights of men who have passed the exam and gained the rank of scholar. Later, no longer able to teach, Zhou Jin becomes a bookkeeper for a merchant. On a visit to the examination hall in the provincial capital, he suddenly recalls the bitterness and anguish he has been forced to spend half his life in, and "His head hit the desk top with a crash, and he lay there rigid, oblivious of all around him." When he is revived he lets out an anguished howl. Little does he know that he will soon have a change of fortune. Indeed, he passes the provincial and capital exams in short order, and is made the director of the Imperial Academy. Then the scholars who once snubbed him become his obsequious pupils, and the people of the village where he was once a humble schoolmaster all turn out to congratulate him on his success. In this way, the novel gives us a glimpse of the fickleness of the world. Fan Jin has failed the lowest exam a score of times, and at the age of 54 he lives in poverty. When he finally passes the exam he becomes virtually insane with joy. Then too, his relatives and neighbors all change their attitude toward him. Within two or three months he is wealthy enough to afford servants and handmaidens. It is with such episodes that Wu Jingzi tears away the conventional curtain, and reveals the various dark sides of his society. He expresses particular condemnation of greedy and corrupt officials who use their fame and wealth to get themselves promoted, and the evil landlords and gentry with who they collude in their wickedness. Yan Gongsheng is a prime example of this class of person. In addition, Wu Jingzi reveals the trickery of bogus scholars who live off their false names and reputations, like Kuang Chaoren, Niu Buyi and Zhao Xuezhai, as well as degenerate Confucianists, like Mr. Ma Er, who have had their brains turned by the eight-legged essay. The author describes them all in a life-like manner.

At the same time, Wu Jingzi also portrayed some positive characters in order to express through them his own ideals. Du Shaoqing is a true and upright Confucian scholar, a simple man who scorns power and wealth. He shows respect for individuality, and is unrestrained by conventional bonds. He also harbors solicitude for the country and the people. In Du Shaoqing, the author portrays a fine person, but he is by no means blind to the fact that society could not be transformed by relying on people like Du Shaoqing alone; and so he turned his gaze to the common townspeople, and toward the end of the novel, he writes about the "four eccentrics" – Ji Xia'nian, Wang Tai, Gai Kuan and Jing Yuan. These four are not officials, and earn their own living with their talents and artistry. They live free-and-easy lives, representing what Wu Jingzi considers to be true elegance.

The Scholars is structured out of a group of separate episodes: The central character in one chapter introduces another, and in the next chapter the first character leaves the stage to the second, and so the various protagonists are linked by a chain of events in a somewhat similar way to that used by the writers of the classical-language novels. The satirical function of *The Scholars* is produced by a very successful use of subtle diction pregnant with meaning.

A Dream of Red Mansions, meticulously composed by Cao Xueqin, represents the epitome of the classical Chinese novel. The tightness of its structure, its vivid language and the freshness of its characters make it superior to all other Chinese novels. It is generally acknowledged that this history of the rise and fall of the Jia family is a representation in microcosm of the China of the mid-18th century. It lays bare the multiplicity of evils perpetrated by the feudal ruling class by focusing on the path to ruin pursued by one feudal clan. This judgment is true enough, but, in my opinion, there is more to the novel than just this simplistic analysis. Through the tragic love affair between Jia Baoyu and Lin Daiyu, which runs like a connecting thread through the story, which also represents the antagonism between beauty and ugliness, the author explores the world on three levels: The first is the relationship between the world outside the walls of the Jia family mansion and that inside it. At the top of society are Beijing Duke and Jia Yucun as the representatives of officialdom; in the middle are Second and Third Sister You and Grandma Liu, as distant relatives. At the lower end are the servants of the Jia family, like Qingwen and Xiren. The second is represented by the Rongguo and Ningguo mansions, with Jia Zheng and Jia She as typical patriarchs. The main protagonists here are the Lady Dowager, Wang Xifeng and Jia Lian. The third is represented by the Grand View Garden, which is presided over by the Lady Dowager. Jia Baoyu is the central character in this small independent world in which he, Lin Daiyu, Xue Baochai, Shi Xiangyun, Tanchun, Xiren, Qingwen and Miaoyu emerge as independent personalities in their own right. These three worlds are connected, but each preserves its own characteristics. The first and second worlds are realistic, but the third contains quite a large number of idealistic elements. The real power of expression of *A Dream of Red Mansions* lies in the way its author vividly brings this beautiful third world to life before the eyes of the reader, and at the same time to have it devoured, destroyed and buried. Jia Baoyu is a prototype of the embryonic democratic thought that was beginning to emerge in the late stage of feudal society in China. He is not prepared to follow the orthodox path, nor do his life values correspond with the traditional understanding of the feudal outlook on life. He pursues individual freedom and values youth and beauty, eschewing feudal norms of morality and the customs and habits of his time. In the end, he is destroyed together with his beautiful fantasies. Destroyed also are the people who love him. Perversely, their love for him is in no way able to ward off his destruction and tragic death. And it is precisely here that the tragic nature of the novel lies. *A Dream of Red Mansions* could be said to be a paean to youth and beauty, but it is also a tragic description of how youth and beauty come to be destroyed. But the destruction of Jia Baoyu and his dreams is also a metaphor for the inevitable fall of feudalism as it attempts to strangle the new burgeoning force that is arising within it. This is a true historical picture of the late period of feudalism in China. *A Dream of Red Mansions* is a song of praise to freedom, youth and beauty, and at the same time a lament for the destruction of that beautiful "dream."

The story of *A Dream of Red Mansions* chiefly deals with humdrum everyday life. Although there are no thrilling tales of heroic deeds or swashbuckling battlefield scenes, nevertheless, the descriptions of daily life contain stimulating impulses which stir the reader's emotions. The subtlety of the style, the directness of the diction and the freshness of the characters all give the reader endless material for contemplation. This is where *A Dream of Red Mansions* differs in great part from *The Romance of the Three Kingdoms* and *Outlaws of the Marsh*. The psychological descriptions in this novel are very precise, and it is in this respect that it represents a big development compared to previous novels. As an example, we can quote a piece of psychological writing from Chapter 32: Daiyu has just heard Baoyu praise her for not "talking nonsense" about "worldly affairs":

> This surprised and delighted Daiyu, but also distressed and grieved her. She was delighted to know that she had not misjudged him, for he had now proved just as understanding as she had always thought; and was surprised that he had been so indiscreet as to acknowledge his preference for her openly. Distressed because their mutual understanding ought to preclude all talk about gold matching jade, or she instead of Baochai should have the gold locket to match the jade amulet. Grieved because her parents had died, and although his preference was so clear there was no one to propose the match for her. Besides, she had recently been suffering from dizzy spells which the doctor had warned might end in consumption, as she was so weak and frail. Dear as she and Baoyu were to each other, she might not have long to live. And what

> use was their affinity if she were fated to die? These thoughts sent tears coursing down her cheeks. And therefore, instead of entering, she turned away, wiping her tears.[3]

The language of *A Dream of Red Mansions* is basically the colloquial language current in the north of China in those days. It is lively and vivid, and clearly descriptive. It also draws on elements of classical Chinese writing, making it elegant and concise, and boundlessly evocative. Another pleasing aspect of the novel is the way it makes the speech of the different characters suit their different personalities and stations in life: The speech of Xifeng is impertinent; that of Miaoyu is refined; that of Qingwen is cutting, etc. All have their innate characteristics. This can be seen in the different ways that the people who visit Baoyu after his beating speak:

> Before his father could beat him any further, lady Wang seized the rod with both hands. "This is the end," roared Jia Zheng. "You're determined to be the death of me today."
>
> "I know Baoyu deserves a beating," sobbed lady Wang. "But you mustn't wear yourself out, sir. It's a sweltering day and the old lady isn't well. Killing Baoyu is small matter, but should anything happen to the old lady that would be serious."
>
> "Spare me this talk." Jia Zheng gave a scornful laugh. "I've already proved an unfilial son by begetting this degenerate. When I discipline him, all of you protect him. I'd better strangle him now to avoid further trouble."
>
> With that, he called for a rope. Lady Wang hastily threw her arms around him.
>
> "You're right to chastise your son, sir, but have pity on your wife," she cried. 'I'm getting on for fifty, and this wretch is my only son. If you insist on making an example of him, how dare I dissuade you? But if you kill him today, it means you want me to die too. If strangle him you must, take this rope and strangle me first, then strangle him. Mother and son, we won't dare hold it against you, and at least I shall have some support in the nether world."
>
> She threw herself down on Baoyu, and gave way to a storm of weeping.
>
> In the middle of this commotion, a maid suddenly announced, "The old lady is coming."
>
> And they heard her quavering voice outside the window: "Kill me first and then kill him. That will be a clean sweep."[4]

The evolution of the concept of the modern novel

With the advent of the modern era and the influence of the Western concept of literature, both the idea and intellectual position of the Chinese novel underwent a profound change. Following the Reform Movement of 1898, Liang Qichao founded a magazine titled, *New Fiction* to promote creativity in novel writing. Articles he wrote for the magazine, such as "An Introduction to the Translation and Printing of Political Novels" and "On the Connection Between the Novel and Mass Politics" became seminal works for the theory of the new novel. His ideas are encapsulated in the following quotations: "The novel is the highest vehicle of literature," "The novel has inconceivable strength to guide human morality," "In its essence and position it is like the air or beans and grains, a social entity that can neither be avoided nor hidden behind a screen," and "These days, he who wishes to transform mass politics must start with a revolution in the world of the novel; he who wishes to remake the people anew must start with the new novel."[5] Tao Zengyou, in his "On the Power and Influence of the Novel," says that the novel "has an inexpressibly great power" and "scholarship relies on it for progress, society relies on it for civilization, the individual relies on it for wholesome ideas and the nation relies on it for progress."[6] But all these views of the novel regard it as no more than a vehicle for the purveying of street gossip. How far this is from the traditional concept of the novel! Wang Zhongqi, in his *Discussion of the History of the Novel Through the Ages*, looking back on the past says "The novel supplies what is lacking in the *Poems* (the original name of the *Book of Odes*) and the *Spring and Autumn Annals*, thereby putting the novel on a par with the classics and histories." He adds, "Novelists in our country are all worthy gentlemen; of the poor and lower classes, there are some who cannot use words, some who dare not use words, and some who can't stop themselves using words, and so come out with roundabout and freakish writings."[7] In this way, he raises novelists to the level of worthies and philosophers, and this is another expression of a new attitude which rebels against tradition

The evolution of the concept of the novel, from one angle reflects the history of the development of the novel itself. The evolution of the concept of the novel from pre-Qin times to the Ming Dynasty was a slow process, and yet was one from obscurity to enlightenment, from confusion to simplicity, and from lowliness to exaltation. The traditional concept was a strong fetter hampering the development of creative novel writing. In fact, without shattering this fetter it was impossible for the novel to develop further.

However, the new concept of the novel did not immediately raise the level of creativity in this regard and lead to a "golden age." The modern era produced such fine "novels of indignation" as *Notes on the Present State of Officialdom* (by Li Baojia), *Strange Situations Observed over Twenty Years* (by Wu Woyao) and *Flowers From an Evil Sea* (by Zeng Pu). There were also novels advocating revolution, such as Chen Tianhua's *The Lion's Roar*. In addition, there were romantic novels such as *The Soul of Jade Pear* (by Xu Zhenya) and *Tide of Guangling* (by Li Hanqiu). But the real new form of creativity in the novel only emerged after the "May 4 Movement" of 1919.

Following the "May 4 Movement," the important social position of the novel became firmly entrenched, and even popular novels attracted wide attention among intellectuals. Lu Xun, for instance, did a great deal of work in classifying and researching classical novels, opening a new page in studies of the history of the Chinese novel.

Notes

1 Zuxiang, Wu: *Collection of Chats*, Peking University Press, 1987, P. 27.
2 [Ming Dynasty] Tianqi reign period: *Annals of Huai'an Prefecture*, Vol.16, woodblock print, P. 1626.
3 [Qing Dynasty] Xueqin, Cao. and Gao, E: *A Dream of Red Mansions*, Chapter 32, "An Avowal Leaves Baoyu Bemused; Disgrace Drives Jin Chuan to Suicide," People's Literature Publishing House, 1982, P. 446.
4 [Qing Dynasty] Xueqin, Cao. and Gao, E: *A Dream of Red Mansions*, Chapter 33, "A Jealous Younger Brother Tells Tales: A Worthless Son Receives a Fearful Flogging," People's Literature Publishing House, 1982, PP. 453–457.
5 "On the Connection Between the Novel and Mass Politics," See the fourth book in the literature collection *The Works of Ice-Drinking Chamber Collected and Collated*, Shanghai Zhonghua Book Company, 1932, PP. 7, 10.
6 See *The Playful World*, 1907, Issue 10.
7 See *Monthly Fiction*, 1907, Vol.1, Issue 11.

14 The structure and style of the novel

The structure of the novel

The Chinese novel can be divided into the two categories of classical and colloquial. In the material they deal with the two have much in common, but in the aspects of concept, origin, language, thought, fields of interest and author and reader, they represent two different novel traditions. The classical novel has its origin in ancient legends, expressed in classical language. In general, it represents the thoughts and interests of the upper-class literati. Both author and reader were comparatively well educated. The colloquial novel, on the other hand, had its origin in the public market performances of the mid-Tang Dynasty, and was expressed in down-to-earth language. In general, it reflects the thoughts and interests of the common townspeople. The authors of the early colloquial novels were intellectuals who had roamed about the alleys and markets of the towns, and their novels were entertainments which catered to the tastes of the common people.

Structural aspects such as the division into short story, medium-length story and full-length story, which are integral parts of the Western concept of the novel, had little meaning for the classical Chinese novel. It is more apposite to discuss the classical Chinese novel as being divided into the five categories of ghost, hero, mystery, *huaben* and *zhanghuiti.* The first three contain classical novels, and the other two colloquial novels. Here we will discuss them under the headings of the five categories.

Ghost novels appeared in an unbroken line from the Wei and Jin dynasties to the Qing Dynasty. Representative works in this genre are *In Search of Spirits* by Gan Bao of the Eastern Jin Dynasty, *Fantastic Tales* by Niu Sengru of the Tang Dynasty, *Investigating Spirits* by Xu Xuan of the Song Dynasty, *New Stories About Trimming the Lamp* by Qu You of the Ming Dynasty, and *Strange Tales from a Chinese Studio* by Pu Songling and *Scribblings from Yuewei Cottage* by Ji Yu, both of the Qing Dynasty. Ghost novels describe weird happenings involving the supernatural, and all of them are short. Much of the material is taken from popular legend, either directly recorded or with more-or-less literary embellishment. With the former type, it is very difficult to perceive the author's individual style, while the opposite is the case with the latter, in books such as *Strange Tales from a Chinese Studio.*

Hero novels appeared from the Southern Dynasties (420–589) right down to the Qing Dynasty. Representative works are *New Words for the World*, by Liu Yiqing of the Song Dynasty of the Southern Dynasties, *Lofty Words of the Sui and Tang Dynasties*, by Liu Su and *New Words of the Great Tang Dynasty* by Liu Su (both Tang Dynasty authors), *A Forest of Tang Words*, by Wang Dang and *Words of Consecutive Ages*, by Kong Pingzhong (both Song Dynasty authors), *A Forest of Words of Mr. He*, by He Liangjun of the Ming Dynasty, and *Words of This Era*, by Wang Zhuo of the Qing Dynasty. Hero novels tend to concentrate on the actions of officials and scholars and suchlike people. We can occasionally glimpse in them vivid descriptions of characters and personalities. They are all short works. Their subject matter is taken mostly from the tales passed down among the upper classes of society, with some attention paid to literary refinement. Novels of this kind had varying value in the course of the history of literature, but not many can be viewed as stylistically outstanding; only *New Words for the World* can be said to be concisely written in a form that ensures that the meaning lingers in the mind of the reader. In *Scribblings from Shaoshi Mountain Cottage* by Hu Yinglin of the Ming Dynasty we read, "Reading his words, we seem to see the real features of the people of the Jin Dynasty flickering before our eyes. The words are full of meaning and deeply realistic."

The mystery novel was a new genre which emerged in the Tang Dynasty, and had its imitators in the following Song Dynasty. Although its content is basically the fantastic and weird, much of its material is taken from real life, and not confined to the supernatural. Overall, the Tang mystery novel is marked by ornate language, convoluted plot, tight structure and rich imagery. The authors often resorted to historical sources, which accounts for the "*chuan*," meaning "transmitted" or "handed down," in the name of this genre. Each story is preceded by an account of the protagonists' names, pedigrees and social position, and some have an appraisal or summing up at the end. This is clearly a technique used in traditional Chinese historical writing. In *Loose Notes of the Cloud-Covered Foothill* we read, "In all these works we can see traces of historicity, poetry and discourse."[1]

The *huaben* are short. They can be recited at one sitting or divided into sections. In the latter, each section ends with a two-verse poem introduced by the words "*zheng shi*," or "It really was a case of. . . " These marked convenient pauses which the storyteller could utilize to collect money from the audience. Sometimes these novels insert a short introductory story before the main story begins, called a "*tou hui*," or "header." Some novels guide the reader or hearer into the main story by means of a stanza called a "ru hua," or "prefatory words." Often poems are inserted into a novel, sometimes in the form of poetry-prose couplets, to bring to life people or scenes. A novel generally winds up with a poem of the order of seven words to a line, to point out the lesson to be learned from the story. *Huaben* that deal with historical stories tend to be longer, and the episodes into which they are divided would have been recited on different days. The style of the *huaben* was colloquial, lively and facetious, which were all typical features of the way the common townsfolk spoke.

The *zhanghuiti* novels are long works, written in colloquial language and divided into sections. Each section is introduced by a couplet. For instance, the first episode of *Romance of the Three Kingdoms* has this couplet to introduce it: "Three Bold Spirits Plight Mutual Faith in the Peach Garden; Heroes Win Top Honors Fighting the Yellow Turbans." Each chapter starts off with the words "The story goes," poems are inserted at various points in the narrative, and each episode ends at a strategic point in the plot, with the words, "If you want to know what happened next, listen to the next episode" or "If you want to know how this turned out, the next section explains." These are relics of the storyteller's technique. As the *zhanghuiti* novels are long ones, their structure is particularly important. In addition, the rhythm of the ups and downs of the plot combined with suitable subject matter and language to produce over a lengthy span of narrative each novel's unique style, either bold, subtle, moving or learned, and thus ensure each one's long-term popularity.

The stylistic characteristics of the novel

The following three points should be included in any discussion of the overall characteristics of the Chinese novel: 1) Reminiscence. Stories are often woven around the life and experiences of an important character or several characters, and the plot and writing method combine to convey their reminiscences. 2) Narrative. The richer in narrative plot a novel is, the better it is able to tell the story. But it should be noted here that the Chinese novel lacks psychological and scenic description, compared to its Western counterpart. 3) Logical structure. The Chinese novel tends to follow a time line in the development of its narrative plot, with a "head and tail."

Among all the different forms of literature, the novel was the easiest to be transmitted as a commodity, especially the colloquial novel. The heyday of the colloquial novel coincided with the flourishing period of the art of printing, in the Song and Yuan dynasties and thenceforth. As the printing of novels became a profitable business, a large number of block-printed copies appeared in the book markets, along with an increased demand from booksellers for people to edit and publish novels. In consequence, the situation in novel creation was marked by the following development: The spread of the reputations of a number of excellent novels was followed by a spate of imitations. For instance, *Journey to the West* was followed by *Journey to the West Continued, A Follow-up to Journey to the West, Supplement to the Journey to the West, Journey to the North, Journey to the East* and *Journey to the South. A Dream of Red Mansions* also had its purported continuations. Some of these imitations were works of real merit, such as Dong Shuo's *Supplement to the Journey to the West*, but most were slipshod and mediocre. At the same time, in the field of poetic creation a school harkening back to the ancient styles appeared, with the object of smoothing away contemporary malpractices in poetry writing, and with no eye to commercial success. The imitators and readers of novels grew in number along with the growth of the commodity economy and the transmission of the novel as a commercial item. This was one of the differences between the novel and other types of literature, and a subject for attention in the study of the history of the Chinese novel.

Interim summary

Compared with Western literature, Chinese literature has tended to be weighted toward the lyrical. For instance, lyrical poetry emerged and reached a high standard as early as in pre-Qin times; in contrast, narrative works emerged comparatively late. Although the origin of the Chinese novel can be traced back to the myths of antiquity and pre-Qin historical accounts, such works were stuck at the stage of "trivial anecdotes and tales" until the Wei, Jin and Southern and Northern Dynasties period, when the novel started to take regular shape. And it was not until the Tang Dynasty that writers began to consciously create novels, with invented story plots. It was only then that the novel reached its maturity in China.

The Chinese novel has characteristics different from its European counterpart. To put it simply, these consist of fulsome description of the story plot and only brief psychological or scenic description, especially avoiding any lengthy departure from the plot itself. As far as plot description goes, it was initially affected by the oral art of the storyteller (taking into account what the listeners were used to and the degree of appeal of each episode). In addition, the Chinese novelist paid great attention to clarity of structure and story line, and beginning-to-end consistency.

Note

1 [Song Dynasty] Yanwei, Zhao: *Loose Notes of the Cloud-Covered Foothill*, Vol.8, Classical Literature Publishing House, 1957, P. 111.

Part 4

Essays

The word wenzhang (essays) literally means a riot of color or confused patterns. In the *Mozi * Condemnation of Music* we find: "So the reason why Mozi condemns music is not because . . . he considers the towers decorated with grandiose patterns are not beautiful."[1] Later, *wenzhang* came to mean simply writing or independent written works. For instance, in the *Records of the Historian * Preface to the Biographies of Confucian Scholars* we find, "They have clarified the difference between the law of Nature and that of mankind. They have brought the concepts of state governance in the past and today together, and written about them in a very elegant and immaculate manner. They are of profound instructive significance and will bestow far-reaching benefits on the state and its people."[2]

We include in the term *wenzhang* all types of writing not classified as *shi*, *fu*, *ci* or *qu* poetry or novels. It mainly includes essays and parallel prose. The *Selected Works of Literature* edited by Xiao Tong, crown prince Zhaoming of the Liang Dynasty (502–557, one of the Southern Dynasties), divides literary works into 37 major types, including *fu*, *shi* and *sao* poetry (The latest research recommends that two more – *yi* and *nan* – be added, to make 39 major categories). This work then subjoins some minor categories according to genre. Among the major categories are some with little literary merit, such as public notices, official decrees, records, orders etc. The *Blooms in the Literary Garden* by Li Fang of the Song Dynasty (960–1279) has 38 categories of literature, including *fu* and *shi* poetry, but also including matter such as annotations, judgments and tables. From this we can see that *shi* and *fu* had already become two independent categories of literature, which, as a concept had a wide and sweeping connotation. At this time there was no distinction between literary style and subject matter, and no unified standard for judging literature.

The essay is the fourth major category of literature discussed in this book, following *shi* and *fu* poetry, *ci* and *qu* verse, and the novel. This category covers both the essay proper and the type of *wenzhang* written in the form of parallel prose. Regardless of subject matter, even if a piece is an official document, so long as it has literary merit it is included in the discussion. The original scope of what was to come under the heading of Chinese literature was indeed broad, and so-called "letters" could not be judged to come completely within the narrow boundaries of what we today call literature. Nevertheless, to exclude certain works from the sphere of literature on those grounds would be to ignore Chinese reality.

Prose and poetry were the first two genres of Chinese literature to appear, and they have developed as literary genres from ancient times to the present. Among ancient writers there were some who could not write novels and some who could not write drama scripts, but there were none who could not write *wenzhang* (essays in the broad sense). It could be said that *wenzhang* is the trunk of Chinese literature, and the other genres are just branches.

Notes

1 *Mozi*, Vol.8, *Collected Writings of the Four Basic Branches of Literature*.

2 [Han Dynasty] Qian, Sima: *Records of the Historian*, Vol.121, Zhonghua Book Company, 1959, P. 3119.

15 The origin and evolution of the essay

The heyday of ancient prose

Wenzhang can be traced back to the oracle bone inscriptions of the Shang Dynasty (16th century–11th century BC). For example:

> Divining on the day Guimao. It will rain today. Will the rain come from the west, east, north or south?[1]

This inscription can be seen as an interesting piece of prose. Besides the oracle bone inscriptions, the inscriptions on bronze vessels of both the Shang and Zhou (11th century–256 BC) dynasties can also be regarded as early examples of prose, and indeed mature prose writing can be traced back to a collection of documents known as the *Book of History*. One part this book, *Book of Shang*, contains oaths, commands, instructions and rescripts issued by officials of the Shang Dynasty, and in the other, the *Book of Zhou*, mostly documents drawn up during the early part of the Western Zhou Dynasty. However, the writing is full of obscurities and is very difficult to understand.

Tradition has it that the *Zuo Zhuan* was written by Zuo Qiuming, chief archivist of the State of Lu during the Warring States Period (475–221 BC). This title is an abbreviation of *Master Zuo's Commentary on the Spring and Autumn Annals*. The *Spring and Autumn Annals* is said to have been compiled by Confucius from the historical records of his home state of Lu. It is a major work detailing the year-by-year events which occurred in that state, recorded in very succinct language. The "Spring and Autumn (770–476 BC) writing style" developed by later generations had a great influence on Chinese historical writing and more broadly on prose writing in general. The basic meaning of this style is described in the *Records of the Historian* * *The Lineage of Confucius* as "Writing only what is essential and leaving out whatever is not"; in the "Commentary on *Zuo Zhuan*" by Du Yu as "Praise or blame – one word only"; and in the *History of the Han Dynasty* * *Records of Art and Literature* as "few words but deep meaning." *Zuo Zhuan* was written to elucidate the meaning of the *Spring and Autumn Annals*. It gives minute descriptions of the events described in the latter from beginning to end, including trifling anecdotes connected with them.

Although it is basically a historical work, the *Zuo Zhuan* has a strong literary flavor; its descriptions of battles, relating of stories and delineations of personalities are all outstanding. Particularly popular are this work's "The Battle of An Between the States of Qi and Jin" and "Death of the Prince of Jin," among others. The description of the battlefield in the former is particularly vivid and impressive:

> In the melee Que Ke received an arrow wound. Blood filled his shoes, but he did not stop beating the drum for the advance.

Que Ke called out to Xie Zhang: "I'm wounded!" Xie Zhang scoffed, "I received an arrow wound from the hand to the elbow as soon as battle was joined. I simply broke it off and kept driving. My blood dyed the left wheel dark red. Wounded? What are you talking about? Put up with it."

Zheng Qiuhuan thereupon interjected with, "Right from the time we clashed with the enemy, whenever our chariot got into difficulties I had to jump down and push it. But it seems that you, sir, did not notice. The flags and drum in this chariot are the eyes and ears of our men; they advance and retreat as we signal. Could one man alone preserve the vital function of this command chariot? How can you endanger the great cause of our sovereign by complaining of a little thing like a wound? When a man dons armor and takes up arms he should be prepared to fight to the death. So long as he has not received a fatal wound he is duty-bound to give of his best." Thereupon, holding the reins in his left hand, Zheng Qiuhuan beat the drum signal for the advance with his right.

His chariot horses galloped headlong at the enemy line, and the whole allied army followed.

The forces of the State of Qi, having suffered a crushing defeat, fled to Mount Huabuzhu, where they were trapped in a threefold encirclement.[2]

The conversation between Que Ke, Zhang Hou and Zheng Qiuhuan, inserted into the heat of battle, describes very well the atmosphere of a battlefield.

The *Intrigues of the States* is a historical work compiled and covering the closing years of the Warring States Period and the Qin (221–206 BC) and Han (206 BC–220 AD) dynasties. It concentrates on the plots hatched by the roving advisers of the rival states, hence its title. It deals with states individually, and mainly tells anecdotes about them. A famous story from this book is "Zou Ji Makes the King of Qi Accept Advice Through Indirection":

> Zou Ji was a man of impressive stature and figure. One day as he was about to attend the morning audience at court, dressed in his official robes, he happened to glance at himself in a mirror. Then he asked his wife: "Who is better looking, myself or that Xu fellow who lives in the northern part of the city?" His wife answered, "You are much better looking than Xu, my dear." Xu was famous throughout the State of Qi for his handsome countenance. Zou Ji was not convinced, but when he asked his concubine the same question he got the same answer. Later that morning, when a guest arrived, and the two

> of them were talking, Zou Ji put the same question to him, and again got the same answer. The following day, Xu himself came to call. Zou Ji looked at Xu closely, and got the feeling that he did not match this man in looks. He then stole a glance at himself in a mirror, and decided that he was far inferior to Xu in looks. That night, when he retired to bed, Zou Ji mused, "My wife said that I was better looking than Xu. But that was because she is partial to me. My concubine said the same thing. But that was because she fears me. My guest also said the same thing. But that was because he wanted something from me."

The following morning, as he attended the morning audience at court, Zou Ji said to King Wei: "Your Highness, I am well aware that I cannot compare with Lord Xu in looks. However, my wife, who dotes on me, says that I am more handsome that Lord Xu; my concubine, who is in awe of me, says the same; and a guest, who wants something from me, also says the same. Now, sire, your realm of Qi stretches for 1,000 *li* on all sides, and encompasses 120 cities. Your palace ladies and attendants all dote on your august person; your court functionaries all hold you in awe; throughout your domains there is no one who does not seek your regal favor. Viewed from this angle, Your Majesty, it can be said, is shielded from much." Thereupon, the king said "Indeed, I see what you mean!" And he issued a decree as follows: "From now on, any official or functionary who tells me to my face of my faults shall receive the highest reward; whoever submits a petition of advice shall receive a secondary reward; and whoever tours the highways and byways to determine my reputation among the common people shall receive a tertiary reward."

As soon as this decree was promulgated the king's officials flocked to deliver advice to their master. The royal gates and courtyard were as busy as a marketplace. But after a few months, the stream of people offering advice to the king had slowed to a trickle, and after a year even those who wished to do so avoided offering advice. However, the states of Yan, Zhao, Han and Wei, hearing of this, all sent envoys to pay homage to King Wei of Qi. This is called winning without leaving the court.[3]

The *Analects*, which records the words and deeds of Confucius, is a collection outstanding among the prose works of the pre-Qin period. The language is pithy and lucid, and mostly in the form of aphorisms. For instance, the first words of the first chapter (Xue Er) of the *Analects* are "To study and continually practice what you study, is that not a joy? To be unruffled when others do not appreciate you, is that not the mark of a gentleman?" In the chapter "Wei Zheng" we find "The gentleman is broad-minded and not partisan; the petty man is partisan and not broad-minded." In the chapter "Li Ren" we find, "I am not concerned that I have no place, I am concerned how I may fit myself for one. I am not concerned that I am not known, I seek to be worthy to be known." In the chapter "Zi Lu" we find, "Do not be desirous of having things done quickly. Do not look to small advantages. The desire of having things done quickly prevents their being done thoroughly. Looking to small advantages prevents the accomplishment of great affairs." The longer of these sayings can be viewed as short pieces of writing in themselves, through which we can get a glimpse of the personalities of Confucius and his disciples. For instance in the chapter "Xian Jin":

> Zi Lu, Zeng Xi, Ran You, and Gongxi Hua were sitting by the Master. He said to them: "Though I am a day or so older than you, do not think of that. From day to day you are saying, 'We are not known.' If some ruler were to know you, what would you like to do?" Zi Lu hastily and lightly replied, "Suppose the case of a state of ten thousand chariots; let it be straitened between other large states; let it be suffering from invading armies; and to this let there be added a famine in corn and in all vegetables – if I were entrusted with the government of it, in three years' time I could make the people to be bold, and to recognize the rules of righteous conduct." The Master smiled at him. Turning to Ran You, he said, "Qiu, what are your wishes?" Qiu replied, "Suppose a state of sixty or seventy *li* square, or one of fifty or sixty, and let me have the government of it – in three years' time, I could make plenty to abound among the people. As to teaching them the principles of propriety, and music, I must wait for the rise of a superior man to do that." "What are your wishes, Chi," said the Master next to Gongxi Hua. Chi replied, "I do not say that my ability extends to these things, but I should wish to learn them. At the services of the ancestral temple, and at the audiences of the princes with the sovereign, I should like, dressed in the dark square-made robe and the black linen cap, to act as a small assistant." Last of all, the Master asked Zeng Xi, "Dian, what are your wishes?" Dian, pausing as he was playing on his lute, while it was yet twanging, laid the instrument aside, and said, "My wishes are different from the cherished purposes of these three gentlemen." Said the Master, "What harm is there in that? Do you also, as well as they, speak out your wishes." Dian then said, "In this, the last month of spring, with the dress of the season all complete, along with five or six young men who have assumed the cap, and six or seven boys, I would wash in the Yi, enjoy the breeze among the rain altars, and return home singing." The Master heaved a sigh and said, "I give my approval to Dian." The three others having gone out, Zeng Xi remained behind, and said, "What do you think of the words of these three friends?" The Master replied, "They simply told each one his wishes." Xi pursued, "Master, why did you smile at You?" He was answered, "The management of a state demands the rules of propriety. His words were not humble; therefore I smiled at him." Xi again said, "But was it not a state which Qiu proposed for himself?" The reply was, "Yes; did you ever see a territory of sixty or seventy *li* or one of fifty or sixty, which was not a state?" Once more, Xi inquired, "And was it not a state which Chi proposed for himself?" The Master again replied, "Yes; who but princes have to do with ancestral temples, and with audiences but the sovereign? If Chi were to be a small assistant in these services, who could be a great one?"[4]

The *Mencius* records the words and deeds of the eponymous philosopher with verve and great oratorical power. As an example, we can cite the first part of the section "King Hui of Liang":

> Mencius went to see King Hui of Liang. The king said, "Venerable sir, since you have not counted it far to come here, a distance of a thousand *li*, may I presume that you are provided with counsels to profit my kingdom?" Mencius replied, "Why must Your Majesty use that word 'profit?' What I am provided with, are counsels to benevolence and righteousness, and these are my only topics. If Your Majesty says, 'What is to be done to profit my kingdom?' the great officers will say, 'What is to be done to profit our families?' and the inferior officers and the common people will say, 'What is to be done to profit our persons?' Superiors and inferiors will try to snatch this profit the one from the other, and the kingdom will be endangered. In the kingdom of ten thousand chariots, the murderer of his sovereign shall be the chief of a family of a thousand chariots. In the kingdom of ten thousand chariots, the murderer of his sovereign shall be the chief of a family of a thousand chariots. In the kingdom of a thousand chariots, the murderer of his prince shall be the chief of a family of a hundred chariots. To have a thousand in ten thousand, and a hundred in a thousand, cannot be said not to be a small gain. But if gain is put before righteousness, there will be no end to snatching. Without benevolence, kin will be discarded; without righteousness, the ruler will be discarded. Your Majesty should speak only of benevolence and righteousness. What necessity is there to speak of 'profit'?"[5]

This passage touches on an important question in Chinese philosophy – the distinction between righteousness and profit. Mencius maintains that the exclusive discussion of profit will lead to clashes, and eventually to war. Only by discussing righteousness, he insists, can the standards of proper conduct be ascertained, and only when man recognizes that righteousness is the basis of his existence, and is bound by it, can society be harmonious. In his discussion of this matter, Mencius is unequivocal, and his argument is forceful and clear. In this passage, the beginning of the book, Mencius' style of argument comes through loud and clear. Another example is the second part of the section "Gongsun Chou":

> Mencius said, "Opportunities of time vouchsafed by Heaven are not equal to advantages of situation afforded by Earth, and advantages of situation afforded by Earth are not equal to the union arising from the accord of Men. There is a city, with an inner wall of three *li* in circumference, and an outer wall of seven. The enemy surround and attack it, but they are not able to take it. Now, to surround and attack it, there must have been vouchsafed to them by Heaven the opportunity of time, and in such a case their not taking it is because opportunities of time vouchsafed by Heaven are not equal to advantages of situation afforded by Earth. There is a city, whose walls are

> distinguished for their height, and whose moats are distinguished for their depth, where the arms of its defenders, offensive and defensive, are distinguished for their strength and sharpness, and the stores of rice and other grain are very large. Yet it is obliged to be given up and abandoned. This is because advantages of situation afforded by Earth are not equal to the union arising from the accord of Men. In accordance with these principles it is said, 'A people is bounded, not by the limits of dykes and borders; a State is secured, not by the strengths of mountains and rivers; the kingdom is overawed, not by the sharpness and strength of arms.' He who finds the proper course has many to assist him. He who loses the proper course has few to assist him. When this – the being assisted by few – reaches its extreme point, his own relations revolt from the prince. When the being assisted by many reaches its highest point, the whole kingdom becomes obedient to the prince. When one to whom the whole kingdom is prepared to be obedient, attacks those from whom their own relations revolt, what must be the result? Therefore, the true ruler will prefer not to fight; but if he does fight, he must overcome."[6]

Opportunities of time vouchsafed by Heaven, advantages of situation afforded by Earth and the union arising from the accord of Men are the three conditions determining success or failure. Mencius lays special emphasis on the latter, on personal power tinged with humanism. This passage has a great deal of persuasiveness through the accumulation of its argument.

The *Zhuangzi*, a classic purportedly compiled by the philosopher of the same name, is rich in imagery, which is bold and immediate. Let us take a look at opening of the section of this book known by the title of "Enjoyment in Untroubled Ease":

> In the Northern Ocean there is a fish, the name of which is *Kun* – I do not know how many *li* in size. It changes into a bird with the name of *Peng*, the back of which is (also) – I do not know how many *li* in extent. When this bird rouses itself and flies, its wings are like clouds all round the sky. When the sea is moved (so as to bear it along), it prepares to remove to the Southern Ocean. The Southern Ocean is the Pool of Heaven. There is the (book called) *A Record of Marvels*, a record of marvels. We have in it these words: "When the *peng* is removing to the Southern Ocean it flaps (its wings) on the water for 3,000 *li*. Then it ascends on a whirlwind 90,000 *li*, and it rests only at the end of six months." (But similar to this is the movement of the breezes which we call) the horses of the fields, of the dust (which quivers in the sunbeams), and of living things as they are blown against one another by the air. Is its azure the proper color of the sky? Or is it occasioned by its distance and illimitable extent? If one were looking down (from above), the very same appearance would just meet one's view.[7]

Zhuangzi himself called his book *The Nineteen Parables* (*The Parables* for short). He included in his "parables" objects from the natural world, stories from social life and even outrageously fantastic stories to produce, as Liu Xizai puts it in his *Survey of the Arts*, "a surreal world of wonder from the tip of his writing brush." The unique artistic effect thus produced is one of rich imagination and gorgeous fantasy, a bold flight of fancy. For instance, the following famous passage from the chapter titled, "The Adjustment of Controversies": "Once, Zhuangzi dreamed that he was a butterfly. This butterfly, flitting around to its heart's content, did not know that it was actually Zhuangzi. Immediately after he awoke, with a pleasant feeling Zhuangzi could not decide whether he had been Zhuangzi dreaming that he was a butterfly or was a butterfly that was now dreaming that it was Zhuangzi. There was obviously a distinction between the two entities Zhuangzi and the butterfly. This is called metamorphosis." In the chapter "Horses' Hoofs," we read, "Horses can with their hoofs tread on the hoarfrost and snow, and with their hair withstand the wind and cold; they feed on the grass and drink water; they prance with their legs and leap: this is the true nature of horses. Though there were made for them grand towers and large dormitories, they would prefer not to use them. But when Bo-le (arose and) said, 'I know well how to manage horses,' (men proceeded) to singe and mark them, to clip their hair, to pare their hoofs, to halter their heads, to bridle them and hobble them, and to confine them in stables and corrals. (When subjected to this treatment), two or three in every ten of them died. (Men proceeded further) to subject them to hunger and thirst, to gallop them and race them, and to make them go together in regular order. In front were the evils of the bit and ornamented breast bands, and behind were the terrors of the whip and switch. (When so treated) more than half of them died." In the chapter "The Floods of Autumn," we read, "The time of the autumnal floods was come, and the hundred streams were all discharging themselves into the Yellow River. Its current was greatly swollen, so that across its channel from bank to bank one could not distinguish an ox from a horse. On this the God of the Yellow River laughed with delight, thinking that all the beauty of the world was to be found in his charge. Along the course of the river he walked east till he came to the North Sea, over which he looked, with his face to the east, without being able to see where its waters began. Then he began to turn his face round, looked across the expanse, (as if he were) confronting the God of the North Sea, and said with a sigh: 'What the vulgar saying expresses about him who has learned a hundred points (of the Dao), and thinks that there is no one equal to himself, was surely spoken of me. And moreover, I have heard parties making little of the knowledge of Zhongni and the righteousness of Boyi, and at first I did not believe them. Now I behold the all-but-boundless extent (of your realms). If I had not come to your gate, I should have been in danger (of continuing in my ignorance), and been laughed at for long in the schools of our great System.'"

Zhuangzi's prose has both persuasive and rhetorical vigor, infused with philosophical wisdom. For example, here is another passage from the chapter "The Floods of Autumn":

> Zhuangzi and Huizi were walking on the dam over the Hao, when the former said, "These fishes come out and play about at their ease – that is the enjoyment of fishes." The other said, "You are not a fish; how do you know

what constitutes the enjoyment of fishes?" Zhuangzi rejoined, "You are not I. How do you know that I do not know what constitutes the enjoyment of fishes?" Huizi said, "I am not you; and though indeed I do not fully know you, you certainly are not a fish, and (the argument) is complete against your knowing what constitutes the happiness of fishes." Zhuangzi replied, "Let us keep to your original question. You said to me, 'How do you know what constitutes the enjoyment of fishes?' You knew that I knew it, and yet you put your question to me – Well, I know it (from our enjoying ourselves together) over the Hao."[8]

The most famous prose writer of the Han Dynasty was Sima Qian. His father, Sima Tan, had preceded him as Grand Historian or Archivist. On his deathbed, he exhorted his son to complete the great work he had started. This Sima Qian did, finishing the *Official Records of the Grand Historian* (later shortened to the *Records of the Historian*), despite in the meantime suffering the physical and mental agony of being cast into prison and castrated, after being caught up in a court intrigue. In another work titled, "A Letter in Reply to Ren An," he explained his purpose in compiling this huge history of China from the most ancient times until his own day: "To investigate the connection between Heaven and Man through the changes occurring throughout history, and thereby form a coherent view of history." From this we can see that he was not content just to record events, but to draw from these the principles lying behind developments and changes. Pervading the whole work are Sima Qian's views of the cosmos and history.

The *Records of the Historian* is the first book to record China's historical tradition. In its incisive descriptions of personages and events, it also has great literary value. In its descriptions of personages the book shows a good grasp of their peculiarities of character. For example, the policymakers Su Qin and Zhang Yi are described differently – the former as having an above-board personality always striving for the success of his master, and the latter as a schemer and plotter. Also, the assassins Zhuan Zhu, Yu Rang, Nie Zheng and Jing Ke are all described as having distinct personalities. Some of the episodes in the book, including those found in the accounts of Xiang Yu, Lian Po and Lin Xiangru, and the prince of Wei, read like novels. An example is the following, from the "Biography of Xiang Yu" and known as "Songs of Chu All Around":

> Xiang Yu's army was entrenched at Gaixia. Their numbers were few and they were low on provisions. In addition, the army of Han Xin and his allies among the feudal lords surrounded it in a tight ring. One night, Xiang Yu heard on all sides folk songs of the Chu area, of which he was the nominal lord. Greatly alarmed, Xiang Yu exclaimed, "Has Han Xin overrun the whole of Chu then? How otherwise could he have so many men from Chu in his army?" He then spent the rest of the night in his tent drinking. His favorite concubine, who accompanied him everywhere, was called Yu, and his favorite steed, which carried him everywhere, was called Zhui. Xiang Yu composed the following dirge: "My power was once mightier than the mountains/ My authority once

> covered the earth/ Fate has turned against me/But Zhui remains faithful/ Zhui remains faithful, but to what avail?/And Yu, Oh Yu, what will become of you?" Tearfully he repeated this several times, accompanied by his concubine Yu. His attendants too wept, unable to raise their eyes to their master's face.[9]

The *Records of the Historian* has plenty of lyrical flavor, and powerful emotions often flow from Sima Qian's writing brush, giving this work something of the appeal of poetry. By way of illustration, let us glance at this scene of Jing Ke setting off from the State of Yan, from the "Biographies of Assassins":

> The heir to the throne [of the State of Yan] and his attendants, knowing full well that Jing Ke was going to his doom, dressed themselves in white mourning attire to bid him farewell. When they reached the River Yi and had sacrificed to the river god, Jing Ke sang a dirge to his companions, which reduced them all to tears. He then sang to them in the *zhi* mode the following: "The wind soughs and the water of the Yi is cold. Once I am gone I will be gone forever." He then switched to the mournful *yu* mode, and sang another dirge. His companions glared at him angrily, but Jing Ke simply mounted his chariot, and drove away without a backward glance.[10]

The emergence of parallel prose and its interaction with prose writing

The thought of the writers of the Wei (220–265) and Jin dynasties (265–420) was not confined within the boundaries of the Confucian classics; their works were marked by an unrestrained directness and a free and lively spirit. Cao Cao's "Seeking Worthy Men" is a piece which departs from the solemnity of similar works of the two Han dynasties, and in which the directness of the poet's thought is most clear. Cao Pi, in his "A Letter to the Zhaoge County Magistrate Wu Zhi" reminisces about a pleasant meeting with an old friend, sighs over today's parting, showing the writer's true nature and sincere feelings. Likewise, Cao Zhi, in his "A Reply to Wu Zhi," writes with fervor and verve. Zhuge Liang's "Memorial on Going to War" is a memorial to the emperor stating Zhuge Liang's intention to lead the Hanzhong garrison northward against Cao Cao's army of the Kingdom of Wei, and forwarded through Liu Shan. In this memorial, Zhuge Liang recommends Liu Shan as an official and general whom the court can rely on, and thereby shows his loyalty to the Shu ruler. In this memorial too, Zhuge Liang reveals his true personality, and its painstaking sincerity and meticulous choice of words make it a model of prose composition in its own right. Besides these, we might mention as outstandingly individual works Ji Kang's "A Letter of Parting to Shan Juyuan" for its merry laughs and angry curses, and pungent style, and Ruan Ji's "Biographies of Noblemen and Learned Elders," which, through the "noblemen and learned elders", subjects people who cling to etiquette to merciless criticism.

Tao Yuanming, who lived in the late years of the Eastern Jin Dynasty (317–420), was a splendid prose writer. His representative work in this respect is "The Story of Mr. Five Willows." It is a self-portrait handed down to later generations which describes the author as a free-and-easy person above worldly cares, merry and content, unfazed by poverty and devoting himself to cultivating the Way. The complete essay is as follows:

> This person's hometown is not known to us, and neither is his name. But since there are five willows beside his house we call him Mr. Five Willows. Calm and of few words, he has no hankering for fame and fortune. He loves reading, but does not strive for any deep meaning. However, when he gets deep into a book he sometimes even forgets his meals. He is also fond of wine, but this is a rare treat because he is poor. Knowing his situation, his relatives and friends sometimes invite him to drink with them. Every time he accepts such an invitation he will quaff to his heart's content, and only go home when he is good and drunk, without being fussy about etiquette. He lives in a shabby house, inadequate to shelter him from the wind or sun; his clothes are ragged; and he is short of cupboards and utensils. Nevertheless, his demeanor is tranquil and pleasant. He often writes for his own amusement, and to express his thoughts. Gaining or losing, he ignores all. In this way, he will live his whole life through.
>
> A eulogy of this person goes as follows: The wife of Qian Lou said, "Don't be anxious about poverty and humble status, and don't crave wealth and fame." Isn't this sound advice worthy to be a boon companion? All one needs for happiness is sweet wine and poetry. Isn't this the life of Mr No Care and Mr Embrace Heaven, and suchlike people?[11]

The whole piece consists of only 160 characters or so, but within this compass it manages to convey a complete picture of Mr Five Willows, making it a gem of prose writing.

Tao Yuanming's "The Story of Peach Blossom Valley" describes his ideal society. The inhabitants of Peach Blossom Valley are ordinary people, not immortals. There, there is no strife whatsoever, no king and no taxes. Life is lived in perfect harmony. This ideal of a utopia exerted a deep influence on later generations:

> In the time of Jin Taizhong, a man from Wuling, who was a fisherman by trade, was traveling along the edge of a creek, and forgot the distance of the route. He suddenly chanced upon a peach blossom forest; keeping by the shore he moved a hundred paces; inside there were no other trees, and the fragrant grasses were fresh and beautiful; the fallen leaves were a mix of colors, and the fisherman found it strange. He continued onwards, wanting to find the end of this forest. At the end of the forest and the creek, he came to a mountain. There was a small opening in the mountain, and it seemed like there was light, so he abandoned his boat and went in. At first it was extremely narrow, and could only just allow a person to pass. After several

dozen more paces, it suddenly opened up. The ground was flat and vast, and there were neatly arranged residences. There was fertile land, beautiful pools, mulberry trees and bamboo, and roads and paths for travel; chickens and dogs could be heard. Within were people working planting seeds, men and women were clothed in strange ways. They had yellow hair in long tufts, and seemed joyful and happy. They were surprised to see the fisherman, and asked where he had come from. He told them his story. They invited him to their homes, brought out wine, killed chickens and made a meal. Once it was noised in the village that this person was there, everybody came to ask him questions. They said: "A former generation fled the chaos in the time of the Qin Dynasty, bringing their wives, children and fellow-villagers to this remote spot. We have never left. And so we have been separated from outsiders." They asked what era it currently was. It turned out they hadn't even heard of the Han Dynasty, let alone the Wei or Jin dynasties. The fisherman was asked about all he knew, and everyone gasped. The other people all wanted to have him back to their homes, and all brought out wine and food. He stayed for several days, then made his goodbyes and left. The people there said: "It would not be good to tell others about us." Thereupon, he left, got into his boat, and returned the way he had come, leaving signs to mark the route. Upon reaching the county seat, he went to see the governor, and explained what had happened to him. The governor then sent people to follow his trail, searching for the signs he had left, but they could not find the way again. Liu Ziji of Nanyang, a renowned scholar, heard this tale and eagerly sought the "Peach Blossom Paradise," but to no avail; in fact, he fell ill and died on the quest. After that, nobody again tried to find it.[12]

The antithetical style of writing appeared in Chinese prose as early as in the pre-Qin period. In the Eastern Han Dynasty (25–220 AD) more attention was paid to this style, under the influence of *ci* and *fu* poetry. In the Wei and Jin dynasties a tendency to embellish prose writing with parallel sentences became rapidly more marked, as the first stage in the development of the fully fledged parallel prose style. This style, in contrast to ordinary prose in China, is marked by three peculiar features: The first is the emphasis on antithesis. Mostly in chunks of four to six lines, the antithetical pairs are likened to teams of horses, which is the meaning of the expression "parallel" or "teamed." The second has to do with euphony, the grouping of level and oblique tones. The third is the use of flowery and ornate language, and obscure allusions. It could be said that parallel prose is a kind of "poeticized" prose. Under the influence of the way of speaking of the Southern Dynasties (420–589) period the structure of parallel prose became tighter. At that time even prose used for ordinary writing was influenced by parallel prose; Liu Xie, in his work on literary theory *Carving a Dragon with a Literary Heart*, uses parallel prose. In his famous "Letter to Chen Bozhi," Qiu Chi of the Liang Dynasty urges Chen Bozhi, who has sought refuge in the territory of the Wei Dynasty, to return to Liang. As a result, Chen Bozhi does give himself up to the Liang ruler, bringing 8,000 soldiers with him. In this work, Qiu

Chi describes the magnificent scenery of their old home south of the Yangtze River in very moving terms:

> In the third month, in late spring, the grass is growing south of the River. The vegetation is sprouting and the trees are budding. Flocks of orioles fly hither and thither. To see the flags and hear the drums of our old homeland reminds us of times long gone. To strum the lyre and mount the city wall is to be overcome by nostalgia. It was only natural for Lian Po to pine for contributing to Zhao and for Wu Qi to weep at West River. Are you, General, alone without feeling?[13]

Some short pieces of parallel prose are particularly delicate and novel, such as Tao Hongjing's "A Letter to Xie Zhongshu":

> The beauty of the mountains and rivers here has been a topic of conversation among people since ancient times. The mountains were so high that they reached the clouds, while the water was so clear that light penetrated to the very bottom of the streams. On both sides of the river stood the precipices, their multiple colors enhancing one another's charm. Trees and bamboos remained verdant throughout the four seasons. Mischievous monkeys whooped while gorgeous birds sang before the fog dissipated in the morning. Fish that had swum deep in the water vied with one another leaping from its surface at sunset. The place proved to be a paradise on Earth. Since Xie Lingyun, however, this fascinating picture has disappeared.[14]

Also, Wu Jun's "Letter to Song Yuansi":

> After the wind spent itself and the mist vanished, the sky and mountains shared the same hue. Boats drifted with the current. Along the 100-*li* watercourse from Fuyang to Tonglu, the beauty of the mysterious water and crags was matchless under Heaven. The light on the surface of the water, which appeared light blue, penetrated a thousand feet down, revealing the swimming fish therein and the tiny pebbles beneath them. On the surface, the current flowed as fast as an arrow and the breaking waves pranced like galloping horses. The cliffs flanking the river were replete with hardy trees. As the terrain ascended, the mountains vied with one another in displaying their heights, thereby forming into hundreds of soaring peaks. Spring water slapped gurgling at the rocks. Singing in chorus, fascinating birds twittered in harmony. Cicadas never stopped their cries, while monkeys would not stop chattering. People pursuing their official careers like aspiring eagles would stop chasing fame at the sight of these captivating ridges. By the same token, those busy planning everyday affairs found it hard to tear themselves away from this tranquil beauty. The crisscrossing boughs of the trees blotted out the sky, making daybreak look like dusk. Occasionally the sun would peep through the gaps left by the branches.[15]

Famous prose works of the Northern Dynasties (386–581) include the *Commentary on the Waterways Classic* by Li Daoyuan and "Record of Luoyang's Buddhist Temple" by Yang Xuanzhi.

Classical and parallel prose from the Tang and Song dynasties on

The literary influence of the Southern Dynasties lingered on into the Sui Dynasty (AD 581–618) and early Tang Dynasty (618–907), including parallel prose. In particular, the two lines "A lone duck with the sunset clouds flies/The autumn river mirrors the blue sky." from Wang Bo's "Preface to the Teng Wang Pavilion" continued to be quoted long after the Tang Dynasty passed from the scene. A similarly famous piece was Luo Binwang's "An Official Denunciation of Wu Zhao Announced on Behalf of Xu Jingye."

The appearance of parallel prose enriched China's range of literary genres, and had a positive meaning for artistic expression. However, the tendency among parallel prose writers to overdo their search for fine diction was a drawback as far as writing style was concerned. This led to the rise of criticism as early as in the Southern and Northern Dynasties period, in works such as "On Scribblings" by Pei Ziye of the Liang Dynasty and *Mr. Yan's Family Admonitions * Writings* by Yan Zhitui of the Northern Qi Dynasty (550–577). In fact, all through the Sui and early Tang dynasties there were constant appeals for reform of the writing style, most notably in the "Letter to Emperor Gaozu of the Sui Dynasty About Reforming Belles-lettres by Li E." In the middle years of the Tang Dynasty, in concert with the rising tide of a Confucian trend of thought to return to the ancient ways, Han Yu and Liu Zongyuan vigorously advocated the classical style of writing and produced a number of excellent works. It was then that the whole face of the world of letters was transformed, leading most literary historians to dub this period one of a "classical movement." Han and Liu were adamant that literature and the way of morality should be fused. Han Yu said, "It is through one's words that one embraces the ancient morality"[16] and Liu Zongyuan said, "The purpose of literature is to burnish morality."[17] What they meant by morality was the orthodox Confucian doctrine of Confucius and Mencius. They strove to create a new type of literary diction completely within the boundaries of natural speech, and use it to form a new style of free-flowing prose.

Han Yu and Liu Zongyuan actually practised what they preached. Han Yu's "On Teachers" and "An Account Complementary to the Biography of Zhang Zhongcheng," and Liu Zongyuan's "Eight Records of Yongzhou" (eight accounts of scenic rambles) won universal acclaim.

Let us take a look at the middle section of Han Yu's "An Account Complementary to the Biography of Zhang Zhongcheng":

> When Nan Jiyun beseeched Helan Jinming to send troops to his rescue, the latter refused because he was jealous of Zhang Xun and Xu Yuan for their superior prestige and exploits. Although he would not listen to what Nan

> Jiyun had to say, Helan Jinming appreciated his courage and stoutheartedness, and therefore tried everything he could to urge him to stay. Asking him to sit down, Helan Jinming offered him a feast accompanied by musical performances. With indignation, Nan Jiyun said, "When I came here, the army and the people in Suiyang had been starving for more than a month. It is unethical for me to eat here. Even if I could place the food in my mouth, I would find it hard to shove it down my throat." Then he drew his sword out of its sheath, cut one of his fingers off, and showed it dripping with blood to Helan Jinming. Everyone present was at first stunned, and then moved to tears. Knowing that Helan Jinming had no intention whatsoever of sending reinforcements, Nan Jiyun galloped away. Before leaving the city, he shot an arrow at the Buddhist pagoda in the temple, half of its length penetrating the wall. He then vowed, "After I vanquish the rebels, I will come back to eliminate Helan Jinming. This arrow is a mark of my resolution."[18]

This piece of writing in the classical language flows naturally, and is a typical example of Han Yu's style. In the fourth part of his *Miscellaneous Discourses* he uses the metaphor of the "thousand-*li* horse" to describe a worthy and talented person. The wording is lucid and succinct:

> Only when there is Bo-le (a famous horse-trainer) can there be pedigree horses with the staying power of galloping a thousand miles in a day. The latter can emerge from time to time, but the appearance of the former is rare. Therefore, a very precious thoroughbred could suffer humiliation in the hands of a servant, having to die in a stable like ordinary horses, never to be known as a horse of great ability. A pedigree horse with the power to galloping a thousand miles a day can eat a hundred pounds of forage in a single meal. A groom normally does not know how to feed a horse in accordance with its capacity. Therefore, if such a horse is so starved that it lacks strength to bring its superb quality into full play, or if its capacity is unknown to the public, or if it cannot even be treated like an average horse, how can it be expected to gallop a thousand miles a day? Spurring it in the wrong way, feeding it without knowing how to make it perform, and hearing it neighing without understanding what it wants to say, one comes wielding a whip to it and complains, "What a pity that there are no good horses!" Alas, is it that there are no good horses in existence? I'm afraid that the truth is that people do not know how to identify them.[19]

In this extremely short piece there are three twists to the argument, which progresses with great impetus and reveals Han Yu's great mastery of words.

As an example of Liu Zongyuan's work, we can cite his "Account of Little Stone Pond":

> Sauntering a hundred and twenty steps or more to the west from the hillock, I heard water gurgling through a bamboo forest like jade pendants jingling,

which cheered me up. I hacked my way through the bamboo forest and, looking down, caught sight of a small pool with crystal-clear water in it. At its bottom there was a single piece of bedrock, which curled up at one side and jutted out of the water like an islet. Along with this "islet" were some rocks of smaller sizes or uneven surfaces. Lush trees and verdant vines covered and intertwined with each other, their branches of different lengths joining and swaying in the wind.

The hundred or so fish in the pool were swimming as if in the air without any medium of buoyancy. The sun shone directly through the water, and cast the shadows of the fish upon the bedrock at the bottom. For a time, the fish remained motionless. Then all of a sudden they shot to the far end, and shuttled back and forth briskly and nimbly, as if to tease the sightseers.

West of the hillock with the pool beneath it, the banks along the stream wound like the Big Dipper or a wriggling snake, part of it visible and part concealed. The serration of the banks made it hard to identify the source of the stream. While I was sitting by the pool in that serene environment where groves of bamboos and forests of trees were on all sides, a sense of loneliness crept upon me, sending a chill down my spine. The solitude and profoundness elicited a sentiment of desolate sadness, which eventually proved too much for me to bear. As a result, I decided not to linger, and left after making these notes.

Traveling with me were Wu Wuling, Gong Gu and my younger brother Zongxuan. Two other participants, namely, Shuji and Fengyi, tagged along.[20]

The title of this piece is "Account of Little Stone Pond,", but its references to the pond itself are confined to "The water is like frigid liquid" and "It tinkles like jade belt ornaments." The author devotes most of his description to the pond's surroundings above and below and to left and right – the surrounding bamboo groves, the variously shaped which make up the pond's floor and walls, its fish and spring source. The composition is minute but not trivial, and the wording is succinct and rich in implication. This is particularly evident in his contrast between the opaque fish and the translucent water; the flickering fish are set against the limpid water of the pond. In his technique of personification of the fish from stillness to movement, the author conveys his own feelings of joy.

Although Han Yu's advocacy of the classical language was influential in his time, he also contributed much to the transformation and development of parallel prose. Lu Zhi, a contemporary of Han Yu and Liu Zongyuan, was celebrated for his memorials to the emperor written in parallel prose in a simple and straightforward style. In addition, in the late Tang period there was Li Shangyin, who was good at writing public notices in parallel prose of four or six characters to the line. These soon became a model for public notices not only in his own time but in the Five Dynasties (907–960) period and the early part of the Northern Song Dynasty (960–1127). In the middle part of the latter dynasty Ouyang Xiu, Wang Anshi and Su Shi revived the classical language movement, solidifying the trend started by Han Yu and Liu Zongyuan. Fine works of this movement are Ouyang Xiu's "An

Account of the Old Toper's Pavilion," Wang Anshi's "A Reply to Sima Guang's Poem" and Su Shi's "Stone Bell Mountain."

"An Account of the Old Toper's Pavilion" was written when Ouyang Xiu had been demoted to become prefect of Chuzhou, having met with woe in the midst of happiness. The writing is temperate and refined, and a mixture of ordinary and parallel prose. The vocabulary he uses here is transcendently concise and penetrating, and the tone is flexible and musical. The first section describes the surroundings of Drunken Old Man Pavilion and how the structure got its name.

> Chuzhou is surrounded by mountains on all sides. With forests and a valley, the ridges to its southwest are particularly gorgeous. The peak that looms over it from a distance, thick with trees, is Mount Langya. Six or seven *li* up the mountain, the gurgling sound of water draws nearer. It is the Brewing Spring, with its water tumbling down into a gorge. The path winds through the mountain and leads to a pavilion high above the spring, its flying eaves tilting in the four directions like the open wings of a bird. That is the Old Toper's Pavilion. Who built it? It was a monk who lived on the mountain. His Buddhist name was Zhixian. Who named it? It was a county magistrate, who used his nickname. The magistrate had a party with some guests here. Unused to alcohol, he became inebriated after only a few cups. As he was the eldest of the group, he good-humoredly called himself an "old toper." The old toper's heart was not in the cup but in the beauty of the scenery. While the heart appreciated the beauty, the cup embodied the appreciation.

The final section describes how Ouyang Xiu and his companions reel home in tipsy ecstasy;

> Before long, the sun descended to the mountaintop, its fading light scattering the shadows of the partygoers, who followed the magistrate down the mountain. With their departure, the animals and birds in the thick forest reclaimed their territory with joy, singing and chattering. However, animals and birds knew only the bliss of Nature, but not people, who in turn enjoyed themselves without knowing what the magistrate was happy about. The one who could share his happiness with his companions in inebriety and jot the happy event down in sobriety was none other than the magistrate. Who was the magistrate? It was Ouyang Xiu of Luling.[21]

The 21 sentence-ending "也(*ye*)" in a total of only 22 sentences [in the whole piece] are what give it its flexible and musical effect.

Wang Anshi's prose diction is powerful and brisk. His "A Reply to Sima Guang's Poem" is addressed to Sima Guang, who had censured Wang Anshi for promoting a new style of writing, terming it "infringement on the domain of officialdom," "troublemaking," "aggressive," "resistant to criticism" and "offensive." All these charges Wang Anshi refutes in a most pointed way.

Su Shi's "Stone Bell Mountain" is a narrative of a night excursion to the mountain of that name. The description of the scenery and the atmosphere which sets it off is a unique accomplishment. Let us glance at a section of it:

> Dusk has fallen and the moon is bright. The sole passenger, I am steered by an aged boatman to the foot of a sheer cliff. The sort of spine-chilling place where wild beasts and goblins are ready to pounce on men. Startled by human voices, the fierce birds which nest on the cliff whirl in the night sky. They croak like an old man coughing or chortling in a valley. Assured that they are only harmless myna birds, I am relieved, and suggest returning. I give a loud shout over the water. The echoes roll on and on, like those of bells or drums, startling the boatman.[22]

Su Shi's "Recalling a Night Excursion to Chengtian Temple" contains no more than 80 characters, but its lyrical description of scenery reaches the realm of fairyland:

> On the evening of the 12th day of the 10th month of the sixth year of the Yuanfeng reign period (1083) I disrobed and laid down to sleep. But as the moonlight came streaming in, I contentedly arose. Reflecting that I had no one to share my joy with, I set off for Chengtian Temple to seek Zhang Huaimin. I found that he too had been unable to sleep, and we paced the temple courtyard together. At the bottom of the courtyard was a pond, its water transparent in the moon beams. In the water could clearly be seen the tangled weeds and the reflections of the surrounding bamboos and willows. What night has no moon? What place has no bamboos and willows? But there were few companions in leisure like we two.[23]

In his essays Su Shi extols Nature, and he is not limited to one way of doing so: "Like floating clouds or flowing water, there is no fixed starting point. He goes where he can go, and he stops where he has to stop. His writing is coherent and natural, and full of pleasant surprises."[24] This is amply expressed in his prose style.

In the three dynasties of the Yuan, Ming and Qing, drama and the novel flourished, but poetry and the other orthodox genres of literature, while they registered some successes, never reached the heights they had reached during the Tang and Song dynasties. Parallel prose in the four- and six-character form was confined to bureaucratic notices and records, as a sort of ossified officialese. The parallel prose used as the format for the "eight-legged essay" employed in the Qing Dynasty (1644–1911) civil service examinations was a special form of this genre, and because its restrictions on the expression of human thought were very rigid, even at its best it cannot be included in the sphere of great literature.

In the field of prose creation, in the Ming Dynasty (1368–1644) seven notables emerged one after the other advocating a return to the styles used in the

Qin and Han dynasties. The "Tang and Song school," including Gui Youguang and Wang Shen, held aloft the classical language of those dynasties. Meanwhile, the "Gong'an School," represented by Yuan Hongdao, extolled the expression of human emotions, and the individualistic thoughts and feelings of writers, and were opposed to what they called slavish copying or imitation of classical writing. Famous works from the Ming period include "Words of a Tangerine Seller" by Liu Ji, "Burial in a Remote Land" by Wang Shouren, "Reply to Liu Yizhang" by Zong Chen, "Record of Xiangji Studio" by Gui Youguang, "Biography of Xu Wenchang" by Yuan Hongdao and "Stele Inscription for Five People" by Zhang Pu. Particularly worthy of attention are the short sketches of the late Ming period, many of which are refreshingly novel, and represent a new direction in late Ming prose. A major characteristic of such works is their down-to-earth individuality, giving expression to the interests of an ordinary individual's life. An example is Yuan Hongdao's short account of his trip to Mount Tianmu:

> For the previous few days rain had been falling, casting a pall of gloom over us. As we approached Shuangqing Village at the foot of the mountain, it stopped. The monks there asked us to stay the night. The room was exquisite, but the gurgling of mountain streams tumbling over rocks could be heard throughout the night. Shi Kui mistook the sound for the pattering of rain. Extremely annoyed, he could not get to sleep. The next morning the monks sent us the breakfast and tea they had prepared, and tried to wake Shi Kui up. With a sigh, Shi Kui complained, "Where can I go in this heavy rain? My only choice is to enjoy the scenery by dreaming of it lying in bed." The monks said, "The sky is clear, the wind is mild and the sun is bright. What you heard last night was but the sound of the stream, not of the rain!" At this, Shi Kui burst into a guffaw. He got up and threw on his clothes. After gulping down few cups of tea, Shi Kui and I departed on our trip to Mount Tianmu.[25]

Of particular interest here are expressions such as "The sound of the stream reached my pillow" (I heard the stream in my sleep) and "The foolish expression on the basket." Another example is Tu Long's "With Friends in the Capital":

> Riding on my yellow horse and wearing my cloak with a masked hood, I galloped along the streets of the capital Chang'an through the dusty sand swept up by the wind. When I returned and alighted from my horse, I found my nostrils as black as soot. When it was dry, human feces and animal dung blended with the dirt on the road. When it was rainy, the streets would be flooded with muddy water reaching to the knees and even the saddles. Common people jostled officials in the streets, as the former vied with one another in spurring their donkeys onward. The announcement of a high-ranking official's arrival sent the crowd bustling into the alleys. They scurried so madly that sweat dripped down to their heels. Those were the sights and smells of the capital. I recalled my small village by the Yangtze River, where boats returning from fishing were being moored, after glow was reflected upon the forests, beach

> sand appeared as white as snow, and fishnets were being air-dried beneath flowering shrubs. A tavern fitted with unpainted door panels and draped with black curtains stood in the shadow of some willow trees. Elderly men walked out of their thatched huts, fish and wine jars in hand. Sauntering with three or five friends on the beach at a moment like this is far better than charging on horseback in the muddy streets of Chang'an.[26]

The writer uses a variety of details to contrast the different moods of life in the city and in the countryside, to express the general emotions of everyday life in a way that transcends the words themselves.

Zhang was an accomplished writer of short sketches in the late Ming Dynasty. His "Gazing on the Snow from a Pavilion in a Lake" has received much praise:

> Snow had been falling heavily for days. Neither people nor birds could be heard in the lake area. Around eight o'clock that evening I paddled a small boat alone to the pavilion in the lake to enjoy the sight of the snow, wearing a fur coat and taking with me a small charcoal stove for heating. The air was filled with flying snowflakes. Everything looked white: the sky, the clouds, the mountains and the water. What was visible were but a trace of the causeway, the outline of the pavilion, my boat (which looked as small as a leaf) and two or three silhouettes in the park.[27]

The composition and language of Zhang Dai's "At West Lake on the 15th Day of the 7th Month" are both notably fresh, and are imbued with the author's lofty and refined sentiments. The piece starts off with "Mid-autumn at West Lake. Nothing worth looking at except for the people of mid-autumn. The people of mid-autumn – I can make out five kinds." He then goes on to describe these five kinds of people one by one. In the final part, he writes about himself:

> We had managed to pull our boat to the lakeshore. The flagstones by the Broken Bridge were cooling off. I set lavish dishes upon them, and invited the guests to drink to their heart's content. The moon looked as clear and bright as a newly polished bronze mirror. The mountains had changed their makeup and the lake had cleaned its face. Those who had been sipping and crooning now emerged. So did those who had been obscure in the tree shadows. We went up to greet them, and asked them to sit with us. Joined by literati friends and famed courtesans, the party reached its climax, utensils clinking and instrumental and vocal music shrilling. The guests did not scatter until the moonlight dimmed and gray dawn broke. Having maneuvered our boat into the ten-mile lake of lotus flowers, we fell into a sound sleep, enjoying our pleasant dreams amidst the caressing perfume of the flowers.[28]

The prose writers of the early Qing Dynasty include Hou Fangyu, Wei Xi and Wang Wan. The first of these was an inheritor of the Tang and Song classical language tradition, and his meticulous devotion to this tradition was very influential.

A leading school of prose writing in the Qing Dynasty was the Tongcheng School, the chief proponents of which were Fang Bao, Liu Dakui and Yao Nai. They all came from Tong City in Anhui Province, hence the name of their school of writing. Fang Bao emphasized "justice," Liu Dakui "spirit," essence" and "syllables," and Yao Nai "reasoning," "textual research" and "implied meaning." The lineage of their school reached back to Han Yu of the Tang and Song tradition. The content of their works extolled the orthodox feudal world-outlook, especially as embodied in the Neo-Confucian works of the Cheng-Zhu school (as taught by Cheng Yi, Cheng Hao and Zhu Xi). As far as form is concerned, these writers strove to establish a set of rules for artistic creation, and advocated a clear connection between writing and scholarship. The influence of the Tongcheng School lasted down to the end of the Qing Dynasty. Famous works of this school are Fang Bao's "Miscellaneous Notes Made in Prison" and Yao Nai's "Climbing Mount Tai." Fang Bao's work records his experiences of prison life after he was incarcerated due to his involvement in a famous court case. The following extract from it is profoundly moving:

> Before a condemned convict was put to death, the executioner would wait outside the door and send his partner in to demand money or other valuables – bribes known as "siluo." If the convict came from a rich family, the executioner would negotiate a bribe with his family members. If not, it would be a face-to-face deal with the convict. In the case of death by dismembering the body, the negotiator would say, "If you meet our demand, we'll thrust our knife into the heart first. If not, we'll cut the other parts of the body before the heart is dead." In the case of death by hanging, the negotiator would say, "If you meet our demand, we'll make sure that death comes at the first strangle. If not, it will take three strangles in addition to tortures with various instruments before death comes."[29]

The following is a particularly splendid extract, describing the sunrise, from "Climbing Mount Tai":

> At the end of a month in 1788, the fifth stroke of the drum told us that gray dawn had arrived. Ziying and I were waiting to see the sunrise from the Sun-viewing Pavilion. Sharp gusts of wind scooped snow from drifts and threw their flakes upon our faces. East of the pavilion, misty clouds filled the space from the foot of the mountain to where it stood. A few dozen white specks faintly visible among the clouds proved to be mountain peaks. The thread-like cloud on the horizon soon presented itself in multiple hues. Then the sun rose as red as vermilion, with a vibrating crimson light. Someone said, "There's the East Sea!" Looking back at the peaks west of the Sun-viewing Pavilion, I saw that some of them were in sunshine while others not; some red, and others white. Clad in mixed colors, they all looked as if they were bowing to the sun in awe.[30]

A major figure in Qing Dynasty parallel prose is Wang Zhong, whose description of the tragic destruction of a salt barge by fire at Yangzhou in his "Mourning for a Salt Barge" is poignantly and most excellently worded: "This ill-fated boat could hold no more than 130 people, but some 1,400 souls were burned to death or drowned."[31] Hang Shijun praised it as "a soul-stirring description, in which every single character values a thousand pieces of gold."

A leading modern prose writer who displayed rich creativity was Liang Qichao. His technique was called by the many people who learned from it a "new style of writing." This style was unassuming and flowing. In the large number of essays he contributed to publications he mixed slang words and even foreign terms – He let his pen go where it would, and the effect was one of great power. His "Young China," "Hope" and "The New People," among other essays, opened his readers' ears and eyes to a new form of self-expression.

Notes

1 *The Collected Works of Guo Moruo*, Archeology Section, Vol.2, *Interpretation of the Oracle Bone Inscriptions*, Science Press Ltd., 1983, P. 369.
2 *Zuo Zhuan * Second Year of Duke Cheng, Commentary on the Thirteen Classics*, World Bookstore photocopy of the Ruan woodblock print, P. 1894.
3 [Song Dynasty] Biao, Bao: *The Annotated Intrigues of the States*, Vol.4 "The State of Qi," *Collected Writings of the Four Basic Branches of Literature*.
4 *Commentary on the Thirteen Classics*, World Bookstore photocopy of the Ruan woodblock print, P. 2500.
5 *Commentary on the Thirteen Classics*, World Bookstore photocopy of the Ruan woodblock print, P. 2655.
6 *Commentary on the Thirteen Classics*, World Bookstore photocopy of the Ruan woodblock print, P. 2693.
7 [Qing Dynasty] Qingfan, Guo: *Collected Works of Zhuangzi Interpreted, Collected Works of the Philosophers*, Vol.3, Shanghai Bookstore, 1991, PP. 1–4.
8 [Qing Dynasty] Qingfan, Guo: *Collected Works of Zhuangzi Interpreted, Collected Works of the Philosophers*, Vol.3, Shanghai Bookstore, 1991, PP. 267–268.
9 [Han Dynasty] Qian, Sima: *Records of the Historian*, Vol.7, *Biography of Xiang Yu*, Zhonghua Book Company, 1959, P. 333.
10 [Han Dynasty] Qian, Sima: *Records of the Historian*, Vol.86, Zhonghua Book Company, 1959, P. 2534.
11 Xingpei, Yuan: *Collected Works of Tao Yuanming Annotated*, Zhonghua Book Company, 2003, P. 502.
12 Xingpei, Yuan: *Collected Works of Tao Yuanming Annotated*, Zhonghua Book Company, 2003, Pp. 479–480.
13 [Tang Dynasty] Shan, Li. and Yanji, Lv: *Selection of the Major Writings of Six Officials*, Vol.43, *Collected Writings of the Four Basic Branches of Literature*.
14 [Tang Dynasty] Xun, Ouyang: *Comprehensive Categories of Art and Literature*, Vol.37, Shanghai Ancient Books Publishing House, 1982, P. 669.
15 [Tang Dynasty] Xun, Ouyang: *Comprehensive Categories of Art and Literature*, Vol.7, Shanghai Ancient Books Publishing House, 1982, PP. 129–130

16 [Tang Dynasty] Yu, Han: "Follow-up Elegy for Ouyang Zhan," Ma Qichang's, *Collected Works of Han Changli Collated With Notes*, Vol.5, Classical Literature Publishing House, 1957, P. 178.
17 [Tang Dynasty] Zongyuan, Liu: "A Letter in Reply to Wei Zhongli's on the Principles of Being a Teacher," *Collected Works of Liu Zongyuan*, Vol.34, Zhonghua Book Company, 1979, P. 873.
18 *The Collected Works of Han Changli Annotated by Zhu Wengong*, Vol.13, *Collected Writings of the Four Basic Branches of Literature*.
19 *The Collected Works of Han Changli Annotated by Zhu Wengong*, Vol.11, *Collected Writings of the Four Basic Branches of Literature*.
20 [Tang Dynasty] Zongyuan, Liu: "Account of Going to the Little Stone Pond West of a Hill," *Collected Works of Liu Zongyuan*, Vol.29, Zhonghua Book Company, 1979, P. 767.
21 [Song Dynasty] Xiu, Ouyang: *Collected Literary Works of Ouyang Xiu*, Vol.39, *Collected Writings of the Four Basic Branches of Literature*.
22 [Song Dynasty] Shi, Su: *Collected Works of Su Dongpo with a Short Biography*, Vol.49, *Collected Writings of the Four Basic Branches of Literature*.
23 [Song Dynasty] Shi, Su: *The Collected Works of Su Dongpo*, Vol.101, *The Complete Four Repositories*, Pavilion of the Imperial Library
24 [Song Dynasty] Shi, Su: *Collected Works of Su Dongpo with a Short Biography*, Vol.49, *Collected Writings of the Four Basic Branches of Literature*.
25 *The Complete Works of Yuan Zhonglang*, Vol.9, Taibei Weiwen Publishing House Ltd., 1976.
26 *Prose Works Selected by Genre*, Vol.265, *The Complete Four Repositories*, Pavilion of the Imperial Library.
27 *The Reminiscences of Tao'an*, Vol.3, Nanhai the Ren's woodblock print, 1852.
28 *The Reminiscences of Tao'an*, Vol.7, Nanhai the Ren's woodblock print, 1852.
29 [Qing Dynasty] Bao, Fang: *The Collected Works of Mr Fang Wangxi * Extra Writings*, Vol.6, *Collected Writings of the Four Basic Branches of Literature*.
30 [Qing Dynasty] Nai, Yao: *Collected Poems and Prose of Xibao Studio * Prose Collection*, Vol.14, *Collected Writings of the Four Basic Branches of Literature*.
31 [Qing Dynasty] Zhong, Wang: "Theories on Learning * Different Records, 'Biographical Sketches,'" Wang Xingzhi, *Collected Writings of the Four Basic Branches of Literature*.

16 The structure and style of writings

The structure and style of prose

Prose is structured using self-contained sentences; it seeks no parallel forms, and eschews rhyme. In fact, it is close to natural speech. However, because speech changes relatively quickly, speech which is written down tends to become conservative and standardized compared to the spoken word. The works of the literary masters of a previous generation then become the models, and so the language of prose shows the phenomenon of being anchored in a form that has departed from the spoken one, and as time passes this disjuncture becomes more pronounced.

The contents of Chinese prose are variegated, so much so that it is often difficult to draw a line of demarcation between what is a work of literature and what is not. Not everything that appears in writing, of course, should be considered of literary value, but Zhuge Liang's "Memorial on Going to War" must be so considered. Therefore, a written work cannot be judged merely on its title and content as to whether it is prose with literary merit or not. Other factors must be taken into account, and in this connection I have singled out four:

1 Imaginative power. This is a quality that both poetry and prose must have. If a written work displays an abundance of imaginative power, then it is of literary significance. Particularly rich in this respect are Ji Kang's "A Letter of Parting to Shan Juyuan," Han Yu's "Elegiac Address for Liu Zihou" and Fan Zhongyan's "Records of Yueyang Tower." All these "descriptions of solitary feelings" sketches from the late Ming Dynasty are endowed with imaginative power.
2 Elegant diction. This expression comes from a sentence in the "Preface to the Selected Works of Literature": "Matter comes from deep thought, meaning from elegant diction." This is the yardstick Xiao Tong used to judge whether or not a piece of writing was qualified to be included in his *Choice*. Although other considerations may be taken into account, "elegant diction" is definitely one of the standards for judging prose and literary works as a whole. "Elegant diction" refers to the expressive power of words, transcending mere rhetorical tricks. We could say that the most important standard by which to decide whether a piece of prose is literature or not is the level of elegance of its diction.

3 The style of the historians. Zuo Qiuming's *Zuo Zhuan* and Sima Qian's *Records of the Historian* are indeed works of history; nonetheless, their style of writing, called "the style of the historians," is outstanding, to the extent that these works can be regarded as gems of literature. In the pre-Qin and Han period there was no clear cut distinction between literature, history and philosophy, and the literary value of some historical works deserves attention.
4 Discussion. The prose writings of the pre-Qin masters were all discursive. From the Han Dynasty onward, such writings were all considered works of literature. Examples are Jia Yi's "The Ten Crimes of Qin" and Han Yu's "Inquiry into the Origin of Slanders."

Each prose writer of ancient China had his own style, and it is difficult to lump them all together under any single criterion. However, if we compare these works with parallel prose works we can discern common points of style: They all pursued graceful diction (for instance, ordered words and sentences, antithetical arrangement, harmonious changes of tone and sound, and fine choice of words), but they are all still less-adorned than parallel prose works. Even so, prose still has its "rules," which dictate that the natural cadence of words be adhered to and that they be arranged in a proper way, as encapsulated in the formula "A piece of literature depends on words expressing their proper meaning."[1] To qualify as a composition, moreover, a piece of writing must have balance, with what follows logically meshing with what went before.

Basically, each type of prose has its own prose style: Discursive prose tends to stress a trenchant, deep-going, clearly expressed and original style. It often uses allegory to strengthen its message. Narrative prose tends to stress clarity, with a clear-cut succession of description from beginning to end, creating tension. Lyric poetry strives to express emotions in a genuine way, and landscape prose seeks to express the interchange of emotions and scenery.

The structure and style of parallel prose

The structure of parallel prose shows the following main features:

1 Antithesis. The chief characteristic of parallel prose is the matching of corresponding sentences that echo each other. In early parallel prose this principle was not strictly adhered to; it was sufficient for the first and second sentences to say much the same thing, and the use of the same words in each was not always avoided. Later, the format of parallel prose became much stricter, and the skill in writing it matured. There arose four types of antithesis: that of words, that of things (human affairs and allusions from the classics), that of alikes and that of opposites. There was also "artificial" or "false" antithesis, which contrasted words with similar pronunciations or shapes. The following example is from Shen Yue's "Epitaph on the Tombstone of Minister of Education Xie Fei": "Attached to this heavenly noble (a pun on the word for 'sparrow')/Is the fragrance of a dragon among men."[2]

2 The antithetical sentences are of four or six characters each. Before the Tang and Song period, five- and seven-character lines were often used, but later this crystallized to four- and six-character lines. For instance: "In autumn what moon is not bright; what autumn is not brightened by the moon?" ("*Fu* Poem on the Autumn Thoughts of a Lovesick Wife" by Xiao Yi, Emperor Yuan of Liang [reign: 552–555]), "Fallen leaves cover half the bed; dancing flowers fill the room" ("*Fu* Poem on Little Courtyard" by Yu Xin) and "The fishermen's evening song fills the banks of Peng Li; the cry of the geese startles the chilly bay of Hengyang" ("Preface to the Teng Wang Pavilion" by Wang Bo).

3 Attention to sound. This concern was gradually strengthened following the period of the Qi and Liang dynasties of the Northern and Southern Dynasties period. Its general outline was similar to that of regulated verse. There were rules, of course, but they were not always strictly followed. For instance, the following can be quoted from "A Letter to Xiao Linchuan" by Xiao Gang, Emperor Jianwen (reign: 550–552) of the Liang Dynasty: "Squally showers herald the end of autumn. The riverside maples wilt at dawn. The leaves of the forest are turning sere."

4 The use of elegant words and classical allusions. Prose writers tend to be fond of verbal ornamentation and allusion. This is especially true of the writers of parallel prose, because this form of composition depends heavily on antithesis and sound effects, and so the result is a particularly ingenious working of such elegant words and classical allusions. For instance, when King Teng (named Di, King Wen of Zhou's thirteenth son) gave Yu Xin a fine horse, Yu Xin wrote to thank him. In the letter, he says. "The willows in the valley have not yet bloomed. The purple swallows flit to and fro. The Ling Rill flows ever onward. Suddenly peach blossoms come into view."[3] Ni Fan quotes *In Search of Spirits* as saying, "Willow Valley stretches open its arms from its rocky entrance. In this piece of writing there are five horses, symbolizing the changeover from the Wei Dynasty to the Jin Dynasty." In *Miscellaneous Records of the Western Capital*, we find, "King Wen had a purple steed from the State of Yan" [Yan can also mean "swallow"]. The next two lines are allusions to Tao Yuanming's famous story titled "The Story of Peach Blossom Valley": "There was a man from Wuling who earned his living by fishing. Suddenly he came across Peach Blossom Forest." The *Erya (Approaching Elegance)* says, "A horse with a coat of mixed yellow and white colors." Guo Pu notes, "A Peach Blossom horse for modern times." It seems that Peach Blossom was also the name of the horse. The four lines resonate: In the first two lines Peach Blossoms brings to mind Ling Rill, and in the second two lines Willow Valley does the same for Purple Swallows. Put simply, Yu Xin's meaning is, "I have never been to Willow Valley but I have seen the Purple Swallows. I have never been to Peach Blossom Spring but I have seen Peach Blossom – a horse worthy to be a royal gift." This is elegant diction and allusion refined by Yu Xin to produce something surpassingly beautiful.

The structure of parallel prose ensures that it is symmetrical, sonorous, attractive and tasteful.

Interim summary

Some of the writings produced in China in the old days would not be included in the sphere of what we would call pure literature nowadays, such things as stele inscriptions, court petitions, etc. Nevertheless, since they come within the purview of the characteristics we assign to Chinese literature itself we have to regard them as literature. The study of Chinese literature necessarily entails the study of all of its prose writings; to simply focus on poetry, drama and the novel would mean failure to unfold the whole picture of Chinese literature.

If we look at the diction used in Chinese literary works, we find that the plainness of the words used to compose essays is one of the foundation stones of the techniques of writing other genres. The wording of the novel is closest to that of the essay, and that of the *shi* and *fu* poems and of the *ci* and *qu* verses is the farthest removed from that of the essay. And the linguistic accomplishments of all these genres are displayed in these very differences.

Notes

1 *The Collected Works of Han Changli Annotated by Zhu Wengong* * *Preface, Collected Writings of the Four Basic Branches of Literature.*
2 [Tang Dynasty] Xiu, Ouyang: *Comprehensive Categories of Art and Literature*, Wang Shaoying ed, Shanghai Ancient Books Publishing House, 1965, P. 837.
3 [Northern Zhou Dynasty] Xin, Yu: "Begging to Express Gratitude to King Teng for his Gift of a Horse," *Annotated Collection of Yu Zishan's Works*, Vol.8, Zhonghua Book Company, 1980, P. 585.

Further discussion

Literature is like an organic entity: Its lifetime involves endless changes, developments and improvements – and once it becomes ossified it loses its life force. These changes, developments and improvements follow one of two paths. One involves the artistic characteristics of one literary genre seeping into and drawing from another, and producing a work of an entirely new nature. Classic examples of this process are the transformations of *shi* and *fu* poetry into *ci* poetry. The other path involves a return of content to old forms to produce a movement for innovation. Chen Zi'ang and Han Yu both followed this path. The reason for Chinese literature continuing in an unbroken stream generation after generation for 3,000 years lies in its constant development – from the *sao* poetry of pre-Qin times down through the *fu* poetry of the Han Dynasty, the parallel prose of the Southern Dynasties, Tang *shi* poetry, Song *ci* poetry, Yuan drama and the novels of the Ming and Qing dynasties. However, prior to the Opium Wars of the mid-19th century, China was a closed-off agricultural country the size of a continent, and its literature, in the later part of the Qing Dynasty, found itself, after 3,000 years of constant changes, unable to produce any fresh development. After the New Literature Movement of May 4, 1919, Western literature flowed like a river into this ancient country. The Chinese literary tradition had no choice but to receive a "transfusion" of Western literature. Chinese literature had to change its old forms, and this, in short, has been the trend of Chinese literature since May 4. This trend is likely to continue. While planting our feet firmly on the land of China, we must cultivate the fertile soil of the Chinese literary tradition and at the same time draw nourishment from the literatures of other peoples to nurture more literary blooms. In fact, since the May 4th Movement there has been a great change in the structure and style of Chinese literature. Based on comparisons between the modern novel and the traditional classical-language novel and the colloquial *zhanghuiti* novel, as well as between modern drama and traditional opera, we can see that after the May 4th Movement a great change has taken place in terms of structure and style. An important conclusion for us to draw is that by discarding our literary tradition completely our literature will have no root, while it will make no progress if we refuse to learn from the fine points of foreign literatures. Of China's traditional literary genres, those of *fu* poetry and parallel prose have withered and it would be hopeless to try to revive them. As for *ci* and *sanqu* verses, it was hoped at one time that new music and forms of presentation would spark a revival, but since the May 4th Movement poets have not paid much attention to creativity in these fields. Much more creativity is needed in the sphere of song lyrics in general. The novel is the genre in which the greatest achievements have been made since May 4. Moreover, the novel has tended to preserve the traditional style compared with other genres. It is the most vigorous field of modern Chinese literature, and great hopes are pinned on it producing breakthrough achievements. Another genre giving rise to optimism is that of essay writing, which has, comparatively speaking preserved its traditional features while adapting its creativity to writing in the modern colloquial language. China has always been a "land of poetry." It has a rich legacy of poetry, but unfortunately since May 4 new poetry writing in China has been in forms completely transplanted from the West, and traditional forms have been virtually discarded, unable to strike firm roots among the general readership. This is the most disappointing field of Chinese literature in modern times, but I am firmly convinced that there is hope for a revival in China, the "land of poetry."

If Chinese literature is to become one of the world's great literatures it must base itself firmly on the reality of reform, learning from the fine points of other countries' literature and art while at the same time fully displaying China's own national characteristics. This is the conclusion drawn from this *Outline of Chinese Literature.*

Afterword to the first Chinese edition

The manuscript of this book was submitted to the Hong Kong branch of the Sanlian Bookshop in October last year (1987), and at the beginning of this year (1988), the copyright was sold by Sanlian Bookshop to Taiwan Wu-Nan Book Company Ltd. In September 1988 the book was published in Taiwan, and a Hong Kong edition was expected shortly. It is reported that the book, not long after publication, was chosen as a textbook by several universities in Taiwan. A Japanese-language edition is planned. This has all been very gratifying to the author, but even more pleasing is the kind agreement of the Higher Education Press to make the book available to the general reader.

Looking back at when I first took up the task, I remember that I was far from confident that I could accomplish it. Keeping in mind the fact that no such book as this had been written in the previous 40 years, I could only rely on my own meager understanding of the subject as I strove to forge a *systematic Outline*. The *Outline* I came up with was different from the standard histories and introductions to Chinese literature, as it was to encompass every aspect and complete course of development of Chinese literature. Also, it had to explain in clear and concise language the theoretical aspects of the subject. It was difficult indeed to complete such a task equipped with only my own limited knowledge. In the course of writing this book I had to keep reminding myself that I was to write from an individual perspective, marked by individual characteristics; I was not setting out to write a general introduction to Chinese literature. And this only added to the difficulties. Now, when I presume to glance over this book with the eye of the general reader I can't avoid feeling a sort of inexpressible regret. However, I do not feel any compulsion to embark on a hasty revision, as only 14 months has passed since the manuscript left my hands, and no revision at this stage would lead to any great improvement. It would perhaps be better to wait until later for revision.

Here the author would like to tender his warmhearted thanks to all the scholars in both China and Japan who have shown interest in this book from the time of writing to its publication, as well as to all the people of publishing circles for their support!

Yuan Xingpei
November 3, 1988

Afterword to the second Chinese edition

In 1987 I was invited to lecture on Chinese literature at Japan's Aichi University. Not long afterwards my lecture notes were published separately by Hong Kong's Sanlian Bookshop, Taiwan Wu-Nan Book Company Ltd. and the mainland's Higher Education Press.

This book has been warmly received by a large number of readers, not only on China's mainland, but in Hong Kong and Taiwan too. It has also been chosen as a textbook for use in several high schools. Last year the Higher Education Press expressed the hope that I would arrange for a revised and enlarged edition of the book. I thought that this was a good suggestion, and I have now finished working on this second edition. I have kept the original format and framework and the points of view which pervade the text, but I have readjusted some of the sections, fleshed out many of the contents and improved the wording in not a few places. Since the first edition came out there has been a great development in the study of Chinese literature, and many of the problems raised in the first edition – such as those of the territorial background to Chinese literature, its types, the evolution of literary works and the characteristics of style, the interactions between different types of writing and some of the rules dictating the course of development of Chinese literature – have all received attention to various degrees from the academic community.

There is one more point which I should bring to the attention of the readers: This book was written from a highly individualistic point of view. Based on my own appreciation as a reader of the works of ancient literature, I have striven to express in simple language the depth of my various related impressions, especially to convey the aspects of such writings that moved me, in the hope that the readers can share my emotions. Since this book is an "outline" of Chinese literature it covers literary works and the aspects of literature that move people, as well as the aesthetic values therein. And because it is an "outline" it is not meant to be, nor is there any need for it to be exhaustive. Moreover, it is not overloaded with discussions; many of the points of view are the author's own. I have concentrated on piquing the reader's curiosity, and this endeavor too is in itself a form of academic pursuit.

In the Afterword to the first edition I expressed my thanks to both scholars and people of publishing circles involved in the work. Since its publication I have received many messages of encouragement from readers, and Mr. Luo Zongqiang and Mr. Lin Donghai have been kind enough to write positive reviews. Not long ago, I happened to read a book review by a scholar I am unacquainted with which recommended my book and he later sent me a very encouraging letter. I heartily thank Mr. Cheng Qianfan. Generally speaking, personal letters usually contain no more than polite cliches, but Mr. Cheng's "The *Outline* is no ordinary work. In fact, it probes into the very marrow of its subjects. Eminent scholars will agree with me" (See *Correspondence from the Leisurely Hall*), I am convinced, is no mere lip-service. It has been scholars of the senior and present generations and the general body of readers who have given me the confidence to expand and revise this work which I completed over ten years ago. I wish to take this opportunity to express once more my sincere gratitude to them all!

Back in 1987, when I wrote the manuscript for this book, I used to rise at 4 a.m. every day, and work on it for over ten hours. I would churn out the pages on an old mimeograph machine, and number the rough drafts with a pencil. Then I would ask my students to help me to check each page. I had plenty of energy in those days, and as I considered this task a worthwhile use of my time I completed the book from start to finish at one go. From 1987 to now 18 years have passed, and I too have passed through middle age to old age. That this book is now presented to the readers in a new format is deeply gratifying. I wish to tell them that of all my published writings the process of writing this one was the most pleasant.

Yuan Xingpei
April 18, 2005

Index

For Product Safety Concerns and Information please contact our EU
representative GPSR@taylorandfrancis.com
Taylor & Francis Verlag GmbH, Kaufingerstraße 24, 80331 München, Germany

www.ingramcontent.com/pod-product-compliance
Lightning Source LLC
Chambersburg PA
CBHW071510110726
47908CB00003B/793

* 9 7 8 0 3 6 7 5 2 8 9 3 5 *